A CULTURAL THEOLOGY OF SALVATION

A Cultural
Theology of
Salvation

CLIVE MARSH

OXFORD
UNIVERSITY PRESS

OXFORD
UNIVERSITY PRESS

Great Clarendon Street, Oxford, OX2 6DP,
United Kingdom

Oxford University Press is a department of the University of Oxford.
It furthers the University's objective of excellence in research, scholarship,
and education by publishing worldwide. Oxford is a registered trade mark of
Oxford University Press in the UK and in certain other countries

© Clive Marsh 2018

The moral rights of the author have been asserted

First Edition published in 2018

Impression: 1

Published in the United States of America by Oxford University Press
198 Madison Avenue, New York, NY 10016, United States of America

British Library Cataloguing in Publication Data
Data available

Library of Congress Control Number: 2018950677

ISBN 978-0-19-881101-5

Printed and bound by
CPI Group (UK) Ltd, Croydon, CR0 4YY

Links to third party websites are provided by Oxford in good faith and
for information only. Oxford disclaims any responsibility for the materials
contained in any third party website referenced in this work.

Acknowledgements

Though this book has an immediate life, having been written mainly in a four-year period from 2014–18, it has had a gestation period of a lifetime. Different phases of my academic and broader professional and personal life have fed into its production, even if there are people who should be thanked for its production as a particular text. I have located a mini theological autobiography in a footnote in Chapter 8. That footnote should be read as an extension of these acknowledgements. But beyond that scholarly support stretching back decades there are many others who have helped me write this text, either by reading sections of the work, discussing ideas, mulling over stuff during meals or by just being personally supportive. These supporters include Mary and Richard Gill, Tom Greggs, Andrew and Sarah Hindmarsh, Hannah, Jill, and Philip Marsh, Michael Nausner, Penny Prestage-Roles, Mandy and Vaughan S. Roberts, Chris Roles, Nicola Slee, Miriam Stevenson, and Natasha Whiteman.

Settings in which I have tried out versions of the material in the book include the Postgraduate Christian Systematic Theology Seminar, Christ Church, Oxford, November 2013; the Music and Theology Seminar, Worcester College, Oxford, May 2015; the Protestantism on Screen Conference, Wittenberg, June 2015; the Society for the Study of Theology Conference, Durham, April 2016; the International Society for Media, Religion, and Culture Conference, Seoul, August 2016; the (Post)secular: Imagining Faith in Contemporary Cultures Conference, Warwick, June 2017; the National Cultures of TV Comedy Symposium, Notre Dame University (London campus), November 2017; the Rutland Theological Society, Oakham, December 2017. I am grateful to all those who either invited me to speak to those gatherings, responded favourably to offers of papers I made, or simply made the events happen. Discussions I had at those events proved invaluable.

The epigram to Chapter 7 from *From More Lay Thoughts of a Dean* by W. R. Inge, published by Putnam, is reproduced by permission of The Random House Group Ltd ©1933. I am grateful, too, to Westminster John Knox Press for permission to use the citation from Serene Jones's chapter 'What's Wrong with Us?' in W. C. Placher (ed.) *Essentials of Christian Theology* (Louisville, KY, and London: Westminster John Knox, 2003), p.142, as an epigram for Chapter 8.

The time during which this book was written became more turbulent than expected. I was 'awarded a Personal Chair' (became a Professor) on April Fool's Day 2016, at almost the mid-point of the writing and editing period. In June 2016, whilst on a period of study leave for which I remain very grateful, the Centre for Lifelong Learning at the University of Leicester, of which I am Academic Head, was signalled for closure. The disruption caused to my writing schedule, whilst severe, was relatively slight compared to the turbulence created in and for the lives, professions, well-being and future prospects of my fellow workers. I am, therefore, especially grateful to immediate colleagues in the Centre, most of whose posts will also have come, or be coming, to an end by the time this text appears, for their continuing work in enabling others to flourish. Most of my colleagues have not read a word of this book, and many will disagree with some or most of its contents. Alongside the many associate tutors with whom we all work they have, however, created a positive, supportive working environment for our students and for each other, in which I, too, 'in spite of all' ('*trotz allem*', as my German family, the Jönssons, would say) have been able to flourish. I thank them all profoundly: Elizabeth Bryant, Patrick Cawley, Adrian Coles, Lucy Faire, Mary Graham, Olivia Harrison, Sophie Havelock, Tina Holt, Nalita James, Risha Jadeja, Crysta Kaczmarek, Claudia Kempinska-Hill, Sue Livingston, Sarah McMullan, Jon March, Kate Moore, Henrietta O'Connor, Tony Priest, Clare Symons, Andy Tams, Katherine Taylor, David Wharton, Sue Wheeler, and Junaid Zico. Tom Perridge and Karen Raith provided invaluable OUP support throughout. The anonymous peer reviewers of the original proposal and early draft chapters, and the peer reader of the final manuscript have helped to make this a better book (I hope!—I did not accept all their recommendations). Donald Watt polished the text and made it much more readable at the copy-editing stage. It has been a long and complicated journey, but, dare I say, I am happy and content to have finished it, and hope that it may prove of existential as well as intellectual benefit to those who read it. I even hope that it may have an impact beyond its readers, who, through their practical involvement in religious, educational, domestic and cultural life, may be helping others to flourish and may see that this has something to do with salvation. Otherwise it will, as they say, have been just an academic exercise.

Easter Day

1 April 2018

Contents

Introduction

Salvation is everywhere. Or, at least, you would think so judging by the ease with which people speak of 'redeeming themselves' or 'atoning for their actions'. Addicts are 'saved' by the intervention of friends or family, or by rehab programmes. Sports stars are 'saved', or their careers 'redeemed', through medical care or rigorous training regimes. Meanwhile, the themes of 'rescue' and 'deliverance' (sometimes, in journalists' accounts, 'on a biblical scale') are prominent in reports on disasters, or from war zones, or when referencing the current migration crisis.

Salvation is also evident everywhere by its lack. Many are plainly not rescued or delivered. People are still abused, manipulated, deceived, or exploited in a wide range of situations where no salvation or redemption seems possible. Evil—be it natural or moral—will clearly not go away. Salvation is, then, clearly not an experience which everyone has, or a reality with which all can identify.

Are all such references to salvation or redemption any more than residual theological language which has largely been uprooted from religious soil and lost much of its original meaning? There being no God—it is easily assumed in the secularized West—there can now be no sense of 'being saved' unless this be solely through the help of others. People can only save themselves. Theology will therefore have little to offer by way of understanding such terms, and probably little to gain from wasting time delving into how such terms are used. Better, it may be thought, to let theology stick to its own world and not be tainted by the complexity of the wider context within which it must do its work.

Culturally astute theology will, however, not let this happen. To dig around in the broader culture within which theology operates will not just be about clarifying the context in which theology is done. Trying to find a way of rendering theological insights comprehensible risks changing theology's content. So this may be deemed a dangerous exercise. However, if theology does change, it does so very slowly. God may not change—though that question must be for another time. But human notions of God certainly do, even if never without feverish debate and in highly contested ways. For those of us who believe theism still to be important, we must hope that our notions of God, as they develop, stay close enough to the reality of God to remain truthful (even true). Theologians of different schools and traditions will inevitably disagree as to how that works, and the extent to which it is possible to tell.

This book is all about how it is possible to speak of salvation in the present in the West, when salvation-type language is in wide use and may or may not be being used in theologically conscious ways. It probes examples of where language, images, concepts, and experience pertaining to salvation appear, and what is to be done with them. It asks whether and how this material may offer something constructive to theology's current work. In Chapter 1 I set the scene by beginning with happiness. In Chapter 2 I offer an exposition of the 'cultural theological' approach I am proposing. Readers not interested in the theory of theology can skip this chapter completely. Theologians, on the other hand, may take me to task for it. I would welcome this, for I think that theology is a crucial discipline for human well-being, so it is important that as many people as possible debate about how it is best done. If my approach is mistaken, then others will need to offer a better way forward. But it will have to be one which connects with what people spend a lot of their time doing (when watching, singing, speaking, thinking, working, and not necessarily in explicitly religious ways).

Chapters 3–6 form the potentially contentious heart of the book. These are a series of case studies: examples of artistic, cultural, and media resources, experiences, practices, and activities which invite theological work, which have fallen into my lap for various reasons over the years. My point is not to argue that these are all especially valuable theological resources. Readers will have their own similar lists. I *am* claiming that these are the kind of things which *are* doing theological work, whether we like it or not. So it is useful to ask what theological freight they carry, and what kinds of theological insight emerge from discussion of their content and use.

In Chapters 7 and 8 and in my Conclusion I present the results of my critical reflection on what the conversations of Chapters 3–6 have generated. Chapter 8 is the true test of whether the method I espouse in Chapter 2 has been worth following. In theory, it should not have been possible to write Chapter 8 and the Conclusion without my doing the legwork of Chapters 3–6. Chapter 8 is still an identifiably Christian theology of salvation. But it is more than just shaped by the current discussions represented by Chapters 3–6. It bears significant hallmarks resulting from those earlier cultural conversations. Salvation has to be espoused in contemporary terms for it to be comprehensible as a contemporary phenomenon, and to be graspable and communicable as a potential experience. That is the basic conviction of this book. This is not theological reductionism. Nor, as a form of contextual theology, does it lose a sense of theology's systematic character. The understanding of salvation I present is aware of its limited character and of its connectedness with other branches of doctrine (Christ, Spirit, Church, and so on). For theologians to do their work, they cannot simply talk to other theologians. Or, if they are academic or ecclesiastical theologians, they cannot simply talk to other academics or church people. Theology is much too important for that.

Part I

Salvation as Cultural Theology

1

Happiness, Redemption, and Flourishing

It was as I began to ask how a Christian notion of salvation can be articulated fruitfully today that I had to begin asking questions about happiness. As soon as you try and articulate why an understanding of salvation is important, you have to explain too what the results of 'being saved' are. Even if full salvation comes later—even beyond this present life—it is at least anticipated now. But how should that be described? Has Christianity been creative and helpful enough in describing that present experience?

Happiness, whilst prominent in contemporary Western culture, politics, and economics, is only one example amongst many terms and concepts used to explore and promote positive aspects of human experience in the West. Prosperity, growth, development, and—as we shall see—especially 'flourishing' are other examples. From a different perspective, 'redemption' also merits consideration. In theological terms, 'redemption' is one particular form of salvation. It remains, however, an often used word in Western culture well beyond religious contexts whether or not it can be said to carry theological meaning where it appears. It is used to indicate that someone has endured a negative experience and come through to a positive, fulfilled form of life. We shall see, therefore, that in picking our way through cultural examples of how human frailties and wickedness are addressed, 'happiness', 'flourishing', and 'redemption' will feature prominently.

In this opening chapter I shall do four things. I shall first map the intensity and range of contemporary interest in happiness. As happiness is the most obvious current Western cultural descriptor of what people might hope for in their lives, it is important to sift through the politics, economics, and psychology of this intense interest. Second, I shall explore briefly some examples of where 'redemption' appears as a term used in Western culture. What is being implied and assumed when the term is used? How does this help frame the questions which a contemporary Christian theologian needs to address when seeking to continue to make sense of 'salvation' today? Third, I shall trace some key features of the 'history of happiness', noting where theological concerns have surfaced and what challenges there may be *to* theology from that history. Finally, I shall turn to a sample of recent writings of Christian theologians to find out whether 'happiness' is much talked about—and if so, how. The purpose of this chapter is to clarify terms and concepts, and draw up a set of appropriate questions to be addressed and issues to be explored throughout the rest of the work.

HAPPINESS: THE CURRENT AGENDA

Happiness is topical in the West. As well as being something which people readily say they seek, and wish for others, there are structures in place designed to measure and promote it. Action for Happiness, for example, describes itself as 'a movement of people committed to building a happier and more caring society'. Its members 'want to see a fundamentally different way of life—where people care less about what they can get just for themselves and more about the happiness of others' and 'make a simple pledge: to try to create more happiness in the world around them'. Though an independent organization, related to a charitable body, it regularly receives positive mentions in the words of UK government ministers, despite having 'no religious, political or commercial affiliations'.[1]

In 2011, Action for Happiness worked along with the BBC to support a 'Happiness Challenge' in which eight volunteers tried out some simple practical actions over a period of time (based on the three key areas 'Be Mindful, Be Kind, Be Grateful'), to see if it improved their sense of well-being. The experiment was presented as 'based on the latest scientific research'.[2] The participants admitted that the experiment had a marked impact on their daily conduct, encouraging them to do things they might normally forget to do (e.g. expressing thanks to others).

---

[1] www.actionforhappiness.org/about-us, accessed 18 December 2015.

[2] www.actionforhappiness.org/about-us/the-happiness-challenge, accessed 18 December 2015. At the time of writing the videos reporting on the results of the challenge remain on the Action for Happiness website.

David Sillito, the BBC arts correspondent who oversaw the experiment and reported on it, was especially struck by how his understanding of happiness itself shifted: from a recognition that there are fleeting pleasures in life to seeing happiness more in terms of finding 'the best way of equipping yourself mentally to cope with life's ups and downs'.[3]

In 2015, Action for Happiness launched 'Exploring What Matters', an eight-week 'Happiness Course', supported by the movement's patron, the Dalai Lama. Again the course is presented as having been devised 'based on the latest scientific evidence'.[4] It is explicitly 'intended for people of all backgrounds', although the introductory video might come over as rather intimidating for those not used to formal, small-group discussions amongst well-dressed, articulate, well-educated, and largely middle-class people.

Happiness indices abound. Measurement of happiness has become crucial for governments, especially in order to examine what the relationship might be between economic and emotional well-being. The Office for National Statistics (ONS) in the UK now conducts an annual 'Personal Well-Being' survey which brings together factual information about people (e.g. whether they participate in sports and the arts, have formal qualifications, levels of income vis-à-vis the median rate) and their self-assessments as to their level of happiness (e.g. feelings of worthwhileness, whether they are satisfied with their health or their leisure time, and whether, overall, they are satisfied with life).[5] Though debates will understandably rage about causality—arguably, all such measuring tools can only detect correlations—it is important to note the likely link between key factors (including material factors) in people's life experience, self-understanding, and personal disposition towards life, something which theologians have not always done.[6] It will be necessary to return to the question of the potential relationship between economics and emotional and spiritual well-being much later in this inquiry. It will also be important to explore the relationship and distinction between happiness and well-being—frequently assumed to be identical in meaning.

---

[3] www.actionforhappiness.org/about-us/the-happiness-challenge (part 5, 3.08–3.13 mins.), accessed 18 December 2015.

[4] www.actionforhappiness.org/the-action-for-happiness-course, accessed 18 December 2015.

[5] Relevant data tables can be navigated to from www.ons.gov.uk/ons/rel/wellbeing/ measuring-national-well-being/personal-well-being-in-the-uk–2014-15/index.html, accessed 18 December 2015.

[6] John Atherton, whose work will be used in Chapter 6, is an important voice here.

Happiness is simply 'there' as a contemporary theme in academic research and needs to be taken account of for that reason.[7] It is in the academic realm, understandably, where concern for the measurement of happiness is prominent. It is also to academics that governments turn for their 'evidence base' when seeking to devise policies which promote happiness and well-being. It is thus not surprising that alongside the expanding number of statistically supported articles appearing in journals such as those just cited, books on the topic also abound.[8] Inside and outside the academy, however, questions are raised about how convincing and persuasive the evidence for happiness can be. For one thing, can the responses to survey questions or answers given to interviewers always be trusted? Are we, in fact, the best judges of our own happiness and well-being?[9] The question of the distinction between happiness and well-being surfaces here. Happiness may or may not be identical with emotional well-being, though it is more likely to be an emotional matter than is the concern for economic well-being. Happiness may at least have something to do with contentment and satisfaction, within which one would expect there to be at least *some* emotional element. Well-being, by contrast—though it, too, may contain an element of satisfaction—could easily have much more of a meaning of material contentedness. It may be as much to do with the objective circumstances of living as it is with a subjective state.

In a searching recent study of 'The Happiness Industry' William Davies has drawn attention to how concern to measure happiness has run alongside the rise of consumerism and the marketing industry in Western culture. His work is replete with sharp observations about, and conclusions drawn from, the historical alliance he maps.

---

[7] There has been a *Journal of Happiness Studies* since 2000, an *International Journal of Happiness and Development* since 2012, and a *Journal of Happiness and Well-Being* since 2013 (the last of these with a colossal editorial board of seventy-seven—presumably happy—members as of December 2015).

[8] The main works consulted for this book were: William Davies, *The Happiness Industry: How the Government and Big Business Sold Us Well-Being* (London and New York: Verso, 2015), Carol Graham, *Happiness around the World: The Paradox of Happy Peasants and Miserable Millionaires* (New York and Oxford: Oxford University Press, 2012), Daniel M. Haybron, *The Pursuit of Unhappiness: The Elusive Psychology of Well-Being* (Oxford: Oxford University Press, 2008), Richard Layard, *Happiness: Lessons from a New Science* (London: Allen Lane, 2005), Martin E. P. Seligman, *Flourish: A Visionary New Understanding of Happiness and Well-Being* (New York: Atria Paperback, 2013; first published 2011).

[9] Daniel Haybron in particular has pursued this insight. See, for example, *The Pursuit of Unhappiness*, 191, 195, 220, 233.

He remarks: 'The current explosion in happiness and well-being data is really an effect of new technologies and practices of surveillance. In turn, these depend on pre-existing power inequalities.'[10] Or again:

> what often begins as a basis on which to understand human flourishing and progress—fundamental ideas of enlightenment and humanism— suddenly reappears as a route to sell people stuff they don't need, work harder for managers who don't respect them and conform to policy objectives over which they have no say.[11]

Questions can, of course, be raised about Davies' own marshalling of the evidence, and the accuracy of the judgments he makes, although his case is compellingly presented. All we need to note for our purposes is that the ways evidence is gathered, the purposes to which it is put, and the evaluations made are far from clear-cut. We need simply note that this is a very lively field of study and activity in the academy, in politics, and in commercial and cultural life. To undertake a study, then, which seeks to explore what the positive side to any religious exploration of salvation/redemption might be cannot ignore what is being said in this field. If it is assumed that salvation has a positive dimension and may not simply relieve misery a little but actually have an impact on people's sense of contentedness or well-being in the world, then it is logical to ask at some point what connection it might have with the contemporary emphasis upon happiness and well-being.

REDEMPTION: A CONTEMPORARY PREOCCUPATION

If happiness and well-being may be regarded the positive pole of contemporary approaches to the satisfied life, then redemption is a key term which seeks to capture a process through which a person is deemed to have to go in order to turn around, or be rescued, from a bad situation in life.[12] It might be expected that the regularity with which

---

[10] Davies, *The Happiness Industry*, 219.
[11] Davies, *The Happiness Industry*, 232–3.
[12] My quest has not been to clarify in Christian understanding what constitutes 'the satisfied life' (or, in philosophical or ethical terminology 'the good life'). I am only concerned to explore this because of the implications of having started the other way

the verb ('redeem'/'be redeemed') or the noun ('redemption') appears should be welcome for any theological exploration. It is certainly striking that the term remains so current even when used without any evident awareness that there may be a theological history to the term.[13] After all, etymologically the term is to do with 'buying back' and hence has a commercial origin.[14] Its theological resonance came later, even if we can now see that this meaning reverberates through many of the ways in which it is now used.

Admittedly, reference to 'redemption' implies that whatever negativity is being referred to has already been overcome. Or, if redemption is being sought, then the suggestion is being given that the way out is known. This may explain why DVD blurb writers, film critics, journalists, and cultural commentators so readily use the term. We like a good tale of someone who was down on their luck—the grizzlier the tale of woe, the better. Better still when we can hear the tale of woe alongside a story of heroic endeavour, or astonishing altruism on the part of others, leading to the rescue and recovery of the person in plight.[15] A happy ending is usually welcome.

Redemption (or salvation) may be needed from a range of things: financial misery, alcoholism or addiction of some other kind, domestic violence, continual failure in life, a major physical injury, natural disaster, low self-esteem, psychological, mental, or emotional illness. Some such states may be within human power (the person him- or herself, or others—family members, friends, health or other professionals)

---

round: if a person is 'saved' or 'redeemed', does this have any positive bearing on life *now*, and if so, what form does that take?

[13] I have quoted David H. Kelsey's observation already in print, but it bears repeating here, given its accuracy and pertinence:

> (A)s an assiduous reader of reviews of fiction, plays and movies, I have been impressed by the frequency with which reviewers comment on the presence or absence of a redemptive note or theme in the work under review or debate whether there might be such a note . . . Although I am often unable to tell just what the reviewer means by 'redemption' or 'redemptive', it is clear that the words are used in the context of certain practices that help make up Western cultural life.
>
> *Imagining Redemption* (Louisville, KY: Westminster John Knox Press, 2005), 5–6.

[14] It was prominent language in the buying back of slaves, and hence is a key aspect of the context within which early understandings and interpretations of the meaning of the death of Jesus were articulated by Christians. In the present, the term 'redemption' is most commonly associated with the use of shopping vouchers.

[15] Interestingly, when others do the rescuing, the term 'saved' seems to be used more.

to do something about. Other states may not seem, or be, capable of being overcome. The nature of the 'redemption' being referred to can therefore take on many forms.

Talking of redemption as a 'contemporary preoccupation' may admittedly be slightly hyperbolic. It is, however, appropriate to draw attention to the scale and range of uses of the term. Even if the term is used mostly from the positive end (redemption has been achieved), it suggests an awareness that to be placed, as a human being, in a perilous state, with a major obstacle to be overcome, is more common than we may often wish to admit. Life is far from easy for a great many people— even in the affluent West—even if the 'redemptions' referred to in cultural and media life concern mostly the lives of celebrities or sports stars. Such recurrent references may simply highlight the fact that the human experience and well-being being explored are common within everyday life.

To substantiate and explore further this claim for the prevalence of references to redemption, consider the following examples. On 16 December 2015, *The Guardian* newspaper in the UK carried an article listing the 'Top 10 books about justice and redemption'. The common bond suggested between the works was the restoration of 'cosmic balance'. 'Redemption', suggests the article's writer, Jeffrey Lent, 'is . . . beyond the law, and thus attainable by each person according to their own efforts and needs'.[16] Three months earlier, in the same publication's sports pages, it was possible to read: 'Aston Villa derby woe leaves Tim Sherwood relishing shot at redemption'.[17] Again there is the suggestion that redemption lies within the power of a human agent, in this case a football manager. A victory would make amends for a previous failure. Two years prior to that, the emphasis lay on the recovery of a reputation in the world of politics. With reference to the disgraced Liberal Democrat politician Chris Huhne,[18] Chris Calland explored what insights those who had managed to

---

[16] Jeffrey Lent, 'Top 10 books about justice and redemption', www.theguardian. com/books/2015/dec/16/top-10-books-about-justice-redemption-jeffrey-lent, accessed 14 January 2016.

[17] Peter Lansley, 'Aston Villa derby woe leaves Tim Sherwood relishing shot at redemption', www.theguardian.com/football/2015/sep/20/aston-villa-west-bromwich-albion-premier-league-match-report, accessed 14 January 2016.

[18] Huhne had been found guilty, along with his then wife Vicky Pryce, of perverting the course of justice in 2012, having asked her to accept a speeding fine on his behalf in 2003.

salvage their reputations might be able to bring to others who needed to 're-brand' themselves.[19]

Lest it be thought that such references appear only in the left-leaning press, consider these further examples from the *Daily Telegraph* and the *Daily Mail.* In the midst of a long list of examples of sporting recovery—all with the term 'redemption' attached to them— Art Spander reported from Pebble Beach, California, for the *Daily Telegraph* that golfer Phil Mickelson had recovered from his failure (a 'meltdown' on the final hole of the US Open) through a better, winning performance in a later, more minor tournament. His confidence was back.[20] Meanwhile, of the 3,453 results from a simple search of the *Daily Mail* online version, Daily Mail Australia reported on the 'personal and professional redemption' of reality TV star Sam (antha) Frost through participation in the TV show *The Bachelorette.* Jason Chester wrote of 'her journey from heartbreak to happiness'.[21]

Outside the world of media reporting on sport, politics, and celebrities, redemption is in use in the world of literary, music, and film criticism. Examples are easy to find. In a review of *God Help the Child,* Razia Iqbal notes that '(s)o much of [Toni] Morrison's writing is about responsibilities and redemption'.[22] *The Light in You,* an album by US rock band Mercury Rev is cited as revealing 'belief in music's redemptive powers'.[23] Guy Garvey's solo album *Courting the Squall* contains a track 'Angela's Eyes' in which Garvey's devotional style is

[19] Chris Calland, 'From rogue to redemption: what can brands learn from persona non grata?' (30 September 2013), www.theguardian.com/media-network/media-network-blog/2013/sep/30/rogue-redemption-brands-reputation-lessons, accessed 14 January 2016.

[20] Art Spander, 'Mickelson finds redemption' (13 February 2007), www.telegraph.co.uk/sport/golf/ustour/2307676/Mickelson-finds-redemption.html, accessed 14 January 2016.

[21] Jason Chester, 'My how you've changed! A look back at Sam Frost's transformation during a life changing year...' (30 December 2015), www.dailymail.co.uk/tvshowbiz/article-3378294/A-look-Sam-Frost-s-transformation-life-changing-year-chart-journey-heartbreak-happiness.html, accessed 14 January 2016.

[22] Razia Iqbal, 'Pain and trauma live just under the skin', *The Independent* (Radar section), 11 April 2015, 23. Iqbal does not quite define what understanding of redemption is being assumed here, however. Does it mean 'pulling through regardless'? Surviving, or even prospering, against a background of trauma? It may be a correct judgement about Morrison, and Morrison may well clarify her meaning much more than her reviewers. But as used in the review, the meaning of the term 'redemption' is left unclear.

[23] *The Independent*, (Radar section), 3 October 2015, 30.

said to 'take more redemptive form'.[24] The 2015 film *A Walk in the Woods* (dir. Ken Kwapis) is said to be 'unabashedly sentimental' and yet to have 'redemptive charm'.[25] Presumably, the focus here is on the impact of music and films on the listener and film watcher respectively. Quite what constitutes redemption is, once more, not fully spelled out. Whether it is any more than about the receiver feeling good is open to debate. More is implied, perhaps, but what, in terms of quality or scale, a listener or watcher experiences in the process of engagement with the music or film is left imprecise.

Redemption is, then, indeed in widespread use as a concept. If we are to speak of an evident emphasis across the multiple usages, then from the first set of examples it appears to be *what people can do for themselves* to rectify an unfortunate or negative occurrence or situation, or to restore a lost reputation. It may take above average effort to turn things round, but because it has been achieved, the bad situation has been rectified. Redemption in common Western usage thus means 'putting things right' when they have gone badly wrong. The dominance of use with respect to sport should perhaps be noted. Sporting stars can 'redeem themselves' because their very existence (their profession, even their vocation) is to excel, and to exceed their previous performances. The quest for perfection is bound up with what they do for a living, and with who they are as people. To return to their calling after a major setback (injury, bad performance, complicated private life) therefore becomes testament to their hard work and (physical) effort. They are their own redeemers, however much they may be supported by coaches, friends, and family members.

In the second set of examples, it might be felt there is the possibility here of redemption being a 'gift' in the sense that something happens for the listener or viewer, more so than a reader. But what it is within the film and music examples particularly which is redemptive, as opposed to what is received, is not made clear.

The question is not, of course, directly being raised in any of the examples as to whether there may be situations which are *irredeemable*, or whether people may be redeemed through the endeavours or intervention of others. We shall need to explore further in due course

---

[24] Andy Gill, 'Garvey goes down a storm with songs straight from the heart', *The Independent* (Radar section), 31 October 2015, 18.
[25] Geoffrey Macnab, 'Old devils charm on a slow voyage of discovery', *The Independent*, 18 September 2015, 45.

how this current common usage and insights from theological use may or may not interweave and be informing each other. We must, though, face squarely the possibility that reclamation or refinement of a theological meaning of the term may be very difficult to achieve in the light of this available evidence. The term may potentially have become so attenuated in meaning that any sense of human beings *not* being in control of their own redemption or simply being *unable* to redeem themselves may simply be incomprehensible. As things stand, to start from the perspective that people cannot, by definition, redeem themselves could instantly be seen as a stark counter-cultural approach to the current use of the concept. We shall have to address this issue directly in Chapters 7 and 8 below.

THE HAPPINESS TRADITION IN WESTERN THOUGHT

So much, then, for current interest in and cultural usage of the terms 'happiness' and 'redemption'. What about past discussions of happiness? To what extent have theologians contributed to those discussions? Darrin McMahon has written a brilliant survey of the quest for happiness in the West.[26] A main conclusion of his study is that the approaches to happiness we now adopt are distinctly modern. For most of Western culture, construals of reality and understandings of the world (this world and beyond) quite different from those we might assume now were in view. McMahon puts it starkly:

> modern conceptions of happiness . . . were born in the seventeenth and eighteenth centuries, in an age we now call the Enlightenment. It was in that period that considerable numbers of men and women were first introduced to the novel prospect that they could be happy—that they *should* be happy—in this life.[27]

On this basis, the shift to understanding redemption as within our power as human beings (even, within our responsibility) makes

---

[26] Darrin McMahon, *The Pursuit of Happiness: A History from the Greeks to the Present* (London: Penguin Books, 2007). I am indebted to McMahon for his historical survey throughout this section.
[27] McMahon, *The Pursuit of Happiness*, 12.

post-Enlightenment sense. From a sense that human destiny lies totally out of our control (resting in the hand of God or the gods, or nature), through the discovery of how much potential human beings have, to the sense that, aside from the quirks and whims of nature, all now lies in human hands, God has largely been left behind for most people in the West.[28] Happiness and redemption may both be deemed to depend on human action.

Prior to that, human action was far from neglected. It was just that the nature of that action—and the way in which it related to human happiness—was rather differently conceived from contemporary Western assumptions.

A series of examples makes clear how these differences took effect. McMahon shows how ancient Greek approaches to happiness were about the steering or controlling of desire through a variety of strategies. Desire had to be 'educated', be it through the control of reason (as in Socrates and Plato, if in slightly different ways), the steering of it towards a good purpose through the cultivation of virtues (Aristotle), or 'strict regulation' (in Epicureanism or Stoicism).[29] All of these tendencies later became evident in Christianity too, interlaced with theological insights into how God would assist in the steering or cultivation of appropriate responses to human drives in the service of a divinely appointed goal. Whether 'happiness' would be talked about explicitly is another matter. In the meantime, three aspects of happiness agreed upon during the classical period can be summarized: (1) it is objective not subjective; (2) it is rational rather than feelings-based; (3) it requires discipline and hard work.[30] From a current perspective arguably only the third aspect might be readily supported (especially by sportspeople seeking redemption), though as an achievement it could perhaps also be considered something 'objective' and hence satisfy the first. In the current 'feel-good' age, however, happiness would scarcely be thought of as a rational goal, reached via rational means. Happiness, rather, is something which you *feel*, attainable through all sorts of experiences which, even if chosen, must be felt to be enjoyed.

[28] Precisely when this became mainstream Western thinking is, of course, debatable (The eighteenth century? The nineteenth century? After the Holocaust? From the 1960s onwards?). The question dovetails with debates about the process of secularization.
[29] McMahon, *The Pursuit of Happiness*, 25–55.
[30] McMahon, *The Pursuit of Happiness*, 64–5.

Interestingly, some of the current emphases are perceived by McMahon in early Christianity. In sharp contrast to classical approaches, Christian happiness 'was unabashedly sensual in its imagined ecstasies'.[31] This theme will recur throughout this study. For whilst the sensuality may have been palpable, whether the sensual 'happiness' envisaged bears any resemblance to what would now be understood by the term remains a moot point. Sharing in the pain and suffering of Christ in a literal sense would not now be expected to issue in a feeling of happiness. Hence, contemporary Western citizens may need some persuading that Christianity can contribute to better, richer understandings of happiness. Indeed, because Christian notions of happiness were largely envisaged as relating to *the next life*, sensual aspects of this-worldly experience may not have been much wanted.[32] Or, rather, what might have been accepted and endured (rather than wanted) was seen as a means to something greater.

From an early phase of its history, however, Christianity was feeding in potentially important insights to understandings of happiness. First, it presented happiness as *a gift*, whether this was to be in this life or beyond.[33] Despite the other-worldly (next world) emphasis, the notion that there may be glimpses (via blessings, good things) in this life of that gift of happiness was still (just!) maintained.[34] Happiness could be enjoyed in an experience of 'transcendence' when a person 'rises above' him- or herself in some way, be this in a deep spiritual experience or an aesthetic encounter (or indeed, where the latter leads to the former).[35] Even so, as McMahon recognizes, such reflection would have been a luxury for the relative few: 'Bonaventure's stress

---

[31] McMahon, *The Pursuit of Happiness*, 95.

[32] McMahon notes the claims of both Augustine and Aquinas that whatever sense of happiness may be enjoyed in this life, 'true' or 'ultimate' happiness lay beyond (McMahon, *The Pursuit of Happiness*, 104 and 128, referring to *City of God* and *Summa contra Gentiles* respectively).

[33] This insistence was echoed throughout Western history. Even when a greater role for human activity was acknowledged in the pursuit and receipt of happiness, if ever 'one knew lasting happiness, it would only be by the grace of a God who intervened from beyond the stage of the world' (McMahon, *The Pursuit of Happiness*, 137).

[34] McMahon, *The Pursuit of Happiness*, 106 (with reference to the ambiguity in Augustine's approach: 'The same author who speaks in the *City of God* of our mortal lives as a "kind of hell on earth" recounts with reverence the "innumerable blessings" and many "good things of which this life is full"').

[35] McMahon on Bonaventure, *The Pursuit of Happiness*, 120. McMahon cites from the *Journey of the Mind to God* (1259).

on lofty transcendence should not allow us to overlook the far greater number who were forced to cling much closer to earth, eking out an existence on the land or huddling together in Europe's crowded cities and towns.'[36] This is an important reminder for this present study: any kind of theological reflection could easily be seen as the preserve of the wealthy rather than a way of fostering positive human experience for all.

The question of human agency in the service of happiness runs throughout McMahon's history. Christianity delivers an ambiguous contribution here, the fault line falling, not surprisingly, especially between Roman Catholic and Protestant perspectives. For Protestants, Aquinas' 'opening up of a space in which "some partial happiness can be achieved in this life"' and his conviction that 'we could pull ourselves higher, partly on our own' would prove anathema to most Protestants in due course.[37] Even in his own day, his insights 'had the effect of narrowing the conceptual distance between man and God, rendering human life potentially more heavenly'.[38] The ghost of Pelagius lurked in the wings. It is perhaps also not surprising that in the present, the rediscovery and reassertion of Aristotelian virtues, which Aquinas had done so much to promote, are fashionable. Where the richness of human possibility is recognized, then Protestant caution born of greater attention to human depravity and disbelief that the human being is capable of much can be politely set aside. That said, in Aquinas' time, in a way that may be less the case for Western citizens now, 'few Christians denied that perfect happiness could be had only by grace'.[39]

It is debatable, historically speaking, where the tipping point occurs in shifting the focus from the life beyond to this world. Even if it could be expected—in the past and now—that there is conscious happiness to be enjoyed beyond this present world, there is without doubt a change towards a growing appreciation of the pleasures of this world, be this as a result of the Renaissance, the Reformation, or the Enlightenment. That three long movements, stretching across many centuries, can all be seen as contenders to have brought about such a change indicates the gradual nature of the process. If Renaissance humanists

---

[36] McMahon, *The Pursuit of Happiness*, 120.
[37] These summaries are from McMahon, *The Pursuit of Happiness*, 130 and 132.
[38] McMahon, *The Pursuit of Happiness*, 132.
[39] McMahon, *The Pursuit of Happiness*, 138.

such as Erasmus and Thomas More, and then, in their different ways, Luther, Winstanley, and Locke all played key roles within this gradual change, it was nevertheless still true that by the nineteenth century, when secularization began to take serious hold across Europe, that most Western citizens were illiterate, were expected to be Christian, had fairly low life expectancy, and could still not wholly appreciate that this life's happiness would amount to much. God was not out of the picture for most, and was assumed to pull the strings (and probably in favour of the well-to-do), whatever people *actually believed* about God or the life beyond. But life was not particularly enjoyable for most.

By the time the Enlightenment began to take full effect, however, it had 'translated the ultimate question "How can I be saved"[*sic*] into the pragmatic "How can I be happy?"'[40] Indeed, the answers to both of these questions 'eighteenth-century men and women increasingly believed, could be found through human effort and understanding alone'.[41] There remains the question as to precisely what this happiness actually comprised. McMahon disputes that it is to be easily equated with classical understandings of *eudaimonia* (well-being/flourishing), and he is probably right in this. But what the human effort is meant to bring about remains at some remove from what current understandings of happiness might assume. General material well-being and physical, metaphysical, or emotional stability and contentment were still a distant hope for the majority of Western citizens. If pressed as to whether pleasure could be considered a key element in happiness, then the judgements between the wealthy and the rural (or increasingly urban) poor, and the definitions of pleasure being used, would have been markedly different from each other.

There is no going back behind this Enlightenment turn. The secularization process has led to fewer people in the West believing in God, and not just to fewer people being church attenders.[42] Even so, this does not now lead to the inevitable exclusion of God and

---

[40] Roy Porter, *Enlightenment: Britain and the Creation of the Modern World* (London: Penguin, 2000), 22, cited in McMahon, *The Pursuit of Happiness*, 209.

[41] McMahon, *The Pursuit of Happiness*, 209.

[42] For all the justified challenges to the full-blown secularization thesis—which proved wrong about the disappearance of religion—Steve Bruce is right that disbelief has increased. Even if it is as much a case of people having the chance to be honest about not believing (rather than, in the UK for example, writing or stating 'C. of E.' for the sake of (avoiding) argument), the shake-up and clarification process, leading to the rise of the 'Nones' (those with no religious affiliation), has been important.

theology from considerations of happiness. Whilst it is possible to show that the Enlightenment did not, after all, 'wholly succeed in separating happiness from its religious and metaphysical past',[43] '(w)hereas for most men and women at the dawn of the modern age, God was happiness, happiness has since become our god'.[44] As a topic worthy of examination, then, happiness really is that important. Whether or not there is a God, what people deem makes them happy—and which drives them and may therefore then function for them as a god—needs careful critical scrutiny.

Happiness thus becomes a key agenda item for theology. To fail to appreciate just how significant discussions of happiness (and related terms) are in contemporary Western culture amounts to trying to articulate theological meaning in incomprehensible ways. Whether or not happiness will ultimately prove a useful term for theology, it has to be grasped and engaged with. Conversely, whether or not God is believed in, all humans have God equivalents—master narratives, key convictions, primary beliefs and drives—by which their lives are structured and steered. Happiness is now one of these. To fail to acknowledge this, as secular cultures at their worst are prone to do, underplays how and why all people (not just religious fanatics) can get worked up about things.[45]

The post-Enlightenment phase of Western culture has brought significant challenges to Christianity with respect to our theme. The long shift towards valuing human agency (as opposed to divine control) and this-worldliness (as opposed to awaiting rewards beyond this life) has led in turn to profound affirmation of the present, appreciation of the natural world, accentuation of the richness of human experience, and attention to the alleviation of misery in this life. Alongside these developments, loss of confidence that there is a 'next life' to be enjoyed has grown. We should thus expect significant changes to understandings of salvation and redemption to result. Though the perpetuation of salvation language *at all* in such post-Enlightenment times could be regarded a retrograde step, forcing a return to pre-Kantian 'self-incurred immaturity', it could equally be

---

[43] McMahon, *The Pursuit of Happiness*, 14.

[44] McMahon, *The Pursuit of Happiness*, 267.

[45] A point I have argued in 'Films, Values, Absolutes: Why Theological Readings of Films are Morally and Politically Essential', *Journal of Religion and Film* 20.1 (2016), article 11, 1–22.

argued that the more appropriate response is to ask how salvation itself needs to be reconceived alongside the changes in the concept and experience of happiness. If 'our image of happiness is indissolubly bound up with the image of redemption' (Walter Benjamin),[46] then it is vital that a more robust, contemporary definition of salvation be found, capable of interpreting and being interpreted by all of the changes which have occurred in the history of happiness.[47] Happiness may not be the result of salvation. Indeed, I shall endeavour to show that it is not, in any straightforward sense. But looking at the histories and potential meanings of the two concepts in parallel, and in their interweavings, will prove fruitful for contemporary Christian thought and practice.[48]

THE (RELATIVE) SILENCE OF THE THEOLOGIANS

As we have just seen, insights from theologians are part of the philosophical and cultural history of happiness in the West because of Christianity's cultural dominance, at least from early fourth to the early twentieth centuries. Christian theologians are less prominent as public figures now. Nevertheless, the question of how current theologians relate to the concept of happiness is significant. Whilst they remain (especially in ethics) keen to explore what it means to live the 'good life', 'happiness' is not a term much used to characterize the human experience of such a life. The history of the concept itself reveals, in any case, shifting understandings of what constitutes happiness. In what ways, then, do contemporary theologians make use of happiness in their thinking? If they do not use it, why is this?

[46] Walter Benjamin, 'Theses on the Philosophy of History', in *Illuminations* (New York: Schocken Books, 1968), 254 (cited in McMahon, *The Pursuit of Happiness*, 401).
[47] I repeat at this point that 'salvation' is the broader theological term, and the doctrine which I am seeking to rework. 'Redemption' is narrower but made use of because of its cultural currency, whether or not in theologically explicit ways. For practical purposes they are largely interchangeable for the moment.
[48] To anticipate my engagement with the work of Klemm and Schweiker (in Chapter 2): the approach connects here already to theirs. A return to uncritical premodern theism would constitute in their terms a form of 'hypertheism' (i.e. being just a bit too confident about what it is possible to say about God), whereas succumbing to the view that humans are capable of all things, having pretty much taken the place of God altogether, would be a form of 'overhumanization'.

Research into recent theological writings suggests avoidance of the term. With the exception of specific academic studies, in Christian theological and religious writing happiness is left largely to popular writings.[49] A study of twelve theological texts of different genres from the last twenty years reveals that if happiness is talked of at all, then it is largely in relation to anthropology and eschatology that the term appears. It is not usually deemed pertinent to salvation.[50] This observation makes no judgement about the inadequacy and inaccuracy of the works consulted, which have diverse concerns and readerships. Indeed, the relative absence of happiness from such theological texts could even be an indication of the misguided nature of an exploration which brings salvation and happiness alongside each other. The evidence does, though, show that the juxtaposition is not viewed within current Christian theology as a most logical fit.

A number of examples indicate what is happening at present. There are two references to happiness in *The Oxford Handbook of Systematic Theology* (2007) both occurring in the chapter on 'Moral

[49] The main recent academic studies are Vincent Brümmer and Marcel Sarot (eds.), *Happiness, Well-being and the Meaning of Life* (Kampen: Kok Pharos, 1996), Sarah Heaner Lancaster, *The Pursuit of Happiness: Blessing and Fulfillment in Christian Faith* (Eugene, OR: Wipf and Stock, 2010), and Ellen Charry, *God and the Art of Happiness* (Grand Rapids, MI: Eerdmans, 2011). Examples of popular texts include (Protestant) John Piper, *Desiring God: Meditations of a Christian Hedonist*, (rev. edn, Sisters, OR: Multnomah Books, 2011) and (Roman Catholic) Christopher Kaczor, *The Gospel of Happiness: Rediscover your Faith through Spiritual Practice and Positive Psychology* (New York: Image, 2015).

[50] The twelve texts examined were Colin E. Gunton (ed.), *The Cambridge Companion to Christian Doctrine* (Cambridge: Cambridge University Press, 1997), Rosemary R. Ruether, *Introducing Redemption in Christian Feminism* (Sheffield: Sheffield Academic Press, 1998), Susan Brooks Thistlethwaite and Mary Potter Engel (eds.), *Lift Every Voice: Constructing Theologies from the Underside* (rev. edn, Maryknoll, NY: Orbis, 1998), Stephen T. Davis, Daniel Kendall, SJ, and Gerald O'Collins, SJ (eds.), *The Redemption* (Oxford: Oxford University Press, 2004), Gareth Jones (ed.), *The Blackwell Companion to Modern Theology* (Oxford: Blackwell, 2004), John Webster, Kathryn Tanner, and Iain Torrance (eds.), *The Oxford Handbook of Systematic Theology* (Oxford: Oxford University Press, 2007), Mike Higton, *Christian Doctrine* (London: SCM Press, 2008), Jeff Astley, *SCM Studyguide to Christian Doctrine* (London: SCM Press, 2010), Kelly M. Kapic and Bruce L. McCormack (eds.), *Mapping Modern Theology: A Thematic and Historical Introduction* (Grand Rapids, MI: Baker Academic, 2012), David F. Ford and Mike Higton, with Simeon Zahl (eds.), *The Modern Theologians Reader* (Oxford and Malden, MA: Wiley-Blackwell, 2012), Dwight N. Hopkins, and Edward P. Antonio (eds.), *The Cambridge Companion to Black Theology* (Cambridge: Cambridge University Press, 2012), Chad Meister and James Beilby (eds.), *The Routledge Companion to Modern Christian Thought* (London and New York: Routledge, 2013).

Theology' by Stephen Long. Long picks up Augustine's and Aquinas' references to happiness, the latter's especially; yet the emphasis is clear that happiness 'is not to be confused with pleasure and the absence of pain' but rather is to do with 'holiness and the vision of God'.[51] There is a 'certain degree of happiness' in everyday life, but 'perfect happiness' lies in the future.[52] Long thus echoes the findings of McMahon noted in the previous section. If we are to speak of happiness in theology, we may need to do so at some stage removed from the way it is used in common cultural usage in the West. Holiness is more the goal and, in theologians' eyes, may not primarily, or at all, be about emotional contentment. Attention to happiness may even obstruct spiritual aspirations.

In the most recent of the texts, *The Routledge Companion to Modern Christian Thought*, the references to happiness appear mostly in the section on individual thinkers, namely Kant, Feuerbach, William James, and Nietzsche. The Feuerbach references are the most numerous.[53] This might cause concern on the grounds that a focus on happiness dilutes theology's content and turns theology into anthropology. There are other short references in the section of the book devoted to theological movements, i.e. in the chapters on Pietism, existentialism, and deism.[54] The only explicit, and quite cursory, references to happiness in the 'theological loci' section are in the chapter on eschatology, all three mentions referring to post-mortem existence.[55] Telling also is the fact that the chapter on soteriology by Paul K. Moser is preoccupied with Pauline soteriology.[56] My concern here is not just that it is implied that there was no later theological discussion about salvation, but also that Paul controls the entire New Testament's understanding of salvation. What I am undertaking in

[51]   Stephen Long, 'Moral Theology', in Webster, Tanner, and Torrance (eds.), *The Oxford Handbook of Systematic Theology*, 456–75, here 461.
[52]   Long, 'Moral Theology', 471.
[53]   Douglas Moggach and Widukind De Ridder, 'Ludwig Feuerbach', in Meister and Beilby (eds.), *The Routledge Companion to Modern Christian Thought*, 49, 54, 57–8.
[54]   Meister and Beilby (eds.), *The Routledge Companion to Modern Christian Thought*, 286, 289, 327–8, 334.
[55]   Philip Tallon and Jerry L. Walls, 'Eschatology', in Meister and Beilby (eds.), *The Routledge Companion to Modern Christian Thought*, 440 and 442–3 (a reference to C. S. Lewis and the fact that human freedom provides opportunity to 'forfeit our own happiness' by not choosing to follow God's way, and two references to happiness in heaven).
[56]   Paul K. Moser, 'Soteriology', in Meister and Beilby (eds.), *The Routledge Companion to Modern Christian Thought*, 482–92.

this book is thus as far away from Moser as it gets. Whilst I shall be indebted to biblical images and insights into salvation in Part III of the book, it is vital that (re)source material for salvation comes from elsewhere, both from the history of Christian theological tradition and from other realms of human experience and culture. It is difficult to see how a living theology can remain active and comprehensible to more than those who are already Christian believers if there are no ongoing points of contact with human experience outside the world of faith.[57]

Happiness makes no explicit appearance in *The Modern Theologians Reader*, a 2012 collection of readings grouped according to individual writers, geography, movements, theological sub-disciplines, and links with other religions and disciplines rather than the theological loci of systematic theology. Significantly, however, attention to 'human flourishing' surfaces in the final section of the book. Significant too, and pertinent for the approach taken in Part II here, is the fact that reference to flourishing appears in the chapter on 'Theology and the Visual Arts, Music, and Film', a bold addition to such a collection, the editors recognizing that theological reflection on the arts has not been prominent in modern theology.[58] I detect the emergence of a theological fashion here: a preference for the language of flourishing over any reference to happiness.[59] It will need to be examined in due course why this preference occurs, and what the substance and significance of assumed differences in meaning may be. For the moment we need take note of a slightly different, earlier strand of theological attention to flourishing in Western Christian theology that offers a direct link to discussion about salvation.

In an important essay 'The Gendered Politics of Flourishing and Salvation', Grace Jantzen issued a feminist theological challenge to then current expositions of the meaning of salvation. Noting the

---

[57] Even accepting that once one inhabits a 'faith world', the whole of life is interpreted through that lens, accessibility to such a world has somehow to be experientially possible for others.

[58] Ford, Higton, and Zahl (eds.) *The Modern Theologians Reader*, 425.

[59] And twenty years after the feminist highlighting of the theme. Recent writings by Miroslav Volf are pertinent here: *Flourishing: Why We Need Religion in a Globalized World* (New Haven, CT, and London: Yale University Press 2015) and, with Justin E. Crisp (eds.), *Joy and Human Flourishing: Essays on Theology, Culture and the Good Life* (Minneapolis, MN: Fortress Press 2015). The focus on flourishing also connects with the reassertion (including in theology) of the importance of the virtues, as identified by Aristotle, for the construction of character and the building of communal life.

disappearance of the language of flourishing in the New Testament (in comparison with the language of the Hebrew prophets), she acknowledged the persistence of notions of fullness and abundance, though considered that despite these lingering motifs, post-Reformation Christian theology succeeded in stifling such imagery. She summarizes her thesis thus:

the concept of salvation has been developed in a manner which marches in lock step with the social and political projects of modernity, from colonialism to capitalism; whereas the concept of flourishing would challenge those projects. Furthermore . . . the emphasis on salvation rather than flourishing discloses and perpetuates the masculinist bias of western theology.[60]

Whether or not Jantzen is wholly accurate in her claims, there are vital insights here for this present study. Her first point serves as a reminder that all doctrinal formulations are meshed with economic and sociopolitical contexts, and salvation is no exception. There can be little doubt that the positive aspects of salvation have been played down in Western discussion. What one is (and needs, desperately, to be) saved *from* has been more important than what one is saved *for*. This may or may not be a male or masculine preoccupation, but Jantzen is right to note the tendency towards the negative. The same explanation could, of course, serve for the relative absence of happiness. Important for our purposes is simply that it would be right, with Jantzen, to argue for an exploration and reassertion of the *positive* dimensions of salvation. Without this adjustment the doctrine becomes distorted in the way it is expounded and thus fails to articulate the route to the abundant life which it seeks to express. Jantzen is not suggesting that the doctrine of salvation is beyond reform, although there are hints to that effect. More especially, she is asking for 'another approach' which tries to 'see how things would be different if, in addition to a theology of salvation, we were to develop a counterbalancing theology of flourishing'.[61] That is what I am seeking to do in this book. I am doing so by means of a reconsideration of the doctrine of salvation itself. Without such an approach, I suggest, we may end up with an inadequate doctrine of flourishing, as well as an impoverished doctrine of salvation.

---

[60] Grace Jantzen, 'The Gendered Politics of Flourishing and Salvation', in Brümmer and Sarot (eds.), *Happiness, Well-being and the Meaning of Life*, 58–75, here 60.

[61] Jantzen, 'Gendered Politics', 61.

Jantzen's feminist theological challenge is a form of liberation theology. There were other works of liberation theology in my sample of texts.[62] A comment is needed as to why it may be that happiness does not feature as such in these works. Jantzen's critique arguably applies here too: the focus on liberation (as another term for salvation) prevents the positive aspects of what it means to be released, delivered, or redeemed from being highlighted. This is not, however, the explanation in this case. Liberation theologies in all their variety *do* emphasize the positive aspects, even whilst providing illuminating insights into what it is that people need saving from, at the same time as challenging individualistic, white, wealthy Western construals of salvation. Happiness does not appear amongst the ways of articulating the positive aspects, perhaps because it sounds too tame a term to describe the exhilaration of being freed from one or more forms of oppression. This observation in turn highlights why liberation theologies easily critique comfortable Western theologies which have lost touch with what it feels like to be 'saved' on multiple levels (economic and social, as well as privately therapeutic). As we shall see in Part II, it is vital to keep in focus the many dimensions of salvation in order to do justice to the multiple aspects of flourishing which need to be highlighted as a fully articulated version of the doctrine is expounded. Whether, on the basis of Part II's exploration, it proves appropriate in Part III to make use of happiness language, thereby connecting with broader, contemporary cultural discourse, remains to be seen.

AN AGENDA IDENTIFIED

This opening chapter has, then, mapped out the terrain within which we are to work, and set the agenda for what needs to be done. Why do Christian theologians not speak much about happiness? We do not yet know and may not find out. At this stage, we simply need to acknowledge that happiness does not appear much in works of theology. It may be because the positive aspects of salvation are not being emphasized. This will need examination and, potentially, some correction. Happiness offers itself as a vibrant cultural contender as a

---

[62] Ruether, Thistlethwaite and Engel, Hopkins and Antonio.

term which might be usable to make sense of that positive dimension. But it will need further scrutiny. Flourishing is a second contender, rapidly coming into more prominent use, in both theology and broader culture.[63]

In the meantime, it is not only theologians who speak of redemption. It is accepted within broader Western culture that negative aspects of human experience have to be addressed and overcome. But how is that to be done? How are terms like redemption—which have theological resonance, yet may not be recognized as such—to be used and what contribution can Christian theology make to that broader cultural discussion? Questions like these become the contours of our inquiry.

Within his history of the concept of happiness, Darrin McMahon notes: 'Steeped as it is in the primary narrative of suffering, the Christian religion may fail to call happiness immediately to mind',[64] and yet 'the promise of happiness lay at the heart of the early Christian message'.[65] In effect, the investigation to follow examines these statements and offers an assessment of whether it is now appropriate or wise to speak of happiness in the same breath as speaking of Christian understandings of salvation. Does 'being saved' make a person happy? Is it even intended to? We shall see.

---

[63] As a further gloss on Jantzen's contribution, Elaine Graham's point is pertinent (Graham, 'The "Virtuous Circle": Religion and the Practices of Happiness', in John Atherton, Elaine Graham, and Ian Steedman (eds.), *The Practices of Happiness: Political Economy, Religion and Wellbeing*, Abingdon and New York: Routledge, 2011, 227):

> *Eudaimonia* is traditionally translated as happiness, although the philosopher Elizabeth Anscombe has preferred the term 'flourishing', a concept that has also recently re-entered moral discourse with the work of Grace Jantzen, who explicitly contrasts it and the worldview it embodies with the language and terminology of 'salvation' (Jantzen 1996). The aim of the 'good life' in virtue terms for Jantzen is not to seek rescue from a fallen and corrupt world, but to promote the values of new life, creativity and justice in ways that propel us towards 'becoming divine' (Jantzen 1998).

[64] McMahon, *The Pursuit of Happiness*, 76.
[65] McMahon, *The Pursuit of Happiness*, 93.

2

Cultural Theology after Tillich

Christian theology works within a broad cultural context. It does not simply speak to itself, for Christians live in a complex world in which their ideas and beliefs constantly become entangled with other world views. Christian theology thus works not only with existing Christian materials. How could it be otherwise? Without interacting with existing non-theological materials, and new material—media comment, artistic productions of all kinds, reflections on social and leisure practices (e.g. sport, tourism), political activity—it could scarcely reshape itself in appropriate ways to be comprehensible for new generations. This is neither a sheer desire for 'relevance' nor an uncritical plundering of what happens to lie to hand. It is an expression of the adaptability or recon-figuration that is required by a tradition to remain accessible. The old hermeneutical rule applies: to say the same thing in a new age, you have to say it differently. Some kind of reworking is inevitable.

The content of Christianity, then, is not and cannot be wholly 'fixed' even if there always needs to be a definable version of Christian faith carried by the Christian tradition. Whether such a definable version counts as an 'essence' of Christianity need not detain us long here.[1] If 'essence' means a generally agreed cross section of what is

---

[1] Stephen Sykes, *The Identity of Christianity* (London: SPCK, 1984) remains an extremely useful study on this question. Of more recent writings, George Newlands, *The Transformative Imagination* (Aldershot and Burlington, VT: Ashgate, 2004) and the contributors to Dwight N. Hopkins and Sheila Greeve Davaney (eds.), *Changing Conversations: Religious Reflection and Cultural Analysis* (New York and London: Routledge, 1996) differ as to whether there is an essence to Christianity, though all are committed to the full risk of Christianity's engagement with the multiple cultures in which it finds itself. Hopkins's statement that 'there exists no metanarrative or static foundation in theology's changing conversations' sets the tone for the Hopkins and Davaney collection (20), and Davaney emphasizes that '(h)istorical traditions, includ-ing religious ones, have no stable and clearly identifiable essences that remain

believed and to be believed, then there *is* such an essence. If one wants to claim that Christians in the fourth century believed exactly the same things as Christians do in the twenty-first, then there is *not*. Be that as it may, Christian theology always has the responsibility to articulate what is believed on a number of key topics, one of which is salvation. Together with others—God/Trinity, Christ, Holy Spirit, Creation and Human Being, Church and Sacraments, Eschatology—the collection of explorations of these doctrinal themes constitute a systematic theology, a roughly ordered coherent statement of all of the convictions and ideas which make up the belief which supports Christian practice.

But such a bald statement of Christian theology's task needs more theoretical underpinning lest such a stance may be regarded as too accommodationist, insufficiently accountable to the church, or, at the opposite pole, still rather too traditional. Despite Gorringe's claim that 'those who argue that "the age of systematic theologies is over" are surely wrong', is not even the listing of theological themes of systematic theology rather old-fashioned?[2]

To address the question of method, I build first on a summary article on 'Cultural Theory' by Kathryn Tanner to spell out the shape and direction of my approach to cultural theology. I then dig deeper into what it is now possible and necessary for a cultural theology to achieve with prompts from three contemporary theologians: David Klemm, Trevor Hart, and George Newlands. Finally, in dialogue with that quintessential of twentieth-century theologians of culture, Paul Tillich, I acknowledge and explore the limitations of Tillich's approach in moving 'beyond correlationism' to a position more apposite for postmodern times. My methodological position respects and makes use of cultural materials which may not be of Christian origin or explicitly Christian intent, yet which nevertheless contribute to Christian thinking, thereby paving the way for the concrete work undertaken in Part II. The critically dialogical approach will also show how attending to the *already existing interplay* between Christian

unchanging over time' (35), although Fulkerson can still speak of 'the core Christian narrative and grammar' (47). Newlands would seem to agree with the general position of *Changing Conversations*, though he refers to 'the values of the kingdom' (*The Transformative Imagination*, 12), a 'core' which is 'non-negotiable' (34), and 'the values of the Kingdom of God . . . [which] are non-negotiable'. (94). The question of Christianity's essence (or lack of) thus remains live.

[2] Timothy J. Gorringe, *Furthering Humanity: A Theology of Culture* (Aldershot and Burlington, VT: Ashgate, 2004), 263.

materials and broader cultural material demonstrates how constructive Christian theology (as cultural theology) works anyway.

In the most recent of a number of works exploring how Christian theology is to be understood *as* a culture, Kathryn Tanner writes: 'A Christian culture is formed through the reworking of borrowed materials; it is the culture of others made odd.'[3] In this summary of a position worked out across two decades, Tanner is here arguing for recognition of the complex assertiveness with which Christian theology has to claw out its material from within a wide range of available resources. Though it works with its own tradition, it never simply repeats what has been said before as if the content of theology could be isolated from culture. But nor does it have nothing specific to say. Otherwise there would be nothing identifiably Christian about Christian theology at all. What it must do, therefore, in continuity with what has been recognizably Christian in the past is to sift, select, interrogate, and shape available materials from contemporary culture. It must do this honestly, transparently, and in a manner true to the materials it uses. But in so doing, and in not simply offering interpretations of its own material—Scripture and texts generated through official ecclesiastical sources, for example—it launches into the public sphere theological readings of freely available material ('texts' in the widest sense of the term).

All theology is thus cultural theology. God-talk in all of its forms— claims to speak *from* God, *for* God, or *about* God—is culturally specific and is contained within particular linguistic frameworks. In being undertaken in relation to cultural products of all kinds, theology's cultural specificity becomes very apparent. Yet all theology is encultured, and always has been. In recognizing that it works out its content not just in relation to the specifically religious resources from the past which are linked to the Church, theology accepts that it interacts constantly with cultural products which it does not directly control and yet in relation to which the meanings of its leading concepts are continually being reworked. Such cultural products are of varying quality, aesthetically speaking. But theology cannot make quality tests on what does or can function theologically. The practical means by which theology is 'carried' in culture, within and outside

[3] Kathryn Tanner, 'Cultural Theory', in John Webster, Kathryn Tanner, and Iain Torrance (eds.), *The Oxford Handbook of Systematic Theology* (Oxford: Oxford University Press, 2007), 527–42, here 539.

identifiably religious communities, means that it relates to a wide variety of materials.

Theology does not simply speak to itself. Christian doctrine is not simply the articulation of religious insights or beliefs from *within* the Church *for* the Church. In order to maintain a claim to truth, theology has to be a public discipline. Theology does not serve, or glean from, only the 'best' of the arts or from broader cultural life. As its concepts are carried across culture, then all places where theology appears are grist to the theological mill.

Theology's content is to be popular without being populist. Criteria for discernment will need to be presented throughout this study as to why particular resources, and not others, are engaged with. Even when it is acknowledged that Christian theology has to range widely and not either simply repeat an 'official version' of the faith or attend only to forms of high culture in looking for its source material more broadly, it is neither simply a cross section of what ordinary Christian believers believe, in any particular time or place, nor a distillation of what is most prevalent, fashionable, or dominant. It is right and proper that theology pay more attention to what so-called 'ordinary Christians' actually believe.[4] It is appropriate too that popular culture be attended to much more than has often been the case in theology. As a critical discipline, however, theology must be critically evaluative throughout, making clear at every turn the basis on which evaluative judgements are being made.

In her succinct statement of how theology works, Tanner indicates how Christian theology creates a space to have a public voice both within and beyond the Church. If it is to speak within the Church, then it has to make clear how it works with tradition. If it is to do

---

[4] A point emphasized by a range of liberation theologies, noted by Kathryn Tanner in 'Theology and Popular Culture', in Dwight N. Hopkins and Sheila Greeve Davaney (eds.), *Changing Conversations: Religious Reflection and Cultural Analysis* (New York and London: Routledge, 1996), 101–20, and put to good effect in the writings of Jeff Astley, Ann Christie and others in their explorations of 'Ordinary Theology'. See, for example, Jeff Astley, *Ordinary Theology: Looking, Listening and Learning in Theology* (Aldershot: Ashgate, 2002), Ann Christie and Jeff Astley, 'Ordinary Soteriology: A Qualitative Study', in Leslie J. Francis, Mandy Robbins and Jeff Astley (eds.), *Empirical Theology in Texts and Tables: Qualitative, Quantitative and Comparative Perspectives* (Leiden: Brill, 2009), 177–96, Ann Christie, *Ordinary Christology* (Farnham and Burlington, VT: Ashgate, 2012) and Jeff Astley and Leslie J. Francis (eds.), *Exploring Ordinary Theology: Everyday Christian Believing and the Church* (Farnham and Burlington, VT: Ashgate, 2013).

more than this, then it will also be interacting with materials from wider culture. Tanner further remarks: 'The distinctiveness of a Christian culture is not so much formed by a cultural boundary as at it.'[5] What is it, though, that goes on at the boundaries? To address that question, we shall eventually seek the help of that quintessential 'theologian of the boundaries', Paul Tillich (1886–1965). First, though, we listen further to three other voices.

TURNING TOWARDS TILLICH: THREE VOICES

In a helpful summary of where a 'theology of culture' does its best work, David Klemm states:

> Traditionally speaking, theology of culture has been the theological subdiscipline which aims at identifying, analysing, and interpreting religious meaning in the various domains of socio-cultural life: science, art, literature, politics, economics, education, law, etc. Theology of culture can be done in many ways, but in every case its strength is in working up a set of categories for interpreting the religious or theological meanings expressed within the various domains of human culture.[6]

Klemm's approach notes the element of *extraction* in the activity. A cultural theology (in his terms 'a theology of culture') is always looking for 'religious or theological meanings expressed within' forms of cultural life. There is truth in this approach, although care is needed to avoid an 'implicit religion' approach to cultural products, as if theological content is simply 'there' to be rooted out. There will be times when legitimate theological dialogue will be engaged in with respect to cultural products when it is not possible to claim that religious or theological meanings are explicitly contained *within* what is being considered. Theological reflection and construction may still be legitimate, but they occur *between* the product and the interpreter. We shall dig further shortly to explore how this occurs. For the moment, Klemm is reminding us that there must be something 'in' whatever artistic or cultural product being interpreted which merits

---

[5] Tanner, 'Cultural Theory', 537.
[6] David E. Klemm, 'Introduction: Theology of Culture as Theological Humanism', *Literature & Theology* 18 (2004), 239–50, here 239.

theological engagement. Not anything will do. Our conversation with Tillich will help us greatly on this point.[7]

Trevor Hart adds a word of caution to such an approach, however. Being concerned about culture and theology dovetailing too neatly, Hart remarks:

> we may . . . allow our own self-diagnostic skills (or those of our culture) to tell us the best and the worst about ourselves, decide what measures must be prescribed to deal with the situation, and then seek suitable biblical terms in which to dress this up as a version of the Christian gospel . . . Whenever the story which the church tells appears to dovetail neatly and without wrinkles with the stories which human beings like to tell about themselves and their destiny, it is likely that the church is cutting the cloth of its gospel to fit the pattern laid down by the *Zeitgeist* [spirit of the age] rather than the *heilige Geist* [Holy Spirit].[8]

Hart's words were not written specifically with cultural theology in mind. They appear in a chapter on 'redemption'. But Hart accepts that the grasping of a contemporary Christian understanding of redemption entails not simply repeating what Christians have said in the past. If a contemporary version of the doctrine is to connect with society today, then more is needed than simply clarifying the context in which the theologian works. 'How is "redemption" language going in any sense to be comprehensible in the West today?' is the question beneath his chapter.

Hart acknowledges that there is a cultural element to the theological task: in what forms is the topic of salvation/redemption going to be raised within Western culture? He is, however, more cautious than Klemm in not expecting too much of 'religious or theological meanings' that might reside within cultural products, which may nevertheless 'tell us the best and the worst about ourselves' and suggest 'what measures must be prescribed to deal with the situation'. The reason becomes clear: we might too easily conclude that current analytical prescriptions of the human condition (and theological corollaries that may suggest themselves) can simply be wrapped up

---

[7] It should also be noted that Klemm and William Schweiker's approach to the task of a theology of culture in *Religion and the Human Future* does qualify too heavy an emphasis on the element of 'extraction'.

[8] Trevor Hart, 'Redemption and Fall', in Colin E. Gunton (ed.), *The Cambridge Companion to Christian Doctrine* (Cambridge: Cambridge University Press, 1997), 189–206, here 191.

in biblical language and stamped with a theological label. They may, however, prove to be no more than the current wisdom of the age. Theology's critical edge (a word from the past or a Word from beyond) may be lost and go unheard. If, then, theology creates no friction between its own content and the cultural product with which it is engaged, there may be something amiss. Thus, though theology's interaction with contemporary culture may indeed be valuable (and here Hart agrees with Klemm), how the appropriate critical distance and Christian assertiveness are to be maintained is going to need some teasing out.

Finally, George Newlands adds a note of realism. Cultural theology demands a lot of work and its agenda could simply be vast. In the Internet age this is especially so. Newlands writes:

> If we were to imagine a comprehensive, full-scale intercultural theology, this would be encyclopaedic in scale, would be constantly upgraded and would occupy a research institute... Clearly such a project cannot easily be realized... it is entirely possible to engage with intercultural dialogue in relation to a limited field.[9]

If, then, a theologian's task is not merely to revisit known authoritative texts or resources but to scour the overwhelming range of available materials through which Western citizens now do their meaning-making, then the task is enormous.[10] It involves sifting, admittedly, but how much to engage even when doing the sifting? Is the theologian now to examine blogs, fan sites, watch more TV, go to a wider range of musical concerts than before, and attend more closely to web postings of all political parties?

Newlands speaks of 'intercultural' theology. His vision is wide-ranging. His approach commends global, cross-cultural, politically engaged theology, as well as recognizing that the media and cultural resources with which theology must work have expanded hugely. In my own case, I cast the net wide. But I accept that I fall short of Newlands's vision in my own selectiveness. Though I shall not ignore culture in its widest sense, my project is very much a Western undertaking. I am seeking to address the question of how Christian theology

---

[9] George Newlands, *The Transformative Imagination: Rethinking Intercultural Theology* (Aldershot and Burlington, VT: Ashgate, 2004), 165.
[10] Vaughan S. Roberts and I have made a contribution in this regard with respect to popular music in *Personal Jesus: How Popular Music Shapes Our Souls* (Grand Rapids, MI: Baker Academic, 2013).

takes shape in Western society, in a context where Christianity has declined in its public influence and where many other media, works of art and culture, and social practices have come into play in the task of meaning-making than the previously dominant Christian Scriptures and doctrinal statements. Religion has far from disappeared, and Christianity remains explicitly within the mix of what Western citizens encounter merely by virtue of living in the West. But such engagement does not deliver an easily identifiable, coherent theological message.

Hence, Newlands's recognition that 'it is entirely possible to engage with intercultural dialogue in relation to a limited field' is apposite. The intercultural element of my own investigation is identification of and engagement with forms of the aspirations and concepts which we saw emerging in Chapter 1 (redemption, happiness, flourishing) as these become apparent in a variety of forms. What, in short, is being made of 'salvation' and all that may pertain to it across the multiple cultural contexts within which a Western citizen is living today? As Newlands sees, the task is vast enough, and I shall need to explain myself in Part II as to why I have chosen my selected cases. What, though, will I be doing with what I choose? That is where Tillich is able to help.

LESSONS FROM TILLICH ON RELIGION AND THE ARTS

Tillich was one of the relatively few Christian systematic theologians in the twentieth century to engage extensively, in theoretical and practical terms, with the arts.[11] Though his reputation waxed at the

---

[11] His main challenger is Hans Urs von Balthasar, whose multivolume *The Glory of the Lord* is perhaps the most important work in theological aesthetics to have been published in the twentieth century. Its usability for theological method has, however, been challenged by Karen Kilby in *A (Very) Critical Introduction to Balthasar* (Grand Rapids, MI: Eerdmans, 2012), whose views have in turn received a vigorous riposte from the von Balthasar scholar D. C. Schindler, 'A Very Critical Response to Karen Kilby: On Failing to See the Form', *Radical Orthodoxy: Theology, Philosophy, Politics*, 3.1 (September 2015), 68–87. Specialist works on the arts by theologians have been appearing in great numbers since the last quarter of the last century from writers such as Aidan Nichols, Frank Burch Brown, David Brown, Richard Viladesau, Jeremy Begbie, William Dyrness, and Graham Howes.

start of the second half of the century, it waned in the final decades in part through questions about Tillich the man (his personal ethics) but also through changing fashions in theological method and outlook.[12] Despite Tillich's early association with dialectical theology and his role in influencing the Frankfurt School, and the potential for sharp cultural critique which came with those associations, for Christian theology in the latter half of the century, his work was often viewed as simply too accepting of the culture in which it was undertaken. His theology could be deemed a form of liberal accommodationism at a time when the limitations of liberal over-optimism were being exposed, and fresh turns (liberation theologies of varying kinds, on the one hand, and Barthian Neo-Orthodoxy, Post-Liberalism, Radical Orthodoxy, on the other) were felt to be needed.

Nevertheless, his body of work remains a valuable resource for any cultural theology. In the remainder of this chapter I shall work towards a position beyond the correlational approach to theology which Tillich espoused, whilst expressing appreciation for the conceptuality his approach made available. In adopting terms of which Tillich made use in his appreciation of, and response to, the visual arts, and in adapting them for a broader purpose, like Russell Re Manning I shall argue for the value of fashioning a contemporary cultural theology in both continuity and critical dialogue with Tillich. Unlike Re Manning I shall place greater emphasis on the limitations of Tillich's execution of his own approach to cultural theology. I shall show that to implement Tillich's approach more consistently than Tillich himself, and to do so creatively and innovatively in the present in Western culture, requires the theologian to be more culturally adept (using a wider range of resources) than has been the case in the past and less prone to assume a false unity behind the potential theological content or import of cultural products under scrutiny.

It is first necessary to become clear about Tillich's contribution to understanding and responding to art/the arts theologically.[13]

---

[12] Donald MacKinnon's essay 'Tillich, Frege, Kittel: Some Reflections on a Dark Theme' proved especially influential (in *Explorations in Theology 5*, London: SCM Press, 1979, 129–37).

[13] Key primary texts are gathered in Paul Tillich, *On Art and Architecture* (ed. John and Jane Dillenberger) (New York: Crossroad, 1989). The full text of Tillich's 1919 essay 'On the Idea of a Theology of Culture' can be found in two different English translations: in Mark Kline Taylor (ed.), *Paul Tillich: Theologian of the Boundaries* (London: Collins, 1987), 35–54 and in Victor Nuovo, *Visionary Science: A Translation of Tillich's 'On the*

To condense his approach to the visual arts in as succinct a manner as possible we must note the importance of three key terms for Tillich: form (*Form* in German), content (*Inhalt*) and 'depth-content' (*Gehalt*).[14] With respect to fine art or literature, it could be said that the content of a work is what it is (superficially) 'about', whereas its depth-content is what it is 'really about'.[15] Its form is more the means by which the self-presentation of a work (its content) achieves the communication or transmission of its depth-content.

This is admittedly to oversimplify, for to talk of art about 'really being about' something different from what a work presents itself as (its *Inhalt*) is to be in danger of committing the cardinal sin of all Protestant interpretation of creative human work: human creativity is dispensed with, and what matters is what is perceived through and beyond the human work, and is recognized as such in the form of words, i.e. as an interpretation of the work of art in question. This would, however, be to misrepresent Tillich. Even though his concern to identify depth, and ultimate concern, in and through works of art was paramount, he sought also to respect the form in which revelation of depth occurred. Furthermore, his exploration of different artistic 'styles' (which he called naturalistic, idealistic, and expressionistic— though not always in keeping with the way in which art critics and historians used the terms) enabled him to make assessments of the relative revelatory potential of different artistic movements.[16]

Idea of a Theology of Culture' with an Interpretive Essay (Detroit, MI: Wayne State University Press, 1987), 19–39. In my work on Tillich's theology I am indebted to Russell Re Manning's exploration in *Theology at the End of Culture: Paul Tillich's Theology of Culture and Art* (Leuven: Peeters, 2005). For readers new to Tillich, a compressed summary of his approach can be found in Richard Viladesau, 'Engagement with the Arts', in Mike Higton and Jim Fodor (eds.), *The Routledge Companion to the Practice of Christian Theology* (London and New York: Routledge, 2015), 404–21, esp. 414–17.

[14] There are various translations offered of *'Gehalt'* ('import', 'substance', and 'depth-content' are all possible). Here I begin by using that suggested by the Dillenbergers ('depth-content'; *On Art and Architecture*, 51), though I shall move beyond it shortly. Both W. B. Green (translator of the version found in Taylor, *Paul Tillich*) and Nuovo offer 'substance' (*Paul Tillich*, 52, *Visionary Science*, 37), though the latter also refers to 'metaphysical content', which Re Manning regards as misleading (*Theology at the End of Culture*, 117 n. 39).

[15] Re Manning, *Theology at the End of Culture*, 117 n. 39.

[16] Tillich favoured expressionism as a primary form of visual art for theological disclosure, and his use of expressionism has major weaknesses. For discussion, see Re Manning, *Theology at the End of Culture*, 148–52 and also Russell Re Manning,

To adopt, adapt, and broaden Tillich's approach to art is, however, both possible and desirable when it comes to looking at how Christian theology is now to engage with culture in more diverse forms than with the high arts alone. Despite having this theoretical framework for looking at the arts—one which should have enabled him to make use of it with respect to a great many other art forms (music, popular cinema, and even television; he did engage with art film to some degree)—Tillich did not have much time for popular culture.[17] Influenced as he was by the Frankfurt School, like Theodor Adorno in his critical assessment of popular music it was difficult for Tillich to be convinced that any mass-produced or populist form of culture or entertainment might prove valuable.

We, by contrast, must. In widening the reach of the potential cultural forms in relation to which theological engagement may take place, it is possible to make use of Tillich's theoretical approach. Theological insight may emerge from consideration of the form of, say, a TV comedy which is 'about' a parks and recreation depart-ment, a mobile army hospital, a group of university friends, or a bunch of flatmates. The depth-content, the *Gehalt*, of the engagement could, however, in principle be as profound as Tillich's recognition of the theological value of a domestic scene by the Dutch painter of peasant life Jan Steen.[18]

Even allowing for the fact that Tillich is limited in the range of cultural resources which he is willing to consider as having theo-logical potential, his position sounds close to that of David Klemm. The *Gehalt* of a cultural product could be regarded as the religious or theological meaning expressed within a work of art or popular culture. I do not, however, think this is quite the case, which is why the greater open-endedness of Tillich's approach proves especially useful.

'Tillich's theology of art', in Russell Re Manning (ed.), *The Cambridge Companion to Paul Tillich* (Cambridge: Cambridge University Press, 2009), 152–72, here 166–9.

[17] For Tillich on popular culture, see especially Kelton Cobb, 'Reconsidering the Status of Popular Culture in Tillich's Theology of Culture', *Journal of the American Academy of Religion* 53 (1995), 53–85; see also Kelton Cobb, *The Blackwell Guide to Theology and Popular Culture* (Malden, MA, and Oxford: Blackwell, 2005), 90–105; Jonathan Brant, *Paul Tillich and the Possibility of Revelation through Film* (Oxford: Oxford University Press, 2012), 83–95.

[18] Tillich, *On Art and Architecture*, 33.

Building upon Tillich's theological approach to art, the methodological claim I am making is that if we are to take seriously the presence and activity of a lively, creative, future-oriented God within the midst of the human realm (the consequence of a commitment both to incarnation and to the presence of God's life-giving Spirit in the world), then we cannot constrain God's presence, or our perception of that presence, to specific practices or aesthetic or social locations. God is not to be discerned, for example, outside identifiable religion only within the forms of art which broader culture has identified as especially aesthetically pleasing.[19] Tillich would have accepted the first statement (no constraints). I am not sure he worked through to the second (even poor art might be revelatory).[20] Adapting Tillich's approach, then, it becomes possible to identify the *Gehalt* of any cultural project as the *theological trajectory* which any work can be shown to contain. In terms of our present enquiry, we shall be asking of any work under scrutiny whether and how it may contribute to Christian notions of salvation, via its views of how human frailty and wickedness are to be handled, and human flourishing enabled.

Identifying, expounding, and exploring the *Gehalt* (depth-content, substance, or import understood as theological trajectory) of any cultural product being interpreted is, therefore, not simply a matter of *extraction*. As a trajectory, it is vital to clarify where the *Gehalt* is heading. In the case of this present inquiry—an exploration of the Christian doctrine of salvation—it will be necessary to explore what sense of a future way of living is being implied, whether or not such an understanding is directly contained within the cultural product being examined. A TV series may, for example, not be explicitly 'about' religion at all, let alone 'salvation', and yet may be exploring guilt, wickedness, evil, fear, repentance, remorse, forgiveness, justice, reconciliation, and mercy in a range of ways. Theological discussion may latch onto such readily available cultural material as a point of connection. There may be no explicitly articulated theological 'point' to the TV material. A cultural-theological approach to the material may, however, produce a fresh range of insights for future

---

[19] And God may, of course, not be able to be discerned within some forms of identifiable religion.

[20] Though note Tillich's remark in his 1919 essay that 'a theology of culture... carries out a general religious analysis of all [*sic*!] cultural creations' (Nuovo, *Visionary Science*, 27). Whilst wholly unrealistic, its intent is welcome. It could be argued that he did not carry through the implications of his own insight at this point.

thought, belief, and action which are not simply to be identified either with existing Christian belief in any straightforward sense or with what the TV series may be taken to 'say'. A meaning (one of many possible meanings) thus results from the interaction between the series as a 'text', the theological interpreter as one who brings theological materials to bear on the series, and the interaction which happens between the interpreter and the text, in the light of broader cultural discussion about the series and the theological tradition within which the interpreter sits.[21]

Methodologically speaking, we can say that all such theological interaction with culture is shaped in the light of what it is believed it is being done *for*. As we shall see in Chapter 7, the framework of being saved 'from, for, by, and into' will prove decisive in this present study as the optimum 'shape' of soteriology. Insights of a number of theologians prove pertinent here. If a cultural theology accepts that what it will articulate is not already wholly contained within what it is interpreting, then questions of criteria and procedure arise. What exactly is a cultural theology looking for? And how will it know when it finds it? If it is not simply repeating or recasting religious ideas of the past, then what steers or determines the future-orientated ideas and convictions it will express? There is an inevitable element of circularity here.

Two theological concepts stand out as being helpful to enable a cultural theology to do its work creatively: kingdom of God and gospel. In the work of Wolfhart Pannenberg and Tim Gorringe these concepts have been put to particularly effective use. Pannenberg spoke of doing theology 'from the future' on the basis of what he saw to be the centrality of the concept of the kingdom of God, and the role of anticipation, for the work of the Christian theologian.[22] Because we have but glimpsed the kingdom of God, and it is not fully realized in this world, though we can see to some extent what God has in store for the world, our task includes recognizing the incompleteness of our words and work, and the partiality of our vision. This is methodologically of profound significance. There remains, as we saw with the

---

[21] This applies, for example, to the work on *Breaking Bad* offered in this present study (Chapter 4). It is not a theological text in an explicit sense, and yet is a profoundly engaging and widely watched contemporary study of human wickedness, presented as occurring in the midst of normal (US) domestic life. It invites theological attention in ways which Chapter 4 will explore.

[22] To cite just one of many examples: Wolfhart Pannenberg, *Theology and the Kingdom of God* (Philadelphia, PA: The Westminster Press, 1969).

ambiguities in Newlands's position, a key question as to what the content of the anticipated kingdom of God is to be (Just what are 'kingdom ethics'? What social forms should human beings be constructing now in the light of the coming kingdom?). Methodologically, eschatological reticence must result. Too much cannot be claimed for the present content of Christian theology or the present forms of Christian practice. Substantively, the kingdom of God must shape what theology looks for.

Discerning the *Gehalt* in any cultural product (including even sacred religious texts) means undertaking a forward-looking task. It is not a task of extraction of fully developed meaning under a theological lens, but an act of discernment, with a view to articulating a practical theological insight which lies in front of the 'text' being interpreted, and also in front of the speaker doing the interpreting. It is appropriate to be reminded that the kingdom of God is 'already but not yet' and that the kingdom of God is not ours to create. Here we see how these convictions take effect in terms of theological method: the conceptuality of the kingdom of God has to be made use of in reminding all theological interpreters of the limitations of their conclusions. That said, the content of the kingdom of God (the *Gehalt* of that concept!) is brought to bear in seeking to determine the *Gehalt* of what is being interpreted: how does what is being interpreted (religious text, painting, piece of music, TV programme) help us better discern and fashion human action in anticipating the kingdom of God which is yet to be? And how does our glimpse, hunch, or vision of what that kingdom of God is—the context in which God reigns—shape what we are articulating as a theological insight or statement? These are the key questions which drive theological hermeneutics.

The second concept which can be used in a similar way to configure methodologically a contemporary cultural theology is that of 'gospel'. Just as the kingdom of God can be seen as the 'eschatological proviso' of all theology, for no church, no social group, no culture can be said to equate to the kingdom of God, so also all human cultures and communities fall short of the gospel, even those which seek to embody it. As Tim Gorringe notes, it is within the framework of sin and redemption that this tension between what could be the case and what is the case is to be understood.[23] The gospel too, then, is worked

---

[23] Gorringe, *Furthering Humanity*, 19.

out within this framework. Yet for the notion of 'gospel' to be effective there has to be some content to it. If assumed to mean 'that which God wills' or 'what God will bring about' (even when viewed as 'that which extends the work of Jesus'), it could still remain rather vague and abstract if not given some more concrete definition. What is more, the gospel must be transcendent of all particular cultural contexts, even whilst capable of being embodied, potentially and partially, within any. To cite Gorringe:

> if we could not identify a coherent cross cultural gospel then the claim that Christianity stood at the heart of the long revolution of humanization would fall to the ground. What, then, is the gospel?... A 'gospel' promises or announces salvation, and we have seen that this includes fundamental aspects of justice between races, classes and between men and women, and also the fulfilment of fundamental human needs.[24]

Gorringe is surely right here. And the consequences of his insight are far-reaching.

These two concepts—kingdom of God and gospel—function, then, both substantively and methodologically to remind cultural theologians to tread cautiously as they do their work. The concepts inform what they are looking for as they 'read' the authoritative materials of their religious tradition, and as they comb the plethora of cultural materials available in an effort to articulate clearly the content of a cultural theology. Christian theologians will always have their Bible, creeds, and a selection of authoritative texts from their own specific denomination in one hand, and—replacing Barth's proverbial newspaper—will now have a notebook/laptop in the other. The task, however, is contemporary and future-oriented: what is to be said about God now, in the light of what has gone before, bearing in mind all that is around us, in a way which enables people to participate in and move towards God's intended future? That, in short, is the primary question being addressed by all (cultural) theology.

BEYOND CORRELATION

Indebted as we are to Tillich, we have moved beyond his method of correlation. Picking up on liberation theology's critique of Tillich,

---

[24] Gorringe, *Furthering Humanity*, 210.

and echoing the findings of Re Manning's thorough and insightful exposition and discussion of Tillich's work, I agree that the most pertinent aspects of Tillich's work are his earlier writings: his initial more self-consciously sociopolitically and economically aware forays into a theology of culture. Even if Míguez Bonino's critique of Tillich is not wholly accurate, the gist of his charge—that Tillich left economic, societal concerns behind in shifting to internal, psychological interests— has some validity.[25] Furthermore, though Re Manning's judgement that Tillich's 1919 essay 'On the Idea of a Theology of Culture' may be regarded as 'perhaps Tillich's most important piece of writing' may be slightly hyperbolic, it was certainly fundamentally significant for the shaping of Tillich's approach, and has proved valuable for others since, this present study included.[26]

By the time of writing his *Systematic Theology*, however, Tillich had moved (1951–63) to framing his work much more in terms of the question–answer form of correlational apologetics. His approach should not be oversimplified.[27] Though apologetic in form and keen to engage with a wide range of other academic and cultural inter-locutors, his three-volume work was a sustained attempt to construct a philosophically coherent theological system. It was less a Christian dogmatics and more a philosophical cultural theology, though with less emphasis on the cultural-theological aspect in the terms which now need to be explored in this present book. The correlational method presented in the first volume of the work did, though, soften somewhat the more open-ended possibilities implied in the method-ology espoused in 1919 and in his ensuing writings on theology and the arts. In sidestepping the correlational method, we are better placed to let Tillich's earlier, more raw methodology take fuller effect. Seeking the *Gehalt* which may serve the task of clarifying the meaning of the kingdom of God and the gospel, the *Gehalt*, which lies

---

[25] José Míguez Bonino, 'Reading Tillich in Latin America: From Religious Social-ism to the Exile', in Raymond F. Bulman and Frederick J. Parrella (eds.), *Religion in the New Millennium: Theology in the Spirit of Paul Tillich* (Macon, GA: Mercer University Press, 2001), 19–33. Tillich, being European, can scarcely be chided for being deeply affected by his life-shaping experience in Europe, and if he did shift from economics more to psychological concerns as time went on, he nevertheless remained consistent in his interest in the interplay between religion and culture.

[26] Re Manning, *Theology*, 8 n. 8.

[27] John P. Clayton, *The Concept of Correlation: Paul Tillich and the Possibility of a Mediating Theology* (Berlin: De Gruyter, 1980) remains the most thorough study.

partially within and partially in front of any particular concrete forms of culture, may actually prove a more risky undertaking than the correlational method permits. But that is where I am suggesting we need to head, methodologically, in Parts II and III of this book.[28] This approach is similar to the 'Theological Humanism' of which David Klemm and William Schweiker speak in their 2008 volume, *Religion and the Human Future: An Essay in Theological Humanism.*[29] For one thing, whilst being respectful of individual religious traditions and of the Christian tradition from which both Klemm and Schweiker come, they see their task as moving beyond individual traditions in their search for a broader, but still theological humanism. God is bound within and by no individual tradition (which would be 'hypertheism') and yet is vital for the sake of human well-being. Second, Klemm and Schweiker emphasize that 'both anti-humanism and post-theism grasp insights that are important for theological humanism'.[30] In other words (to switch to the Tillich-inspired terms I am using), the *Gehalt* which grasps hold of glimpses of the kingdom of God or the gospel—sought from a dialogue with any product of human culture and seeking to capture that which lies between the object being interpreted and the vision of a humanity yet to be—may derive from anything which humans produce, and come from anywhere. Not only religious resources count. That is not to say that all human productions are equally fruitful for producing kingdom of God or gospel insights. It does mean that no prior judgements can be made as to what will

---

[28] In proposing this way forward I hope to have addressed adequately the accurate and helpful questions posed by Elaine Graham, Heather Walton, and Frances Ward to all such attempts to 'speak of God in public', including Tillich's correlational method and David Tracy's continuation of that in his revisionist approach (*Theological Reflection: Methods*, London: SCM Press, 2005, 154–61, and esp. 167–8). Interestingly, in their follow-up volume (*Theological Reflection: Sources*, London: SCM Press, 2007) my own earlier work is referenced within the chapters on 'Speaking of God in Public' and 'Theology in the Vernacular' (302, 411). This is tellingly accurate. The juxtaposition of those two locations accurately reflects what I am seeking to do here: develop the critical correlational approach well beyond Tillich and Tracy, though not only by attending to what ordinary believers believe. The way in which ordinary citizens—believers included—make meaning has to be acknowledged, and it is in this way that the resource material for theology is expanded and in relation to which appropriate criteria for theological use have to be devised.
[29] David E. Klemm and William Schweiker, *Religion and the Human Future: An Essay in Theological Humanism* (Malden, MA, and Oxford: Wiley-Blackwell, 2008). Schweiker's chapter, 'Theology of culture and its future', in Re Manning, *The Cambridge Companion to Paul Tillich*, 138–51 is also important here.
[30] Klemm and Schweiker, *Religion and the Human Future*, 16.

produce such insights. For example, it is not necessarily the case that an interpretation of fine art, whether it has religious subject matter [*Inhalt*] or not, has a greater chance of being a medium of disclosing or creating a divine *Gehalt* than a dialogue with a TV series.[31]

A third area of common ground is the recognition that attention to theological humanism does not inevitably mean a focus only on human beings, or that humans have it within their power to save either humanity or the earth as a whole. Humanism as Klemm and Schweiker understand it is about respect for humanity as a whole, within a concern for 'the integrity of life'.[32]

Despite these common features and the broad appreciation I wish to express for Klemm and Schweiker's proposals, I do have a number of reservations. First, despite the point just made about transcendence, I am not convinced that the concept of 'integrity of life', so central to the Klemm/Schweiker project, can sustain the important ambiguity of the term 'transcendence'. Retention of a strong sense of 'otherness' is vital to prevent the development of the 'religious narcissism' which Klemm and Schweiker recognize that Christian or theological humanism might become.[33]

Second, despite the openness to many contributors to the theological humanism they seek, their position is insufficiently attentive to the potentially radical diversity of cultural resources which may be engaged with in order to discern what such humanism should be like. It is strong on qualifying Christian exclusivism. It is strong too on challenging anthropocentrism as it seeks to do justice to the whole created order. It remains weak, however, in the potential range of cultural resources which could inform their project. Their humanism feels a little too middle-class and comfortable.

Nevertheless, both my own approach and that of Klemm and Schweiker's theological humanism together stress the open-ended nature of the exploration which all of us recognize has to occur as theology undertakes its work within and in relation to the broader culture(s) of which it is a part. The result is that it is more possible to be true to Tillich's aspiration to undertake 'a general religious

[31] Klemm and Schweiker, *Religion and the Human Future*, 64.
[32] References to transcendence, for example, have to accept the ambiguity of the term but do potentially take us beyond what we know in this life alone. Transcendence may not only be 'lateral' (Klemm and Schweiker, *Religion and the Human Future*, 36).
[33] Klemm and Schweiker, *Religion and the Human Future*, 60.

analysis of all cultural creations' than Tillich himself was able.[34] Added to this, a cultural theology can also be more respectful of and attentive to human experience in all its diversity and social and political complexity. In this way, cultural theology can address the reservations expressed by Míguez Bonino about Tillich's theology, and develop a revised cultural theology above and beyond the charges of liberationists whilst taking into account their justifiable concerns.

'CULTURAL THEOLOGY' REDEFINED

We are now in a position to define the form that the cultural-theological method to be followed in Parts II and III of this book will take. In presenting a list of summary statements about what cultural theology is *not*, and what it *is*, I am both recapping on the material from this chapter and drawing out further implications of what has been said. I am also setting the scene and providing a rationale for detailed explorations of specific cultural resources and movements pertinent to our inquiry which comprise Chapters 3–6.

What cultural theology is *not*:

- *A simple distillation of features of culture which cohere with an already existing theology*

Cultural resources and movements to be examined in Part II do not simply become hooks on which to hang a compendium of theological convictions which have no need of the four chapters' worth of material. If this were so, then they would be but illustrative of a doctrine of salvation drawn up wholly on other grounds. An understanding of salvation will admittedly not simply emerge from the cultural resources and movements to be examined. Our critical examination is for a purpose ('How does this resource contribute to a better understanding of the kingdom of God and the Christian gospel?'). But what is brought *about* the doctrine of salvation *to* the materials has to be considered incomplete for present needs. There is enough to go on, but the critical dialogical process enables God to reveal more as the *Gehalt* (substantive theological trajectory) resulting from the dialogue is disclosed through the interpretative act.

- *A compilation of what is deemed, culturally, to be the 'best of what is believed and thought'*

A cultural theology's job is not to deal only with what a society considers most aesthetically pleasing, most morally uplifting, or most culturally refined. In the UK scene such an approach is often associated with the work of Victorian literary scholar Matthew Arnold.[35] Arnold could not have had a concept of popular culture anything like today's definition.[36] He lived prior to the onset of mass culture, and might have valued 'folk culture', though been critical of 'pub culture'. As a champion of 'high culture', however, Arnold's basic intention was educational and moral (and thus also political). In essence his central question was: how are we to behave better and create better human structures, and how does the culture we consume facilitate that? It is logical that he saw the aesthetically best as being more likely to be more educational and more morally effective. In the present we are less convinced, knowing that all manner of cultural resources can be educationally useful. The same applies for their theological value too. To say that not all materials are of equal value is not the same as saying that only those deemed of the 'best' value (however that is defined) are theologically useful or important. As we shall see in Chapters 3 and 4, this confusion has been a major cause of the reservations about popular culture as a valuable theological resource, and of the implicit—sometimes explicit—favouritism towards that deemed especially aesthetically significant ('high culture').

- *A summary of what happen to be the most dominant features in a society*

Cultural theology is also not interested in simply trying to distil from contemporary culture all of its leading ideas or dominant theories and calling them 'theology'. There is a sense in which those things which a

---

[35] Matthew Arnold, 'Culture and Anarchy: An Essay in Political and Social Criticism', in *Culture and Anarchy and Other Writings* (Cambridge: Cambridge University Press, 1993), 53–187 (first published 1867).

[36] I am grateful to Richard Gill for helping me see this, and thus encouraging me to work on its implications.

culture emphasizes function as its 'gods'.[37] It is important to discern
these lest they fail to cohere with, and actively obstruct, what it may be
wise and therefore advisable to commend as beliefs, ideas, and actions.
But mere compilation of such a list is far from a culture's 'theology' in
any other sense than the identification of what is most publicly apparent. For theology to be allied too quickly with such dominant emphases
would indeed be to make the fateful step of marrying the 'spirit of
the age'.[38]

• *A ventriloquist's theology*

The notion of theological ventriloquism comes from Gerard Loughlin.[39]
It is a helpful image, though a little harsh, as any form of dialogical
theology has to make the attempt to work out what a 'text' being
interpreted is trying to say. And if the writer, painter, poet, director is
dead, or unwilling to say, what she or he 'meant', then the interpreter
has to step in. In fact, the interpreter has to step in anyway, for as we
know well in postmodern times, authors, painters, and directors do
not control the potentially multiple meanings of their works. Interpreters have to speak on others' behalf in order to do their work. Ventriloquism, though, suggests deception, not just entertainment. And here
Loughlin has a point. In the task of undertaking creative cultural
theology, it is essential that theologians do not pass off their own
work as if it is someone else speaking. The charge of ventriloquism is
justified when I begin to imply that 'this is what Luther said' when it can
be shown by others that I am merely voicing what I would like him to
have said. The critical debate amongst interpreters, acknowledging the
contexts out of which critics speak and the assumptions and ideological
worlds within which they work, is vital. Appropriate caution and

[37] As Luther suggested, 'Whatever it is that makes a man do something, that
motive is his god' ('A Sermon on the Three Kinds of Good Life for the Instruction
of Consciences', cited in Klemm and Schweiker, *Religion and the Human Future*, 71).
Similarly, as Tillich recognized, the identification of what drives a person indicates
their 'ultimate concern'. Both could be held to apply to cultures or societies as well as
individuals. Hence, capitalism may be seen as the god of the West. McMahon notes
'happiness' as a further contender (see Chapter 1, p. 21 n. 44).
[38] And thus, in the overused but still pithy and memorable quip from Dean
William Ralph Inge, 'will find himself a widower in the next'. I have been unable to
locate the original source of this well-known quotation.
[39] Gerard Loughlin, 'Cinéma Divinité: A Theological Introduction', in Eric
S. Christianson, Peter Francis, and William R. Telford (eds.), *Cinéma Divinité:
Religion, Theology and the Bible in Film* (London: SCM Press, 2005), 1–12, here 3.

critique are needed. This applies especially in a theology which seeks to engage actively with non-theological resources.

• *A 'generally theological' theology*

Finally, it is important to be realistic and humble about what is achievable. Lack of confidence can sometimes be mistaken for humility. Equally, overconfidence can seem supercilious as well as ending up claiming too much. Theology seeks to speak of God and, at its best, tries to speak from and for God, though it cannot ever guarantee to do so. And as all theology is particular, then it speaks out of specific contexts and traditions, even whilst seeking to speak of (from, and for) God. The notion of a 'generally theological' theology is therefore misplaced, even if it is understandable why such an aspiration informs the theological task. 'Theological theologies' take two forms at present: those that seek to rise above the particularities of specific religious traditions and those that accept the specificity of the traditions out of which they emerge and yet assert themselves forcefully. Klemm and Schweiker's theological humanism arguably features amongst the former, alongside attempts to speak of a theology of religions.[40] Examples of the latter include forms of critical Barthianism—such as the writings of John Webster—or the 'outnarration' practised by John Milbank and others influenced by the Radical Orthodoxy movement.[41]

What cultural theology *is*:

• *A religiously specific (in this case, Christian) theology*

As the cultural theology I am proposing is not a 'generally theological' theology, I have to accept the specificity of its Christianness. Whilst

---

[40] This may also apply to endeavours in the field of 'comparative theology' such as the work of Keith Ward, Francis Clooney, SJ, and Michelle Voss Roberts, though Ward's work does remain identifiably Christian even as it draws on insights from other religious traditions.

[41] Significantly, the Festschrift for John Webster is entitled *Theological Theology* (ed. R. David Nelson, Darren Sarisky, and Justin Stratis, London and New York: Bloomsbury T&T Clark, 2015). Milbank's initial presentation of his basic position appeared in *Theology and Social Theory: Beyond Secular Reason* (Oxford and Cambridge, MA: Blackwell, 1990). His position has been very influential and finds echoes in discussions about evangelism where outnarration becomes an assertive declaration of the Christian story, though not necessarily in verbal form. The church may lay claim, in a sometimes dangerous way, to embody Christian faith in order to prove it is 'better' than all other stories (see, for example, Ross Hastings, *Missional God, Missional Church: Hope for Re-Evangelizing the West*, Downers Grove, IL: IVP Academic, 2012, 81).

occupying a position between the Christian, ecclesial community and the many and diverse cultural resources which can potentially contribute to contemporary theological thinking, I am nevertheless making explicit, focused use of Christian resources as I do my work. I may, of course, have to accept that I am 'privileging' Christianity here. But I do so not because I think Christian theology is the only possible version of what can be done with religiously informed meaning-making in the West, but because it is the tradition I know best and which has made the dominant religious contribution to the culture in which I live. Christianity needs careful and constructive critical scrutiny but it also challenges the cultures in which it sits.

* *A communicative theology*

I adopt a term here from Matthias Scharer and Bernd Jochen Hilberath, without also adopting the full theological method that they propose.[42] I use their term to signify that a cultural theology has an internal, communal component. Rather than denoting the presence of an ecclesiastical element in the sense that a theology is officially authorized and carried by a church, and its constituent congregations, the notion of communicative theology recognizes the concrete communal ways, formal and informal, in which Christians converse and reflect on their faith, in the light of, and with reference to, the multiple non-ecclesial contexts in which they live and work. Formal structures for enabling such potentially rich conversations to happen within churches are all too rare. House groups are less common than in the past and church lectures, seminars, workshops, and conferences do not appeal to all, having their own kind of culture. It also has to be acknowledged that virtual communities have begun to appear which enable theological reflection to occur online in many fresh ways. Scharer and Hilberath's approach by contrast presses the significance of embodied encounter.[43] To recognize that a cultural theology is a communicative theology is to acknowledge the hard work of conversation—in multiple registers, across social, ethnic, economic, and political boundaries *within* the church—as Christians open up and reflect together on

---

[42] Matthias Scharer and Bernd Jochen Hilberath, *The Practice of Communicative Theology: An Introduction to a New Theological Culture* (New York: Continuum, 2008).

[43] A cultural theology is also a 'practical theology'. I cannot at this point raise the further range of theoretical questions or concerns which arise as a result of noting this. My point is simply that the ecclesial dimension of any Christian theology cannot be lost and that it must relate to actual lived experience of Christians.

what faith means, how the world shapes faith and how their worlds are shaped by faith. Scharer and Hilberath express it starkly: 'theology is not "some thing" that then is to be communicated; rather, *communication* is the central content of theology'.[44] Communication within the church is reflection on the response of God's self-communication to and within the world. Conversation cannot, however, be only about something defined as particularly Christian experience. It has also to be about experience in the whole of life. As such it is conversation about participation in culture in the widest sense.

- *A broad, dialogical theology*

With apologies to Gerard Loughlin, and accepting the risks of the charge of ventriloquism, the cultural theology I am developing is unashamedly dialogical. Accepting that there is no art or culture 'in its own right' and that works of art, media, and popular culture do not simply 'speak for themselves', it is still necessary to do some sustained listening rather than impose Christian meanings onto, or offer Christian verdicts about, the cultural products being interpreted. This does not happen in a vacuum, and hence the dialogue process is fraught with difficulty. That said, allowing for the complexity of what it means to interpret and to discern or construct meaning in the 'in-between' space between a text and a receiver, it is vital to 'let a "text" speak' and to let it ask a question of what believers believe and why. Similarly, it is reasonable, essential even, to allow one's own convictions to be brought openly into play in the interpretative process. Honesty in handling the dialogue is essential, as are the communal contexts (ecclesial, academic) in which such dialogue occurs. This heading embodies the intercultural theology for which George Newlands argued.[45]

- *A critical theology*

A cultural theology is critical in two senses: *analytical*, in that it analyses a product of culture through a theological lens, and a theological insight

---

[44] Scharer and Hilberath, *The Practice of Communicative Theology*, 13.

[45] It is also the specific heading under which the approach to theology and culture suggested in my chapter 'Film and Theologies of Culture' should be understood (in Clive Marsh and Gaye Ortiz, *Explorations in Theology and Film*, Oxford: Blackwell, 1997, 21–34, esp. 27–32). In many ways, twenty years on, this present work implements in practice the theological method implied there, as applied to a single theological theme and using a wider range of cultural resources.

in the light of what is received from the product of culture; *evaluative*, in that it seeks to assess the adequacy of the results of either analysis in the service of human flourishing. To put it another way, the search for the *Gehalt* of any cultural product, religious or otherwise, is a critical undertaking which is constantly asking: how does the result of this particular interpretative task facilitate a form of belief, thought, or action which will contribute to an understanding and impending embodiment of that which Christians call, but do not own, and do not themselves yet fully grasp: 'the kingdom of God'?

- *An eschatologically oriented theology*

As already noted with respect to the input of Pannenberg and Newlands, a cultural theology has to be eschatological in two senses: awaiting the kingdom of God, which is not wholly here but only partially glimpsed and embodied, and methodologically reticent in not claiming too much for either its conclusions or the adequacy of its approach. This heading can be summarized in terms of cultural theology being methodologically cautious and substantively patient.

- *A Gospel-focused theology*

Though caution is needed and incompleteness has to be acknow-ledged, there is nevertheless good news to be celebrated here. Reference to the Gospel is the Christian way of characterizing the possibility of human flourishing before God. An adequate cultural theology is there-fore always seeking to glean from whatever sources and resources with which it engages all that describes and promotes human flourishing. Whether or not, with respect to the doctrine of salvation, this will be best done through attention to the dynamics of salvation and be expressed positively in terms of happiness has yet to be seen. A cultural theology can, however, only be *theology*, as opposed merely to the study or philosophy of culture, by being Gospel-focused.

- *A politically and ethically responsible theology*

Graham, Walton, and Ward identify as one of the weaknesses of much theology constructed in the correlationist and revisionist tra-ditions a tendency to address 'existential dilemmas rather than pol-itical concerns'.[46] They are right to be worried about this. Liberal

---

[46] Graham, Walton, and Ward, *Theological Reflection: Methods*, 168. Ruether is considered exempt from this charge, being one of the few revisionists to provide a

forms of correlationism do indeed often 'retreat into forms of personal, cognitive belief'.[47] It will be for readers to decide after reading Part II of this work whether the same charge applies to this present endeavour. A broader resource base does not of itself secure a more sociopolitically engaged or economically aware approach to a cultural theology, but it will undoubtedly help. To put it differently: the more theology looks beyond high-culture resources in the way it engages with non-ecclesial culture, the more likely it is to attend to the issues which arise in daily life for a wider range of citizens. There is still the question of what is then done theologically *with* what is encountered. Graham, Walton, and Ward may still be right that 'personal, cognitive' concerns remain the sole or primary focus. By including Chapter 6 in my investigation, and by linking the inquiry conducted there with what will have gone before, however, I believe I will have addressed the weakness identified. It is indisputable that a cultural theology is bound up with social, economic, material, and political factors.[48] These are not merely *consequences* which flow from prior inquiry into belief; social, economic, material, and political factors are wrapped up with belief from the start. But nor is belief to be reduced to such factors. If theology and faith are to shape factors like these, then it must also be possible to define a cultural theology capable of connecting with such daily concerns and of influencing daily living in a way which serves human flourishing.

Our task, then, from here on is to get at the content of an appropriate understanding of salvation which negotiates its way through the (allegedly) secular construals, suggestions, glimpses, hints, articulations of human frailty, corruption, depravity, and evil, as well as human creativity, self-transcendence, and flourishing.[49] In Christian understanding, this will never be simply a bartering process of human voices arguing rationally, or semi-rationally, in some supposedly

---

bridge to the more liberationist method which the authors consider necessary to correct liberal correlationism.

[47] Graham, Walton, and Ward, *Theological Reflection: Methods*, 168.

[48] In addition to writings by a wide variety of liberation theologians, I have been greatly helped by James R. Cochrane, 'Salvation and the Reconstruction of Society', in Vincent Brümmer and Marcel Sarot (eds.), *Happiness, Well-Being and the Meaning of Life* (Kampen: Kok Pharos, 1996), 76–98.

[49] I say 'allegedly' merely to indicate that at least *some* of what we shall explore in Part II is entangled with (the rich history of Western) religious thought, even if it may not appear to be at first.

neutral space over the meaning of words and actions. If God has reality, then the embodied Holy Spirit of God is in the mix. But neither in this book nor beyond will it be possible to *prove* that this is the case. There can be no guarantee in an academic book like this that God is truly spoken *for*. We may only be speaking *about* God. In such a book as this we have to accept that we remain at the level of narrative and discourse, arguing about terms and concepts and whether these do or not assist us in the search to enhance human flourishing. But it is an argument, I contend, that it is vital to have and is of crucial importance not only for those who say they believe.

Part II

Salvation within Western Culture

3

Salvation in Art and Music

The two works chosen to open this second part of the book, Grünewald's Isenheim altarpiece and Handel's *Messiah*, carry a broad cultural-aesthetic role. They are examples of lasting art which are appreciated as such by many people, religious or not, the former constituting also a major tourist site, the latter regarded a 'popular classic'. That this is so makes them suitable to be considered from the perspective of their aesthetic merit and function. The goal of the chapter is to assess each work's theological *Gehalt*: its potential to offer a trajectory for human flourishing which takes into account how each work 'works', and how it may contribute to a contemporary Christian understanding of salvation.[1]

MATTHIAS GRÜNEWALD: THE ISENHEIM ALTARPIECE

My first example of 'salvation articulated' dates from the early sixteenth century. It can be seen in its original form at the Musée Unterlinden, in Colmar, north-east France, though may be known and viewed by many readers in the form of a printed or on-screen reproduction.[2] Though not now located in a context similar to the

---

[1] For the full exploration of '*Gehalt*' I am working with here, I refer the reader back to Chapter 2. For those who may have skipped Chapter 2, it can mean 'import', 'substance', or 'depth-content'. I am also using it to denote the 'theological trajectory' of any cultural product, whether or not any explicit theological meaning may have been intended originally.

[2] Visible online, for example, at www.wga.hu/html_m/g/grunewal/2isenhei/1view/, accessed 7 January 2016.

hospital chapel for which it was painted—it is now viewed in a gallery, as a piece of fine art—at least the circumstances of its original location and likely purpose are known.[3] I use the altarpiece as one of my cases because of its known artistic merit, lasting impact as art, and proven influence in the history of Western Christian thought and practice. The altarpiece continues to be considered by art historians as a masterpiece of Western art.[4] It receives extensive coverage from scholars of religion and theology who explore the interface between theology and art.[5] It features prominently even in the work of theologians who are less sanguine about the value of art for theology.[6] As a work of classic religious art, then, engaged with by religious and non-religious viewers alike, it is a helpful case study for exploring how the theme of salvation takes shape in relation to a work of beauty.

Art for a Hospital

The nine paintings which make up the altarpiece were painted at some time between 1510 and 1515.[7] They constitute the major life's work of Matthias Grünewald, whose real name was probably Mathis

---

[3] That said, much of the Musée Unterlinden's collection is housed in a former convent, and the Isenheim altar panels are, in fact, on display in the former chapel of the convent. Hence, even in its gallery setting, a concerted effort has been made, five centuries on, to put the work 'in context' as much as possible.

[4] Arthur Burkhard, *Matthias Grünewald: Personality and Accomplishment* (New York: Hacker Art Books, 1976; first published, 1936); J.-K. Huysmans, 'Two Essays on Grünewald', in *Grünewald: The Paintings* (London: The Phaidon Press, 1958), 7–25; Pantxika Béguerie-De Paepe and Magali Haas, *The Isenheim Altarpiece: The Masterpiece of the Musée Unterlinden* (Colmar: Musée Unterlinden and Paris: Artlys, 2015).

[5] Grünewald is, for example, considered in many of the now standard treatments of Christian theology and the arts, such as John Dillenberger, *A Theology of Artistic Sensibilities: The Visual Arts and the Church* (London: SCM Press, 1987), Richard Viladesau, *Theological Aesthetics: God in Imagination, Beauty, and Art* (Oxford and New York: Oxford University Press, 1999), Frank Burch Brown, *Good Taste, Bad Taste, and Christian Taste: Aesthetics in Religious Life* (Oxford: Oxford University Press, 2000), and Patrick Sherry, *Images of Redemption: Art, Literature and Salvation* (London and New York: T&T Clark, 2003).

[6] The obvious example here is Karl Barth, whose fifty-one references to the work are studied in detail by Reiner Marquard, *Karl Barth und der Isenheimer Altar* (Stuttgart: Calwer Verlag, 1995), 23–64.

[7] Key texts in exploring the original setting for the panels are Andrée Hayum, *The Isenheim Altarpiece: God's Medicine and the Painter's Vision* (Princeton, NJ: Princeton University Press, 1989) and Béguerie-De Paepe and Haas, *The Isenheim Altarpiece*.

Gothart,[8] the entirety of whose surviving *oeuvre* is devoted to religious subjects. The panels are prefigured by earlier, similar work of his, and influenced later work. This is especially true of the crucifixion panel, there being three other similar paintings still extant.[9] It appears he was a devout Christian, probably with Protestant convictions (Lutheran materials being found in his surviving possessions after his death), whose major work stands as a 'Catholic Monument at the Threshold of the Reformation'.[10] Countless academic articles and many scholarly books have been written on the Isenheim altarpiece alone. My purpose here is not to offer anything new by way of art-historical exposition, but simply to say enough about what the panels portray to make them comprehensible, and then to ask the 'so what?' theological question about how they are, and are to be, understood, received, and used today.

The nine panels were painted to be used in different combinations ('states') on the altar of the hospital chapel at Isenheim in north-east France, with folding wings able to produce the different states.[11] Commissioned by the Order of St. Anthony, the panels present a graphic visual portrayal of a Christian understanding of the drama of salvation, supplemented by paintings of relevant saints (in this case, Anthony—three times, Sebastian, and Paul the Hermit). Five main panels present a version of the Christian story of salvation, comprising Annunciation, Madonna and Child and Incarnation, Crucifixion, Lamentation, and Resurrection. Crucifixion and Lamentation are visible when the altarpiece is in its closed state, and the others (running from Annunciation through to Resurrection) as a triptych in its second, open, state. In short, it is a sixteenth-century equivalent of a Jesus film, though painted for a highly specific context and with a precise purpose, and inevitably constrained in its impact—until the age of visual reproductive technology—to very local viewing, even when moved elsewhere.[12]

---

[8] Burkhard, *Matthias Grünewald*, 5, confirmed in Béguerie-De Paepe and Haas, *The Isenheim Altarpiece*, 22–9.

[9] Viewable in Basle, Washington, and Karlsruhe.

[10] Hayum, *The Isenheim Altarpiece*, 53–88.

[11] 'Chapel' is in some ways misleading, as it may, in present context, imply 'small building (or even room) within large complex'. We need, instead, to imagine the scale of a church building within a monastery, bearing in mind that the order running the monastery was devoted to care of the sick. It may be a more a case of the 'chapel' functioning as a significant part of the 'monastery as hospital'.

[12] The story of the panels' movements is told in Béguerie-De Paepe and Haas, *The Isenheim Altarpiece*, 50–1.

As the work was to be used in a hospital setting, it is important to grasp how this may itself have influenced the artist's vision and intent, and even what may have been commissioned from him.[13] The lifeless body of the crucified Jesus is gangrenous, accentuating, theologically speaking, the extent to which God in the person of Christ identifies with humankind. The Incarnation, though portrayed in the form of an image of Mary and the child Jesus as a separate panel, is recognized to extend through and beyond the cross within the full drama of the story of Christ. The graphic nature of the crucifixion portrayal, however, makes it clear that the horror of disease as an aspect of human life must be faced. Indeed, the artist recognizes that many of the intended viewers of the painting would be suffering from ergotism.[14] In the care of the monks, patients facing inevitable death from the disease would see in the figure of Jesus one who suffered as they were suffering.[15]

Placing the awfulness of crucifixion within the broader Christian understanding of the drama of salvation, however, locates the suffering at a point in a continuum. Resurrection remains a hope for the diseased. Whatever understanding may have been held as to a potential relationship between sin and suffering, all human beings stood in need of redemption, and the patients in the Antonine monastery would feel this keenly. The cry for salvation was thus very real: a cry of freedom

[13] This is the focus of Hayum's study. See esp. ch.1.

[14] It is usually assumed that the twisted, bloated, gangrenous figure on the bottom of the Temptation of Saint Anthony panel is a portrayal of a typical sufferer of ergotism. Ergotism is 'a toxic condition produced by eating grain, grain products (as rye bread), or grasses infected with ergot fungus or by chronic excessive use of an ergot drug' (www.merriam-webster.com/dictionary/ergotism, accessed 28 December 2017).' It was also called 'St. Anthony's Fire' because of 'the burning sensations resulting in gangrene of limbs' (J. Battin, 'Saint Anthony's Fire or gangrenous ergotism and its medieval iconography' (in French), *Histoire des Sciences Médicales* 44 (2010), 373–82, cited (in English) in www.ncbi.nlm.nih.gov/pubmed/21598563, accessed 28 December 2017).

[15] It is intriguing that in both the current museum audio guide to the paintings and the accompanying book (Béguerie-De Paepe and Haas, *The Isenheim Altarpiece*) emphasis is placed on the fact that viewers would be led to think that however much they were suffering, Christ had suffered *more*. ('Such an image could only enjoin the sick to communion with the Saviour by reminding them that their own suffering was negligible compared with that endured by Christ,' Béguerie-De Paepe and Haas, *The Isenheim Altarpiece*, 61). This may or may not be so, and cannot be confirmed. I doubt, though, that either artist or monks would have thought that the patients' or pilgrims' suffering was 'negligible'. Even so, no comparison of levels of suffering need be assumed. The theological point is that Christ suffered *with* and *for* those who looked at the painting.

from suffering, a freedom looked for beyond this present life, the monks having no medical remedy for ergotism. Prayer for healing would have been offered. But for the most part, Grünewald had painted an altarpiece designed to assist the monks in their task of palliative care.

A 'Theology of Hope'

What notion of salvation is such a work of art offering (both when originally painted, and now)? At its most basic we can simply receive Grünewald's as one of many thousands of works across the history of world art which portray the Christian story visually. If, though, such a work is to function in any way other than an illustration (or prompt) for a verbal or propositional belief, then we need to ask how the work functions aesthetically as well as cognitively. Reiner Marquard's wrestling with Karl Barth's engagement with Grünewald is telling at this point. Marquard knows that Barth is reluctant to attribute too much theological value to the work's intrinsic artistic merit. As beautiful and artistically magnificent as it may be, the work cannot become for Barth a direct source of revelation or a resource for natural theology. Hence, Barth's references to the work frequently emphasize the elongated pointing finger of John the Baptist in Grünewald's crucifixion panel. It is not the art which matters, but rather the one whom the art points towards.[16]

That said, the art is so accomplished, and the form of the visual story so compelling, that more is being offered theologically than Barth can control. Barth may have his reservations, but—exasperating though it is for word-based theologians—a stark, if sometimes elusive Gospel of salvation is being presented in the Isenheim panels. Its content is generally clear (it is the Christian story of salvation); its form is that of a series of works of art which fit into the rhythm of the liturgical year and are (literally) shaped to be used in an ecclesiastical setting. But what is the *Gehalt* of these panels? What are they drawing the viewer towards?

If we were to stay with the crucifixion scene, then, visually speaking, there is little hope. As interpreters rightly note, it is vital to see the

---

[16] On Barth's particular resistance to Christ portrayals, rather than a hostility to art itself, see Marquard, *Karl Barth und der Isenheimer Altar*, 76–96. Thirty-one of the fifty-one references to the altarpiece in Barth's work include reference to John the Baptist, his facial expression, his foot, or—more prominently—his pointing finger (Marquard, 64).

Isenheim altar panels *as a whole*, so that Grünewald's imaginative, brightly coloured, pictorial vision of the Resurrection receives its due weight. It is the full range of the panels which makes the altarpiece, despite the gruesomeness of the crucifixion, a theology of hope. The resurrection hope can only be imaginatively portrayed. Its possibility lies only as an action of God. But 'if God can raise this Jesus, this putrefied body, then there is hope' is the *Gehalt* of these panels.

The gruesomeness of the crucifixion deserves special comment. Art historians have accentuated the point that the horror presented goes beyond all other versions of the crucifixion painted by Grünewald himself:

> the marks from the brutal blows that caused His death are portrayed with realistic and even repellent detail on the dead body. Broken bits of wood still stick in the flesh, blood drips from the wounds, the hands are convulsively cramped, the feet frightfully deformed, the parched yellow skin beginning to take on a greyish-green hue . . . The dread splendor of the presentation is incomparable; Grünewald himself nowhere else approached it, either in the earlier *Crucifixion* at Basle . . . or in the later one at Karlsruhe.[17]

Artistically speaking, the technical brilliance of Grünewald's work forces us to linger, to be stunned by, and to reflect on what he has painted and to feel the full force of the horror of the crucifixion even whilst receiving and interpreting it, as viewers, within a set of images. Engaging with the sheer horror of this portrayal of the crucifixion occurs on two levels. First, the awfulness of crucifixion cannot be dodged. Theologically, the self-giving and self-emptying of God was that extreme. Whatever complexities result from the conviction that 'God was in Christ reconciling the world to himself' (II Cor. 5.19), the pain was that real. God suffered. Visual art expresses this insight in a way in which word-centred theologies have often avoided.

At a second level, given the commission and context of the artwork in its original location, the awfulness of the situation of the viewers is being acknowledged, and thus being taken account of theologically. To be stark: the shittiness of life as being experienced by the sufferers of ergotism has to be addressed by any claim to offer a theology of

---

[17] Burkhard, *Matthias Grünewald*, 28–9. Huysmans may be prone to hyperbole, but he is also clearly wanting to make a point: 'no painter has ever gone so far in the representation of putrefaction, nor does any medical textbook contain a more frightening illustration of skin disease' (19).

salvation.[18] Most of the pilgrims and patients will have ended up at the Isenheim monastery in a state of dire suffering because they ate contaminated food. Even if, in Grünewald's day, there was a belief in a closer link between human conduct and illness than there would be today—and disease thus more easily assumed to be a consequence of sin—we cannot escape our own knowledge (of our own situation and of that of the Isenheim patients): sometimes a dire human situation, even when explicable, cannot be avoided. Suffering is inevitable. Death is, too, but premature death may become inevitable as well. Any doctrine of salvation has to face such a stark reality, not through any glib notion that 'there is always someone worse off than you'—a strategy used in everyday Christianity to enable a person to face their suffering or, more problematically, to accept their suffering without protest. When we recall the original context, in responding to the art now, we are to remember the scale of the horror contained within the drama of salvation. The crucifixion panel enables the viewer to confront the fact that life experience really may be dire, even if interpreted in the light of, and towards a Christian hope of, resurrection.

There is, then, a theology of hope here in Grünewald's work. We now need to explore further how that theology is presented, with respect to the process of work's reception.

Saving Beauty

How does Grünewald's art work *as art*? How might it be said to *save* as art? Two aspects of the work—its artistic brilliance and its Christian subject matter—are inseparable.[19] The bright colours of the

[18] This is true whether or not the original viewers may have engaged with the work in these terms. I acknowledge I take a risk in being so linguistically blunt in an academic text, but I think it is necessary. I am here introducing a theme which will run through this present work, as it is an expression which a great many have voiced to me in recent years, along the lines of 'Does Christianity really help people deal with the shittiness of life?' (implication: it does not). If I were not to face this in an attempt to speak of salvation today, especially with respect to happiness, then I, too, would be dodging the awfulness of what Grünewald presents here and with which he appears to be grappling, both as an expression(istic portrayal) of the crucifixion itself and as a means to acknowledge the level of undeserved suffering of those who would view his work at Isenheim.

[19] Even its 'brilliance' is two-layered: the technical quality of the work and the shining colours (of the *Resurrection* panel in particular) become the focal point of the work as a whole, despite the awful intensity of the *Crucifixion*.

resurrection panel are prompted by the Christian story portrayed. Yet the work may still be appreciated and responded to as art, in its colourful brilliance, whatever the theological or philosophical convictions of the viewer. One could, for example, have no particular sense of transcendence external to human experience and nevertheless find the work as a whole uplifting and hopeful. But why call such a response in any sense 'redemptive' or believe that it has anything to do with 'salvation'? Why not call it 'uplifting' and be done with it?

I suggest that we persist with the language of salvation not only in order to be true to Grünewald's work as theology but also in order to explore how his art is working. It is not only the subject matter which invites the viewer to interpret the work salvifically. The aesthetic quality of the work and the nature of the aesthetic-affective reaction invited to it together suggest a framework of response which echoes any theological framework of response to it. In sixteenth-century terms, it would be assumed that a viewer would locate their response within a confessional Christian framework. A viewer (patient or caring monk) would recognize that one was being saved, or would be saved, by God from the horrors of ergotism—or any other disease—or *from* sin, *for* (and in) a resurrected life. Such a life would have to be beyond this present earthly life, no cure for ergotism being available. Grünewald's imaginative vision of the resurrection of Christ would, however, have been seen as real in the sense that the visual portrayal communicated the hoped-for reality of God's recreation of physical life beyond this earth. This would have been as true for the pilgrims in their gangrenous state as it was for the gangrenous, crucified, but then resurrected Christ portrayed before them. The monastery hospital was thus a temporary holding place, an interim community of sufferers and carers, within which those responding to the art could feel that they belonged. There would almost certainly have been no physical release before death.[20] Seeing and responding to Grünewald's art enabled fleeting imaginative escape from the awfulness of their situation whilst allowing them also imaginatively to anticipate that which they believed was to come. His art represented imaginative release (achieving some mental alleviation of physical suffering) or imaginative

---

[20] Soothing treatment appeared to be the most that could be provided, the range of plants painted on the Meeting of Saints Anthony and Paul panel portraying those used in the concoction of a soothing drink given to the sick (Béguerie-De Paepe and Haas, *The Isenheim Altarpiece*, 98).

escape, in enabling some measure of avoidance of pain. Either of these responses could have been accompanied by faith or doubt—whether people might have doubted the existence of any kind of afterlife, whether pain-free or not, is simply not known—but *as art*, Grüne-wald's work at least enabled imaginative detachment and the possibility of glimpsing hope.

How does a comparable response play out in the present? Clearly there is a kind of equivalence for current Christian viewers. No longer bound to a monastery hospital, the panels portray what one desires to be saved from—be it physical suffering, lack of well-being, mental torment, sin. For most the crucifixion portrayal will function metaphor-ically, even though the reality of what one experiences will not be.[21] Many viewers now, Christian or not, will bring experiences of physical or emotional torment to their viewing. Such suffering is real, but Christians among them will be reminded of the belief framework within which they live their lives.

Similarly, the resurrection hope will be real, whatever the means by which Christians of different persuasions relate to Grünewald's imaginative vision, and whatever Christians deem the precise form and content of resurrection life (particularly beyond this life) to be.[22] It is no longer the case that all Christians hold to a straightforward conviction that they will receive a new body, or a resurrected material body, identifiable physically as themselves, beyond this present life. Yet the conviction that God, as the source of life, goes on supporting and giving life even beyond physical death is the substance of resur-rection hope. One is saved *for* resurrection life in some sense. And the anticipation of that ongoing life begins with an awareness of, and participation in, the quality of divine life now.

The *communal* dimension of the work's original context and purpose may, though, be obscured in the response of Christian viewers to the Isenheim panels today. If viewed largely in the form of a reproduction

[21] It should, though, be acknowledged that the panels' portrayal of acute physical suffering (in the figure of Christ and in the gangrenous figure in the St. Anthony panel) may still be identified with by those suffering acute physical pain in the present.
[22] Paul's characterization of the resurrection body and ensuing discussion of the key texts (I Cor 15 in particular) are at issue here. Resurrection and the form it may take can, though, ultimately only be God's business. For treatments of the topic, see Gavin D'Costa (ed.), *Resurrection Reconsidered* (Oxford: Oneworld, 1996) and Stephen Davis, Daniel Kendall SJ, and Gerald O'Collins SJ (eds.), *The Resurrection* (Oxford and New York: Oxford University Press, 1999).

by individual viewers, then clearly much of the significance of the original location will have disappeared. Even if the original is viewed in its current location, the status of the work of art, and its tourism function, can deflect from the communal setting in which it was originally displayed. The sense that resurrection is God's continuing gift of life, potentially for the whole of humanity and all of creation, rather than a hope of mere individual survival, is lost somewhat.

But what of contemporary viewers who profess no Christian faith or have little grasp of the content of such beliefs? Is there an aesthetic response to Isenheim which comes anywhere near to matching the Christian viewing? I referred earlier to an 'aesthetic-affective reaction' to the work. This picks up on insights voiced within art-historical discussion of the altarpiece. Burkhard suggests that Grünewald's works 'appeal almost exclusively to our emotions and very little to our reason' and that his aim 'is not the creation of beauty or the revelation of truth', but 'expression', and that 'to attain it he is willing to resort even to extreme exaggeration'.[23] We can qualify this contention with the observation that Grünewald surely wanted to be more than merely technically proficient and that he has produced a fine work of art even whilst portraying ugliness and decay. We should also counter Burkhard's claim of Grünewald's lack of interest in truth. Grünewald may not have been wholly focused on realism (in the sense of historical truth), but without doubt wanted to be truthful and theologically sensitive in portraying what happened to Jesus in a manner which would also make sense to Grünewald's own contemporaries.

Where Burkhard and others are undoubtedly correct, however, is in noting the importance of Grünewald's bypassing of formal conventions, undermining them by expressionistic means in order to provoke visceral reactions in his viewers. In this respect it is clear how and why Grünewald is seen as a forerunner of twentieth-century expressionism. The possibility of salvation, for Grünewald, has to be *felt*: what one is saved *from* and *for* is experienced affectively and does not come solely as the result of cognitive insight, aesthetic appreciation, or even religious knowledge. Hence, in terms of viewers today, unless they have seen and felt, they have not 'understood' Grünewald. Whether this comes from Grünewald himself or from those who

---

[23] Burkhard, *Matthias Grünewald*, 74.

commissioned the work (or both), there is a theological vision being expressed here: theology can be no mere cerebral exercise.[24] Does art, then, save? No clear answer is possible at this stage.[25] Grünewald's work does, though, show how art creates the space within which salvific activity proves possible. Art can be seen to console, to stimulate vision, to evoke transcendence, to distract, to empower the sense of sight. In doing all of these things, the Isenheim altarpiece suggests, too, that art can graphically suggest what one needs saving *from*, and imaginatively indicate what one may be saved *for*—leaving open the question whether this may be in this life or beyond.

Confronting Horror

A reservoir of art-historical literacy could, of course, be drawn upon to 'get' the altarpiece. The more one understands the symbolism, the significance of colour, the detail of the story of salvation, the more one 'appreciates' the panels in terms of the cognitive content contained within them and extractable from them. But, whilst informative, such gathering of insight might distance some viewers, past or present, from what the panels achieve aesthetically and affectively. In the same way that religious faith finds expression and stimulates growth through its creeds, symbols, and practices without there being any need for a believer to acquire a university qualification to understand 'what is really going on', so also art has the capacity to function by *being art*. A work of art may command attention and respect through technical brilliance, provocation, humour, telling location, careful juxtapositions of forms of media. In the case of the Isenheim panels, an affective response is evoked because of both the beauty and brilliance of the art and the drama of its subject matter. Technical mastery and affective impact, supported by a general cultural familiarity with the themes being explored, are key constituent elements in creating the aesthetic milieu within which the panels work.

---

[24] This does not mean that faith is reduced to practice, or theology is reduced to spirituality. Theology still has a cognitive task to do. But it must explicitly relate to how a faith is experienced.

[25] Nor can a conclusive answer be given as a result of all that is presented in this book. Can God save in and through art? Yes, certainly. But extensive theoretical investigation of what part the art plays, and what art achieves this, and how, and why, is not a primary focus of this enquiry.

Whether it is received religiously or aesthetically-affectively (or both), the viewer is drawn into the confrontation with an inevitable human reality (decay and death) and its hoped-for overcoming. For viewers for whom there is nothing beyond this life, the imaginative vision remains that: a vision which may provide uplift, however temporary. The art will still have had a positive impact, even if it may be considered a form of escapism from death's reality.

If we follow through what Grünewald's work achieves, then, we see that in the secular West beauty is offering a salvation of sorts through inviting viewers to consider how it is possible to live humanly in a tough world. It provides in itself aesthetic resources which enable viewers to resist negativity and gloom. These need not be seen as dependent on the content of Christian faith, though the Christian content fills out the basis and nature of that resistance much further. The work invites viewers to imagine how they might confront what they experience, however awful that may be, within a framework of potential hopefulness.

Methodologically speaking, then, and moving beyond this particular work, a contemporary approach to the doctrine of salvation which acknowledges an aesthetic dimension to its task will be open to any work of art which is deemed hopeful or to contain a vision of hope. In continuity with Grünewald's art, works of art which explore and express hope whilst also facing the horror of life will attract particular attention. To continue the theoretical terms used in Chapter 2, such works of art may not have crucifixion and resurrection as their subject matter (*Inhalt*) but may be grasping for a vision of human flourishing as their end goal (*Gehalt*). If so, they will be able to be worked with as theological resources. They may work in the same way that, for example, war poetry and war art function as acts of defiance and hope, even whilst portraying episodes of almost unspeakable brutality.

GEORG FRIEDRICH HANDEL: *MESSIAH*

As 'high art', the Isenheim altarpiece has become, through its place on the tourist trail, an example of almost popular religious art. If true of Grünewald's work, this applies all the more to Handel's *Messiah*. From its mixed reception in its early years to becoming a staple in the repertoire of so many choirs across the world, and a fixture (in full or part performance) at Christmas time, Handel's oratorio is a 'popular classic' which functions as an example of how a quite traditional piece of classical music both holds its own in multiple musical worlds and continues to present in an engaged way a version of the Christian drama of redemption within Western culture.[26] How, though, does it achieve this, and what can be gleaned from the way in which it works, for understanding in the present both the *content* of salvation, as understood Christianly, and how that theological content is now carried and worked out afresh within Western culture?

How *Messiah* Works

> *Messiah* . . . is sufficiently rich and complex to speak to a range of human needs and emotions, irrespective of its immediate Judaeo-Christian framework.
>
> Donald Burrows, *Handel: Messiah*, viii

> [Part Two of *Messiah*] would be incomprehensible to an audience without prior knowledge of the subject.
>
> Ibid., 58

It is over twenty-five years since Donald Burrows published his study of Handel's *Messiah*.[27] Whether he would be able to make such a bold claim as the first statement cited above, despite the fact that it is a work which continues to be performed somewhere in the world every year since its first performance (nearly 280 years, and counting), is now questionable. This is especially the case given the second statement cited above. As general cultural knowledge of Christianity declines, in the West at least, and thus as the 'Christian story of salvation' functions less as a piece of common cultural currency—accessible to believer and unbeliever alike—perhaps Burrows underestimated the level of knowledge needed for the oratorio to 'work' even in his first statement above.

In this section of the chapter, however, I argue that *both* of Burrows's claims remain true. I shall defend Burrows's first statement, whilst qualifying his second. The reason that *Messiah* functions as an ideal (classical music) case study in this book is precisely because Burrows's

---

[26] Calvin R. Stapert's statement is telling: 'since its first performance in Dublin in 1742, there has been no year in which it hasn't been performed', *Handel's Messiah: Comfort for God's People* (Grand Rapids, MI, and Cambridge: Eerdmans, 2010), 53.
[27] Donald Burrows, *Handel: Messiah* (Cambridge: Cambridge University Press, 1991).

first statement still stands. *Messiah* works theologically *as music*. Twenty-five years on, we must accept that much more can be gained for the listener or singer who has 'prior knowledge of the subject'. But the music still works musically, as an uplifting and invigorating experience for listeners with even the most rudimentary familiarity with the background story of redemption. As such, the example of *Messiah* raises questions as to where any uplifting piece of music may leave a listener, and thus what may be possible theologically when reflection on a listening experience enables one to 'work back' from the affective state into which one is brought.

To hear *Messiah* is to be put through a nearly three-hour experience of fluctuating emotions.[28] Allowing for the fact that some kind of practice might be needed to get the hang of what is required to listen to such a work,[29] it is nevertheless possible to distil from the structure and evident impact of *Messiah* the aesthetic-affective purpose and function of the oratorio as an artistic work.[30] My purpose here is not to offer extensive commentary on or analyse the lyrics (libretto) of the work, to assess their truthfulness or legitimacy as biblical interpretation, or to identify from its words alone what its theological intent might be.[31] That has been covered by others.[32] I wish simply to respect the shape of the piece, and to explore that shape in terms of how it works aesthetically and affectively. The words which are 'set to music' are far from irrelevant: they are

[28] I say 'hear' and 'put through', thus accentuating the experience of the listener. I accept that a singer experiences things differently. Whichever way readers have experienced the work, however, I emphasize the role of 'participation' in the musical experience. There is no wholly 'passive' listener.

[29] I resist the terms 'training' or 'education' here. Though such preparation would indeed enhance the listening experience, it cannot be a requirement. It would be intriguing to undertake empirical research amongst a variety of listeners who normally listen to other forms of music experiencing *Messiah* live for the first time, securing their responses and reflections, and undertaking analysis of these.

[30] As in the section on Grünewald, I deem it impossible to speak of aesthetics in isolation from affective response. By speaking of 'aesthetic-affective', however, I am seeking to acknowledge in the first place the artistic quality of what evokes the affective response in the listener, as opposed to a cultural production which merely manipulates, whilst having little technical or artistic value.

[31] Though that it *has* a theological intent need not be in doubt. Whether this is solely or mostly that of the librettist Charles Jennens, who may be making a defence of orthodoxy in the face of deism, need not detail us here (see Stapert, *Handel's Messiah*, 75–8; Burrows, *Messiah*, 58–9).

[32] Stapert, *Handel's Messiah*, and Roger A. Bullard, *Messiah: The Gospel According to Handel's Oratorio* (Grand Rapids, MI: Eerdmans, 1993).

being dramatized, and the music carries and interprets them. But it is *as music* that Handel's contribution has its impact upon the listener, and through which the words are received. If Burrows is right, then the musical shape should enable the work to function emotionally despite the religious background of listeners. It will function salvifically for the listener at least in some way through its aesthetic shape and affective impact independently of the words which have led to that musical shape being constructed.

Messiah enables the listener to encounter the Christian story of redemption musically in a single sitting. It does so by transporting the listener from the anticipation of the Messiah's coming to the celebration of his ultimate triumph in three acts (parts), with sixteen 'scenes' in total. Not being a theatrically staged performance—and hence not supported by visual imagery—the scenes are thus pictures evoked in words and music.

Part I prepares the listener musically for what is to come. An expectant, meditative beginning leads into a declaration of what is ultimately envisaged ('Ev'ry Valley shall be exalted').[33] A jubilant choral anticipation of the fact that 'all Flesh shall see it [the Glory of the Lord] together' closes the first scene. Warnings about how challenging the journey towards this glory will be for humankind are, however, quickly sounded. Threatening sounds denote judgement, matching words about the shaking of both the heavens and the earth, and the purging effect of God's assessment of human activity ('He is like a Refiner's Fire . . . He shall purify the Sons of Levi'). Into this arena of anticipation will enter a salvific figure ('Emmanuel, God with us') who will relate to Jews and Gentiles alike. This Son of God will be light-bearing and carry many significant names ('Wonderful Counsellor . . . Prince of Peace'). The lowly (represented by shepherds) will bear witness to him as the one from amongst the Jews who will nevertheless be for all. The impact of the Messiah's work will be huge ('the Eyes of the Blind [shall] be open'd . . . the Ears of the Deaf unstopped'). In anticipation of this, his followers ('his Flock') can be reassured. They will be able to rest their souls in him. Restful music provides this reassurance within the performance, and the first part concludes with a lightness of touch ('His Yoke is easy, his Burthen is light') to confirm that those who ally themselves with

---

[33] From here on the citations from the libretto are taken from Burrows, *Messiah*, 86–100.

the saving figure will indeed be released from their cares. The contextualization of what is to come, then, is represented musically in terms of warning and reassurance. Things are not as they should be, and there should be concern about this. We should tremble as listeners, but not ultimately be afraid.

Part II forces the listener to eavesdrop on the suffering of the salvific figure, and to endure imaginatively with him, through musical experience, the cost of his carrying the burden which should be borne by others. In looking upon him ('Behold the Lamb of God'), we share in the sadness ('He was despised and rejected . . . He was wounded for our Transgressions'), and yet, despite our 'giddy silliness' ('like Sheep . . . we have turned ev'ry one to his own Way'[34]), are nevertheless healed by or through him ('with His Stripes we are healed'). At the only point in the work where the chorus becomes the voice of the crowd, instead of carrying through the prophetic narrative, the chorus shares in the mocking ('He trusted in God . . . let him deliver him').[35] The suffering figure appears abandoned ('He is full of Heaviness . . . neither found he any to comfort him'), sorrowful in the extreme ('Behold, and see, if there be any Sorrow like unto his Sorrow!'), and dies. As listeners, we share in the mourning. He is, however, resurrected ('Thou didst not leave his Soul in Hell') and ascends to be with God ('Thou art gone up on High'), the message of which has to be sounded across the world ('into all Lands'), a declaration reflected in proclamatory musical sound. Turbulence follows, however. At a point in the oratorio which sounds always contemporary ('Why do the Nations so furiously rage together?'), the opposition of a warring world to the prospect of God's judgement and salvation is embodied musically. The sheer affrontery to God of the vanity of human rulers is real, although the reminder of God's sovereignty will soon follow in the rise and fall of staccato notes reflecting a chopping sound ('thou shalt dash them in pieces like a Potter's Vessel') and then, triumphantly, in the celebration and anticipation of God's eternal reign

---

[34] The helpful phrase 'giddy silliness' is from Bullard, *Messiah*, 82, accurately capturing the mood of Handel's music at this point.

[35] I owe this observation to Bullard, *Messiah*, 87. Though it is true that 'the audience is not, unlike the congregation of Bach's Passions, implicated in the denial of Christ' (Stapert, quoting Ruth Smith, *Handel's Messiah*, 132), this is a point at which the audience is caught up in the mocking. The audience may not be rendered too uncomfortable by *Messiah*. But the experience is not meant to be wholly devoid of discomfort.

('Hallelujah! for the Lord God omnipotent reigneth'). At this point, both performers and audience need a short break before the work's final part.

In the third and final part of the work, the resurrection of all is celebrated. All now leads to the consummation of all things ('Worthy is the Lamb...Amen'). Before that, the solace of knowing that the redeeming work of God will be done in and through the salvific figure ('I know that my Redeemer liveth') is acknowledged in a soothing melody. To follow are the urgency and suddenness of resurrection, contrasted with the gloom of death ('Since by Man came Death, by Man came also the Resurrection of the Dead'). The triumph of God is celebrated in resurrection, in the transformation of the body ('the Dead shall be rais'd incorruptible') and in the crushing of death ('O Death where is thy Sting?'). Musically, the trumpet has made the announcement and led the celebration ('The Trumpet shall sound'). All that is left is thanks ('But Thanks be to God') and worship of God ('Blessing and Honour, Glory and Pow'r be unto Him').

The listening experience leaves the participative listener exhilarated. There is a happy ending, both narratively and emotionally. But the journey has been tortuous and emotionally demanding. Theologically speaking, *Messiah* is a compressed eschatology, presented musically. It can undoubtedly only be fully appreciated with knowledge of the Christian story. But as well as looking, in the next section, at what it contains explicitly as a piece of theology, we shall also explore how its effectiveness and function as a piece of musical entertainment—which is how it began, and to a large degree remains—enable it to carry a cultural theology of salvation, whether or not there is full awareness of the Christian narrative to which it relates.

Messiah's Musical Shape

The theology of *Messiah* is not simply the sum of its component biblical parts. It is possible to list the biblical extracts which the librettist Charles Jennens has used to create the composite text. There are extracts (to cite them in canonical order) from Job, Psalms, Isaiah, Jeremiah, Lamentations, Haggai, Zechariah, Malachi, Matthew, Luke, John, Romans, I Corinthians, Hebrews, and Revelation. In terms of biblical books used, then, there is representation of less than a quarter of the books in the Protestant canon. Even then, the material used from these biblical books is slight and highly selective. The libretto of *Messiah* is by no means a full summary of Christian doctrine. It is one man's interpretation of a single doctrinal theme—redemption—offered in continuity with mainstream Christian doctrinal orthodoxy about its central redeemer figure (the Christ), using carefully chosen biblical material to elaborate upon and elucidate the role of that figure. In particular, creative use is made of prophetic material from the Hebrew Bible, most of the extracts used already being established Christian interpretations (including 'readings back' into the Jewish texts), accepting too that some of the texts used seemed originally to point to Israel as a people, rather than a Messiah figure as an individual.

That said, the result is a powerful, orthodox statement of Christian soteriology. If limited in scope linguistically, it is broader in scope theologically as a musical work than the words alone imply. By judicious use of verbal snapshots of Christianity's salvation narrative, and locating them within a well-structured interpretative framework, Jennens handed to Handel a starting point for the construction of a major work of musical theology. The music does not simply illustrate the words. It adds to them as it makes the words come to life. The emotional impact of the music takes listeners beyond the biblical words used, inviting them to inhabit the spaces created by the music's emotional effect. In the same way that films lure viewers into drawing—consciously and subconsciously—on their life experience in order to engage with what is seen on screen and heard via sound (dialogue, music, and other sounds), so also the theological content of *Messiah* is constructed in part between what is performed and what a listener brings to a performance, or act of listening, and then draws out as a result.[36]

We shall explore more in the next section what this means for a cultural theology methodologically. What can be said, though, in terms of theological content beyond the text of the libretto? What is being declared by its music? What is its *Gehalt*, granted that its content (*Inhalt*) is the Christian redemption narrative and its form (*Form*) that of an oratorio? Even to address such questions runs the risk, of course, of reducing the oratorio as art. Theological engagement with the arts is always in danger of implying that a work is

---

[36] This occurs in what can be termed the 'affective space' created by *Messiah* as a musical work, a concept I shall refer to further in due course. Vaughan S. Roberts and I introduce and explore the concept in *Personal Jesus*, ch.2.

dispensable en route to a desired belief statement. That is not my intent. The purpose of this section is to clarify what is communicated theologically through the interaction between the work as music and the aesthetic-affective response of the respondent (as listener or singer). My simple contention is that, having set the scene in Part I, the musical shape of the work is intended to connect the listener emotionally to the experience of the suffering Messiah in the early scenes of Part II (sections 19–28). The music is meant to evoke sadness. In the process, in operatic fashion (though without the visual props), it both lures listeners into contemplation of the Messiah's suffering and death and prompts reflection on when they have experienced the death of others or begun to consider the prospect of their own death. This is imaginative mourning potentially touching on memories of genuine grief—depending on what a listener brings— evoked without the distractions of on-stage scenery.[37] The advantage of the performance being operatic without being opera is keenly felt here: the oratorio format presses the listener to undertake 'inner work' as they participate in the performance through their listening.

Only, I suggest, when *Messiah* has enabled in the listener a point of emotional connection with the Messiah's suffering can it be said that the piece has begun to undertake its theological work. In other words, the primary means by which the work operates is affective rather than cognitive, and yet it is still functioning theologically. A listener is not being asked by the libretto of the work 'Do you believe that Jesus of Nazareth was and is the redeemer promised within the Jewish tradition, and celebrated as such by the Christian Church?' A listener is, instead, being invited by the music to feel the experience of the redeemer's suffering and death, connect with it emotionally, and then on that basis move around within the libretto's words, carried by the music's mood changes, to work out what to do with that experience. This unpicks, I believe, in theological terms what Burrows thinks is true of the work's emotional impact: 'Jennens and Handel together created an oratorio which, although dealing primarily with the abstract idea of "the Messiah", presented a well-known story through a series of musical tableaux whose emotional progressions can still be appreciated by believers and unbelievers alike.'[38] Theologically, my

---

[37] *Messiah* being an oratorio and not opera. On the circumstances of Handel's switching from opera to oratorio, see Stapert, *Handel's Messiah*, 24–36.
[38] Burrows, *Messiah*, 59.

contention connects with Simeon Zahl's exploration of the 'affective salience' of doctrine.[39] In effect I come to a similar conclusion to Zahl's, but from the opposite end. Rather than seek to reintroduce recognition of an element of the affective into the practice of 'holding to' a doctrinal conviction—the core of Zahl's argument—I disclose how a doctrinal conviction may be moved towards from within a musical exposition of a doctrine. In other words, doctrines matter very much but are not always approached cognitively, only then having emotional (and spirituality-shaping) effect. In this case, the affective precedes the cognitive, though both elements would be held together for any listener who said that she or he believed what the oratorio expressed and celebrated.[40]

To put this another way: doctrines have to be felt at the same time as they are believed. Simply saying, as a *Messiah* listener, that 'I make an emotional connection' with the opening scenes of Part II does not of itself mean that one holds to the Christian doctrine of redemption. But holding to the doctrine without feeling it would not amount to professing Christian faith. Unless it is felt, salvation cannot be known and experienced in personal terms. 'Feeling salvation' is not a momentary, temporary emotional kick. It is not a collection of warm feelings—performances of *Messiah* plus other cultural and liturgical high spots, for example. We shall need to explore in due course what 'feeling salvation' may amount to, especially with respect to the question of whether it should in any sense be described as a form of happiness.[41]

How, though, is one to feel the last judgement, or feel the resurrection? That is an affective-theological challenge issued by the experience of listening to the later scenes of Part II and to Part III of *Messiah*. Unlike having something experiential to work with in connecting emotionally with the suffering of the redeemer, and mourning the Messiah's death, anticipation of divine judgement and eschatological fulfilment require

---

[39] Simeon Zahl, 'On the Affective Salience of Doctrines', *Modern Theology* 31 (2015), 428–44.

[40] I shall need, in due course (Chapter 7), to explain and defend my position against the charge—to use a category introduced by George Lindbeck (*The Nature of Doctrine* (London: SPCK, 1984))—that such an approach to doctrine is 'experiential-expressivism', and, as such, is to be resisted. By contrast I suggest that such an approach to doctrine is simply appropriately affectively astute.

[41] Below, Chapter 7. To anticipate: if, as we shall see, at least three forms of happiness may be identifiable, then not all may easily be usable or useful as characterizations of salvation. The emotional uplift one may receive from any experience of art or entertainment may be called 'happiness' but denote a temporary pleasure. Whether and how this might relate in any way to lasting salvation will need further exploration.

something different. Once more, as was the case with Grünewald's vision of the resurrection of Jesus, such eschatological elements of faith need to be *imagined*. If their ontological security—the fact that Christians believe that these are real—is dependent upon God alone, anticipatory participation of them has to include an imaginative element.

What we experience in this life, and claim to be anticipations of glory, judgement or resurrection, are real in so far as they are experienced affectively. But they are present experiences, explicable also in other ways (psychosocially, psychologically, and culturally). This does not alter the legitimacy of claiming them as glimpses of ontological divine reality: anticipations of the kind of flourishing which God promises for the future.

Participating in *Messiah*'s Beauty

From the perspective of a contemporary concertgoer who pays for a quite expensive ticket to hear *Messiah* performed in a modern, acoustically well-designed concert hall by a top-class professional choir it is perhaps true to say that any 'redemptive' element in the listening experience is more likely to come from the exhilaration created by musical quality than the content of the libretto. A Christian ticket purchaser can more easily enjoy the work at two levels. But for many concertgoers, it is the feel-good factor created by the musical experience which could be said to carry the hopeful content. As an immediate response to a musical experience, flourishing results from aesthetic appreciation and the concomitant feel-good factor more than from in-depth knowledge of the pieces of music played. Whether this is in any sense salvific remains to be seen.

Musical performance can, though, be distinguished from listening. Participation as a choir member in a performance of *Messiah* adds a further dimension to the experience of exhilaration, whatever the level of musical knowledge of the singer. It has always been so, and some of the tales of local choirs engaged in performances of *Messiah* make compelling, and entertaining, reading.[42] To be engaged in the

---

[42] See accounts, for example, in Kenneth Young, *Chapel* (London: Methuen, 1972), 95–6 and Oliver A. Beckerlegge, *A Methodist Life* (Loughborough: Teamprint, 2000), 50–1, and also reference to parish church attenders 'slipping away early from evening service so as to hear the closing numbers of *Messiah* done at the Methodist chapel' (John Hibbs, *The Country Chapel*, Newton Abbott: David and Charles, 1988, 115; I am

production of a sound which in turn may move others is itself profoundly moving. Such a consideration shifts us to reflection of how music works, be it for performer or listener. Even though we have been looking at a piece of religious (specifically Christian) music as a point of access to the doctrine of salvation, at this point the words have been left behind.[43] Music as sound is neither immediately religious nor non-religious.

A form in which the key question arising from the second half of this chapter must be posed, then, is this: where music creates a sense of human flourishing (through uplift, exhilaration, or a sense of transcendence), is this the place where salvation's positive aspect is being wrestled with and disclosed? And is this always true? Following on from this, if the creative, affective space produced in the listener or performer by aesthetically rich music is an indicator of where salvation is found, how might it be possible to work back from the point of exhilaration (or ecstasy, or euphoria) to a sense of what is being escaped, or what a person is being saved *from*?

The fullest answer to these questions which this book can provide can only be offered later, after the further case studies of Chapter 4 in particular, and the constructive chapters at the end of the work (Chapters 7–8). But methodologically we must note what is happening here. *Messiah* always *was* entertainment. This can easily be forgotten in how the work is received now. It is a religious work and has a clearly Christian libretto which was meant to undertake a specifically Christian task when first performed (i.e. to take on the deists). But it was always intended to make people feel good too, to rouse their emotions, to keep them riveted whilst being entertained, to send them away happy. It did confront them to some degree with aspects of their selves which might need some attention (and also, if

indebted to Martin Wellings for drawing my attention to these examples). It is important to highlight here, of course, that the value of such practices is not simply to do with the aesthetic quality of what is performed. Local choirs may or may not reach dizzy aesthetic heights (any more than weekly worship in churches may always be regarded as 'top-quality', aesthetically speaking), but they *aspire* to, in praise of God, and know they are engaging with, works of high quality as they do so. But aesthetics is not the *only* point at issue. Aspiration to do justice to a work of high aesthetic quality gives way to achievements in other realms (affective and therapeutic, the substance of Chapters 4 and 5 of this present work) and will certainly deliver successes in terms of social and cultural capital (addressed in Chapter 6) for those who listen and those who perform.

[43] Vaughan S. Roberts and I have explored the point that popular music works as much (if not more so) via sound as by lyrics (*Personal Jesus*).

not in a direct way, the society of which the listeners were members):
a saviour was needed, for they *would* be judged. There was a challenge
at work here. *Messiah* carried a religious message with considerable
moral freight which may be less easily heard today. But it was, admittedly, also a comfortable, even comforting discomfort which they
experienced as listeners.[44]

Messiah can still carry, musically speaking, many of the same
functions it originally had for religious and non-religious performers
and listeners alike, even if, in its cultural reception in the secular West,
the full force of its religious and moral message may have weakened
somewhat. For our purposes, however, it is both legitimate and
important to ask what contemporary *equivalents* are of such a work
as *Messiah*. In very different times, when more people (though far from
all, even in the West) have access to live musical performance, and to
recorded music through a variety of means (CD, MP3, online streaming), there are a great many more opportunities than were possible in
the mid-nineteenth century to encounter directly beautifully crafted,
technically well-performed, uplifting music.[45] Where do people now
go to for such uplift? Large-scale concerts and gigs may well have a
similar emotional effect, though without the religious content. In truth,
though, because of technology, listeners do not need to 'go' anywhere,
unless they wish consciously to choose the communal experience of
listening.[46] The basic point to note here is that there are equivalents of
Messiah in terms of emotional impact. It is just that in secular times
such aesthetic experiences are less likely solely to be classed as high art
and will be just as entangled as was always the case with affective
responses. Performances of Wagner's *Parsifal* will work for some as
artistic encounters with redemption and experiences of flourishing,
whilst repeated attendance at, or viewings of, *Les Misérables* or a Bruce
Springsteen concert will work for others.[47] Let us be clear: art is not

[44] And accepting that most early listeners of the paying performances would have
been the well-to-do.
[45] It should also be said that music moves not necessarily only when well-
performed or deemed aesthetically satisfying. Here, though, in a chapter focusing
more on aesthetics than affectivity (even though the two dimensions of life are
inseparable), I am emphasizing the quality of music.
[46] We have explored the impact of technology on, and resulting individualized
practices in, music-listening in Robert and Marsh, *Personal Jesus*, 49–50 and 109–13.
[47] On theological responses to *Parsifal* see, for example, Claus-Dieter Osthövener, *Erlösung: Transformationen einer Idee im 19. Jahrhundert* (Tübingen: Mohr
Siebeck, 2004), 162–76, and Brian Horne, 'The Legacy of Romanticism: On Not

the same as religion or theology, but nor can theology and religion be detached from what the arts and popular culture have done, and are doing, in human culture. Locating points in culture where redemptive moments are being suggested or produced and/or where human flourishing is celebrated is a way of identifying crucial spaces in the realm of aesthetic life from which theology can undertake fruitful work, regardless of whether a work or product is specifically religious.[48]

Messiah as Popular Music

I have chosen a 'popular classic' which also happens to be a Christian work in this opening chapter of case studies. It should be received within the content of Chapters 3–6 as a whole, in which we look at case studies which are not specifically Christian, and alongside which, therefore, *Messiah* jostles for attention. Even accepting its Christian content, however, does not mean that *Messiah* is always heard simply as a Christian sacred work. Respect for its origins, history, and current functions means that we have been opened up more generally to how music works and how forms of music are received and consumed. *Messiah* remains a powerful, aesthetically satisfying vehicle for carrying the Christian story. It will not work for all. Importantly, many other aesthetic productions will bring people to a place where the issues and concerns which theology identifies as those to do with flourishing and salvation will surface and need to be addressed. The attention I have paid to *Messiah* sharpens the question whether the salvific experience which Handel's work invites a listener to inhabit imaginatively, through aesthetic-affective means, can only

Confusing Art and Religion', in Stephen Holmes (ed.), *Public Theology in Cultural Engagement* (Milton Keynes, Colorado Springs, CO, Hyderabad: Paternoster, 2008), 153–69, here 162–6; on *Les Misérables*, see Ian Bradley, *You've Got to Have a Dream: The Message of the Musical* (London: SCM Press, 2004), 15, 145–68; on Bruce Springsteen and fandom, see Daniel Cavicchi, *Tramps like us: Music & Meaning among Springsteen Fans* (New York: Oxford University Press, 1999).

[48] Theologically speaking, Christian doctrines of creation, incarnation, and pneumatology all enable such an approach to be defended as they identify where and how, in the material world, God's creativity is active and present. Holmes, *Public Theology*, Kevin J. Vanhoozer, Charles A. Anderson, and Michael J. Sleasman (eds.), *Everyday Theology: How to Read Cultural Texts and Interpret Trends* (Grand Rapids, MI: Baker, 2007), and Steven R. Guthrie, *Creator Spirit: The Holy Spirit and the Art of Becoming Human* (Grand Rapids, MI: Baker: Baker, 2011) are recent examples of such theological explorations.

be created when allied to Christian discourse. It is unlikely that such a view is sustainable. In due course, through and beyond the multiple examples within contemporary Western culture which will be considered, an overall perspective will need to be taken on how Christian theology interweaves with, learns from, interacts with, and challenges key examples of cultural engagements with salvific themes.

We would not do justice to God if we did not look for God in and through works of beauty, either in the natural world or in works fashioned by human creativity. Not all such human creativity will be explicitly seen as divinely inspired by artists themselves, whatever theological interpreters may claim. Not even all works explicitly deemed to be divinely inspired will necessarily sit easily with Christian theological readings of the creative task. In this chapter I have started very cautiously in selecting two well-known examples of aesthetic activity which are also Christian works of art. I have, however, sought to show how even in their Christian orthodoxy they are works which, in the way they function, do not simply repeat the Christian message *for Christians*. As public works of art they both invite the orthodox to look again at how public art works and encourage all respondents, religious or not, to receive and make use of their content at the intersection of aesthetic and affective response. We are meant to feel something in the gut—even be shaken to the core—as we respond to their beauty.

That is what great art does and is therefore why Christian theology cannot simply draw up, in any lazy fashion, lists of useful sacred works, or define what is theologically valuable simply in terms of its subject matter (to use Tillich's terms: when its *Inhalt* is Christian). The *Gehalt* of any work of art cannot be presupposed and can, in theological terms, only be discerned when it is permitted to do its work artistically, and when it is brought alongside the question of where it is heading (How, if at all, does this work contribute to an understanding of human flourishing? How, if at all, does it help us better to understand what it means to be a 'saved' or 'redeemed' person?). Both of the works considered here continue to make a contribution to such discussions. In ensuing chapters the contributions will be less clear. It will, though, be important to consider the way in which Chapters 3–6 *as a whole* provide an impression of how Western culture is experienced, and thus map the context in which Christian theology is undertaking its current work.

4

Salvation in Film and Television

Oscar-winning films are not necessarily great films, aesthetically speaking. Nor do they inevitably prove popular. They are likely to be technically good, especially those that win the awards for cinematography, costumes, and the like. And they are likely to be popular enough to have surfaced in public life prior to securing an award and sure to get publicity afterwards. But they may not prove to be 'classics' and stand the test of time. This applies to a great many cultural products. They may 'have their day', prove hot property for a while, suggest that they are going to be influential over a long period, but then fade, soon to appear (in the case of films, as DVDs) in second-hand or charity shops or to be obtainable cheaply online.

This may be the long-term destiny of both of the products of popular culture considered in this chapter. Such a future would merely highlight the risk of undertaking any form of theological enquiry in critical dialogue with current works of art and culture. But that would be beside the point as far as this present book is concerned. A living, cultural theology has to take such risks and work with what is 'just there' in culture, and which demands consideration given its own interests and the seeming similar interests of the products with which it engages.

In this chapter we take a sharp turn from the kind of material examined in Chapter 3 by seeking the *Gehalt* and reflecting on the significance of two case studies from popular culture. One is an award-winning film based on a late twentieth-century novel, which is claimed, on the cover of its DVD, to be about 'redemption'.[1] The

---

[1] To be precise, the DVD cover states that it is 'the powerful story of a country music star's rocky road to redemption' (*Crazy Heart*, 20th Century Fox Home Entertainment, 2010).

second is a compelling TV drama which offers one of a spate of recent
lengthy examinations of human wickedness and evil. It is, then, an
example of what contemporary Western culture at least implies one
needs to be saved from.

In each case we shall explore both the content of the work and its
impact on viewers, recognizing once more that how artistic products
work is in the 'affective space' which they produce around the work
in question for the viewer.[2] In contrast to the previous chapter I am
making no great claim for the aesthetic magnificence of either work to
be examined. *Breaking Bad* is admittedly a very creative and technically
well-made product. But rather than construct an aesthetic-affective
argument on the grounds of these works' proven influence, I am letting
the affective response to them take the lead here.[3] This is in keeping
with how films and TV very often work (in the gut first, rather than in
the head, even if got at via the eyes).[4]

CRAZY HEART

The film *Crazy Heart* (2009) is based on a 1987 novel by Thomas
Cobb and secured Oscar-winning performances from its lead actor
Jeff Bridges and from Ryan Bingham and T Bone Burnett for their
song 'The Weary Kind'. It is the story of the later years of Otis Arthur
Blake, more commonly known as Bad Blake, a country singer who
has fallen on hard times because of alcoholism, and is four times
married, and four times divorced. The film follows his attempt to

---

[2] The concept of 'affective space' is introduced and put to work in Clive Marsh and
Vaughan S. Roberts, *Personal Jesus: How Popular Music Shapes Our Souls* (Grand
Rapids, MI: Baker Academic, 2013), 16–21. Affective activity has already been noted
in Chapter 3, as inevitably entangled with aesthetic response. The distinction between
Chapters 3 and 4 ends up, then, as largely one of emphasis or starting point rather
than sharp disjuncture. Aesthetics and affectivity *are* different, but belong together.

[3] It is still too early to assess their lasting influence. Scholarly discussion of *Breaking Bad* is just beginning. *Crazy Heart* is less likely to attract such attention, formal
responses to it taking the form of published reviews.

[4] I am, of course, making a considerable theoretical claim here. But, as in my earlier
study *Cinema and Sentiment: Film's Challenge to Theology* (Carlisle: Paternoster
Press, 2004) and in keeping with recent theoretical work such as Crystal Downing,
Salvation from Cinema: The Medium is the Message (New York and Abingdon:
Routledge, 2015), any form of theological interaction with the arts cannot evade the
responsibility of acknowledging how art forms actually work.

recover his career and recreate the experience of his earlier life through returning to a life of touring. In the process of doing this he meets Jean Craddock, a journalist with a small son who interviews him for an article she is writing and with whom he falls in love. Though she helps him to reassess his life and enables him to resolve to become sober, they do not end up staying together, parting on good terms.

There is a significant difference between the film and the book. In the book, Blake returns to drink. He is not released from, nor does he appear to be able to live with, his alcoholism. The film, by contrast, is more positive. There is no suggestion that he remains mired in his alcohol addiction. Why, though, is the film said to be about redemption? Is it simply because there is a happy ending?

At its simplest the film is said to be about redemption because it presents a story of a life turned round from destructive tendencies to a more hopeful and healthy way of living. The 'narrative shape' or 'arc' of a story which attracts the verdict that it is a redemption narrative plots the movement from a negative situation to a more positive state, with ups and downs on the way, external (human) intervention, but also some kind of inner change in the life of the main character. The film's plot could, then, be said to slot into a basic soteriological shape: a character is saved *from* something (here, alcoholism), *for* an amended life (here, an alcohol-free existence, with restored relationships, rediscovered creativity and improved material well-being), *by* external intervention (here, the goodwill and emotional attention and support of a new friend and then lover), *into* a more supportive network of professional contacts and friends.[5]

The film is therefore seen as a redemption story because of this turnaround. Yet, as we shall see shortly, there appears to be little, if anything, in the film version of the story which makes any connection to theological readings of redemption. Nor can it be said in any unqualified sense that the book on which the film is based is about redemption understood in a religious sense. I shall show that the book contains more resources than the film that invite a theological

---

[5] Neither 'salvation' nor 'redemption' features explicitly as a main theme in Christopher Booker, *The Seven Basic Plots: Why We Tell Stories* (London and New York: Continuum, 2004), though a number of the 'basic plots' Booker considers inevitably contain redemptive elements (e.g. rags to riches, the quest, voyage and return, rebirth) and considerable attention is paid to 'dark versions' of the plots examined. This always explains why, even when approached theologically, the 'redemption' motif can function so easily as an overarching narrative for human experience.

interpretation of what the story presents. But even so, it will be difficult to claim that there is much that is explicitly theological about *Crazy Heart's* redemptive element.

Given the commercial aspect of the concept of redemption, however, it is at least pertinent to ask what redemption *costs* any of the characters in the story. The answer to that question is 'not much'. There is little in the way of self-sacrifice endured by any of the characters around Blake who enable him to turn his life around. Jean Craddock takes something of a risk in allowing Blake to come close to her son, a risk which seems to go badly wrong when Blake temporarily loses the child in a shopping mall. But this ends happily when the child is found. Tommy Sweet, a former supporting act for Blake who then, to Blake's annoyance, becomes the main attraction, has to tame his ego in approaching Blake to ask him to record music with him. But this is scarcely sacrificial. And as Roger Ebert rightly notes: 'This is a rare story that knows people *don't* always forget those who helped them on the way up.'[6] Though the support of friends needs to be noted, therefore, Blake's story is mostly one of a person being enabled to turn his own life around. In this respect it fits in with the sketch of contemporary culture's understanding of redemption as outlined in Chapter 1. Human agency is paramount.

Crazy Heart as Film and Book

In an earlier study I show that five standard elements in a Christian understanding of redemption receive short shrift in *Crazy Heart* the film.[7] In two respects there are points of contact. Blake is certainly a man in need of redemption; otherwise he will self-destruct. His experience thus embodies what Christian theology deems is true of all human beings, i.e. all people stand in need of redemption in some way. The film does not, however, reflect the full scale of this universality of sin, as Blake clearly has a particular need, a more intense struggle than many other characters, and has for some considerable time not recognized the depth of his need.

[6] Roger Ebert, Review of *Crazy Heart* at www.rogerebert.com/reviews/crazy-heart-2009/, accessed 14 April 2016.

[7] 'Protestant Themes within Secular Models of Salvation—"Redeemed" or just "a bit Happier"?: The Example of *Crazy Heart*', paper delivered at the 'Protestantism on Screen' Conference, Wittenberg, 25 June 2015 (unpublished).

Second, he demonstrates amendment of life. This occurs in a number of ways. Blake begins to seek to repair damaged relationships—with Tommy Sweet, the performer with whom Blake had fallen out over the years, and with his long-lost son Steven, with whom he makes contact after twenty years of silence. Both of these subplots do not wholly end happily. With Tommy Sweet there is greater hope. Blake and Sweet do start to work successfully together again. With the son Steven, contact is made, but that is as far as it goes. Steven wants no further contact.

In addition to these examples of the attempt to repair relationships there is also Blake's resolve to be sober and stay sober. If the recovery process just seems a little too easy, at least a clear resolve is shown.[8] The amendment of life takes shape in the fact that Blake looks after himself more, and looks better physically as a result of his getting on top of his alcoholism.

In three other respects, however, the film's linkage with Christian insights into redemption is slight. The characters around Blake who are willing to help and support him and ask him awkward questions about his lifestyle and challenge his basic assumptions are, of course, human agents. Any sense that in their offering of help they may be an incarnation of divine action is, however, not drawn out. There is therefore, in turn, no indication of such human agency as the work of God (let alone of God being seen to be at work in and through Christ). Whilst it may be a relief to discover that no lazy evocation of a 'Christ figure' is posited in the film, the relative failure, already noted, to explore the costliness of saving activity on both Blake and those around him does, though, limit the extent to which the redemption motif is appropriate in any other than a superficial way. Finally, the amendment of life theme is far from any notion of being a road to perfection. It is a road to improvement, recognizing the support of others, but very much based on an inner resolve, a human act. External agency is confined to the context of interpersonal support provided by friends old and new. Blake is much happier at the end of the film, potentially a little bit happier at the end of the book—though this is unclear—but quite why and how he is 'redeemed' in any other than a

---

[8] Though there is reference to the help provided by membership of an Alcoholics Anonymous group, which suggests recognition of the need for time and discipline as well as the support of others.

quite conventional narrative 'recovery story' kind of sense is open to challenge.

If the film has not, then, wholly eliminated the resonant theological depths of the potential of Blake's story to be interpreted as redemptive, it has pushed them to the edge of the story. Or, if it can be argued that by its happier ending, in comparison with the book, the film has brought redemption more to the fore, what it does not do is make explicit the basis on which redemption is an appropriate term to use.

Redemption Sold Short

To take us a stage further in our exploration of why a film such as *Crazy Heart* is deemed by critics and viewers alike to be about redemption, and what this might mean in practice, it is, though, important to dig deeper into the differences between the book and the film and note what happens in the transition. In the passage from book to film we see the clear *reduction* of explicit theological content. Blake's Protestant background, the motif of his wrestling with religious imagery from different directions, and his decision whether or not to support a right-wing Evangelical politician are all excised from the plot. A 'secularization of penance' occurs in so far as an important feature of Protestantism (how theology and spiritual practices are interwoven with, and evident in, ordinary everyday life) is allied so closely with secularizing tendencies prevalent in Western culture that the lack of explicit theological reference turns the residual motifs into human works. Protestantism ends up producing, in a secular context, forms of the 'works righteousness' its very existence is meant to oppose.[9]

---

[9] 'Works righteousness' is the term used to characterize human effort to please God, i.e. to seek to earn salvation. Martin Luther's theology in particular—and all theological traditions influenced by the Reformation followed his lead—challenged the view that human effort made any contribution to the work and experience of salvation. Though good works were deemed to be part of a Christian life, they followed the acceptance of justification which God brought about in Jesus Christ, received by faith alone (*sola fide*), and were effected in the Christian disciple by the Holy Spirit. Human activity thus allied itself with the will of God but did not bring salvation about. For a summary of Luther's theology, see Markus Wriedt, 'Luther's theology', in Donald K. McKim (ed.), *The Cambridge Companion to Martin Luther* (Cambridge: Cambridge University Press, 2003), 86–119. For a gripping recent account of how Luther's belief and thought related to his life and functioned as a radical influence upon the religious movements around him and the politics of his day, see Lyndal Roper, *Martin Luther: Renegade and Prophet* (London: Vintage, 2017).

To summarize my earlier findings about this film, there are three cases of the elision of a theological context to the change in Blake's life which are pertinent to this present discussion.[10] In the transfer from book to film there appears to be only one clear residual reference in the film's dialogue to the complex interplay which exists between the religious motifs inherent in the country music of the southern US—a reference by Jean Craddock to Blake's retention of Gospel music as part of his playlist. Removed in the film is an entire level of explanatory background as to how and why Bad Blake became a singer and how he relates to the kinds of music he performs.

Second, the film fails to reflect a number of points in the book where it is clear that Blake remains connected to his evangelical past. Third, there is no reference in the film to a scene in the book where Blake wanders into a cathedral where he is struck by 'a crucifix with a twisted, tortured Christ'. It becomes clear that, despite the huge emphasis upon the redemptive significance of the figure on the cross in Protestantism, the version of Protestantism in which he was brought up has not enabled him to be faced with the full import of what the crucified figure was deemed to achieve.[11]

These observations are not to be heard as a simple complaint that 'the film is not as good as the book'. When books become screenplays, all films have to make tough choices and be selective in capturing a story's essence and turning it into a compelling visual and aural experience. My basic point, rather, is that the country music of the southern states of the US is being decontextualized and the broader interpretative framework within which country music is to be understood slips from view. This process in turn symbolizes a cultural tendency to remove any theological framework surrounding a claim for a 'text' (novel, film, piece of music, play) held to be 'about' redemption. Hence, whilst it may be adjudged acceptable and appropriate to apply the term redemption to any narrative about a dramatic turnaround in a person's life, the question arises whether use of the term redemption invites consideration of what is added to an understanding of the person and the change of life described.

---

[10] I note four in my earlier study, of which the first three are summarized in what follows.

[11] The reference in the original novel is from Thomas Cobb, *Crazy Heart* (London: Corsair, 2010), 66.

As things stand, the story being told is sold short precisely because of what is removed, perhaps simply for commercial reasons, in the shift from book to film. The question may still remain as to whether novelist Thomas Cobb has done full justice to the theological framework surrounding Blake's story, though that is not our concern here. For our immediate purposes it must simply be noted that the film functions as a redemption story, which is in explicit ways connected to religious roots and a theological context, and yet which is deracinated from that context.[12] This has consequences on two fronts. First, theological content is not brought to bear in understanding what is entailed when a life experience is described as redemptive. Second, in the process of reception of an artistic work, the potential depth of what it is possible for the viewer to engage with is truncated.

Crazy Heart is, then, sold as a redemption story. In significant respects, especially in filmic form, it functions as such. Blake's life is turned round in a number of ways. Viewers, too, are invited to reflect on their own lives through engagement with the story and emotional response to it. (From what must I be rescued? In what ways is my own life off-beam? Who are those who steer me into healthy and constructive ways of living?). But the redemption label is misapplied in so far as it leaves the story working solely at the level of Blake's own efforts (self-help) and the support of some good friends.

Beyond Book and Film

What are the consequences of a film such as *Crazy Heart*'s function as a piece of popular culture, its designation as a film 'about redemption', and yet its limitations when brought within a theological penumbra? It is first necessary to note that such films fulfil an important cultural and psychological function in providing, in addition to entertainment, a vital arena within which people can undertake cognitive work in an affectively engaging setting.[13] Such films help people cope with life constructively. The designation of the film as being 'about redemption'

---

[12] The theological aspects are thus hidden from view. Though the soteriological shape of the plot's narrative arc is clear (what Blake is saved 'from and for', 'by' whom, and what 'into'), why it is declared as soteriological is played down.

[13] The 'affective space' referred to earlier (see n.2). There is also valuable discussion to be had about the 'religion-like' function of cinemagoing (see my *Cinema and Sentiment*).

is not wholly misplaced. Like many other such films (e.g. *The Shaw-shank Redemption, Awakenings, Patch Adams, The Fisher King, Good Will Hunting, The Green Mile, Gran Torino, Rain Man*[14]) *Crazy Heart* tells a story with which viewers are meant to identify and through which people are, whilst being entertained, intended to be moved, and potentially to be provoked to reflect. There is no need to argue that *Crazy Heart* is a 'classic film' for these to be aspects of its achievement or usefulness. I am not making any claims for the aesthetic quality of the film. If it lasts, it lasts. If it fades, it fades. Other films and other forms of art and media will take its place in Western culture to undertake similar affective and cognitive work. In this study, I highlight the film simply in order to take note of an example of where redemption is being deemed, culturally and commercially, to be explored.

Arguably, though, a story of redemption requires greater clarification of what one is saved *for*, and in particular what one is saved *into*. What is the nature of the new life which results from being rescued or retrieving oneself from a destructive lifestyle (of alcoholism and self-absorption)? What is the new supportive context within which the recovered, amended life is going to be sustainable? Furthermore, to what extent is the Christian insight that one *cannot* save oneself reflected in any sense in the film? What may be added if such an insight is brought alongside the film so that, for example, at the very least the crucial role played by the supportive friends is highlighted as the film is received affectively and interpreted cognitively?

This engagement with *Crazy Heart* opens up a number of dimensions of the question of what salvation might mean today which need addressing. At a point within Western culture where an example of redemption is identified and promoted *outside* an explicitly religious context we are compelled to ask about the extent of human activity. Is redemption the result of human agency alone? If a contemporary claim is made for divine agency alongside or within human action, how is this identified and in what does it consist? And if the claim that there is *nothing* human beings can do to effect redemption—as much Christian thought has declared—then how does this connect, if at all, with apparent contemporary assumptions that human beings are themselves the agents of redemptive change? To express the matter

---

[14] See, for example, the list at the Ranker website, www.ranker.com/list/best-movies-about-redemption/ranker-film, which includes some of the films I list here, accessed 15 April 2016.

in terms of historical theology, it begins to look as if we are all Pelagians now. Indeed, not only is there a sense that human activity *contributes* to salvation, but it looks as though humans are now deemed to be *solely* responsible for what has been known as salvation in the past. The secularization reflected in the movement through Cobb's novel to Cooper's film has begun to leave God out of the redemptive process altogether.

Second, related to this is the question of individual and social elements in salvation. Christianity has itself devoted much attention to redemption/salvation as inner change. In this respect it has focused on the life of the individual. It is therefore not surprising that the focus of such a film as *Crazy Heart* rests upon Blake, and thus on actor Jeff Bridges' performance as Blake.[15] Even so, there is limited depth to Blake's character. As viewers, we want him to address his alcoholism and recover. But we are not wholly clear about what inner change may have happened. Nor, despite elements of evident gratitude which Blake shows to those who support him, are we invited to explore in any depth the nature of his ongoing dependence upon his supportive friends. Craddock will have moved on with her son, having been a broker of his recovery. Wayne Kramer (Robert Duvall) will still be running his bar. Will Blake drop in, whilst remaining sober? Jack Greene (Paul Herman) may or may not continue to be Blake's manager, but will he be there to pick up the pieces if Blake's career crumbles again? Sweet (Colin Farrell) will enable Blake's career to be resurrected, but how long will the new partnership last? Other new, lasting relationships will be needed for Blake to remain healthy and buoyant, and his decline in the book version of the story perhaps reflects their absence. In short, though the film version of the story is designated a story of redemption, loose ends are left hanging in the relation between what happens to Blake the individual and the social contexts within which a redemptive experience occurs and is fostered. In formal terms, the human dynamic here is similar to the process for a person 'coming to faith' not being supported or finding a group within which such a faith can develop healthily.

In terms of the conceptual framework of this study, then, we can ask in what way this cultural example of redemption conceives

---

[15] This is also reflected in the relative weakness of the character of Jean Craddock (Maggie Gyllenhaal), as recognized in reviews of the film.

human flourishing, and whether happiness is in view as an aspect of redemption. It is evident that if Blake's story is about redemption, then much that is painful is carried within it. Blake is a recovering alcoholic and does not end up in a significant new intimate relationship with a 'significant other'. His relationship with his son is not restored, and he must live with the knowledge that he did not maintain a good relationship with the late mother of his only child. His 'flourishing' thus amounts to restored *physical health*, the emotional and mental capacity to resist his addictive personality with respect to drink, a new found creativity (his rediscovered songwriting), and the resulting material benefits of the changes in his life. It is easy to see how viewers would consider such a notion of redemption as flourishing as 'real' and 'grounded'. It is true to life. Blake is happier in the sense that he is more emotionally stable and better equipped physically to deal with life. The adequacy of such an account of a life story as one of redemption, and whether such a story constitutes flourishing (and should also be deemed as happiness), will be examined further in due course. For the moment it has been valuable to note that such a story is culturally defined as one of redemption, and what such a definition entails.[16]

This discussion of *Crazy Heart* thus leads to a few simple conclusions. First, the notion of 'redemption' is alive and well in popular culture. Whether ever intended with theological overtones, its presence means, nevertheless, that the concept is needed to denote an important aspect of human experience. Second, Western culture clearly struggles with the religio-theological dimensions of the concept. Though recognizing a need to address the concept, we find a novel, and then more so a film, offering a rather thin take on the components which make up the concept and experience of redemption. Third, then, a challenge is issued to those of any religious persuasion who wish not just to keep alive the theological dimensions of the concept, but to offer insights into how the term may be better used and understood to work out how, in the secular West, this is going to be possible.

---

[16] In terms of the working definitions of redemption within Western culture identified by David Kelsey, Blake's experiences count as 'making up for a bad performance' and 'redemption from alien control' (*Imagining Redemption* (Louisville, KY: Westminster John Knox Press, 2005), 18–19).

BREAKING BAD

Everyday Storytelling

It is difficult for readers whose childhoods may have been steeped in biblical stories and ideas, and whose lives were thus decisively shaped by biblical narratives and texts, to appreciate what it may be like to be dependent on a wider range of stories the authority of which may need to be argued for and earned rather than simply assumed. For a great many Western citizens up until the 1970s this has, however, been the case. Biblical stories and insights carried a weight which few others could. Despite the historical-critical questioning of the truth or truthfulness, rather than just the historical accuracy, of biblical narratives, stretching over two centuries throughout the post-Enlightenment period, it was the second half of the twentieth century before the full impact of the challenge to the assumed authority of biblical texts was felt in the West. Since then, the cultural dominance of biblical concerns and themes has waned. Whilst insights from the Hebrew and Christian Bibles may be claimed to have a timeless quality, it is now often not to Bibles that Western citizens may turn to encounter and wrestle with key questions of human living. Here is not the place to explore the full implications of this cultural turn. Suffice to say that the range of resources through which Western citizens may ask questions about their life has been broadened out. TV dramas, films, novels, plays, and comics may all command attention, entertaining and informing, whilst also keeping some key existential questions alive, though authority has to be earned and cultural canonical status is not easily won. Bibles no longer carry the weight they did. Viewing and sales figures in practice count for more than positive weighty reviews.[17]

This proves ethically problematic, for how is one to know who to trust? It also highlights the fact that even existentially significant materials have to be attractively and engagingly presented. It has been known

---

[17] High production values, dense and complex plots and scripts, leading to a demanding viewing experience have, however, led to the identification of 'quality TV' amongst scholars and critics (e.g. Janet McCabe and Kim Akass (eds.), *Quality TV: Contemporary American Television and Beyond* (London and New York: I. B. Tauris, 2007); Daniela Schültz, *Quality-TV als Unterhaltungsphänomen* (Wiesbaden: Springer, 2016)). 'Quality-TV' is itself a contested term, however, as it immediately introduces a 'high' and 'low' culture division within the medium of TV, at potential cost to attention to how TV actually works and is received regardless of the quality of its programming.

for some time that Shakespeare might be preferred to the Christian Bible simply because, even with his own dated language, he may have expressed some crucial human issues in more telling a fashion. In the twenty-first century, some forms of popular music and TV dramas play the contemporary Shakespearean role.

Whether or not this can be confirmed, my next case study offers a contemporary reading of the practical effects of sin. Even if one does not hold to a doctrine of original sin, I invite the reader to receive, interpret, and explore the TV drama *Breaking Bad* as an exposition of the way in which the propensity for radical evil lies latent in every human being. Such a possibility of evil is able to be drawn out, extended, and brought to bear not only in the destruction of an individual's life, but also in the damaging impact of their conduct upon people around them, and on the social structures within which they operate. And because such a propensity for evil dwells within each human being, and each may therefore cultivate the evil in another, we are reminded of the structures of evil (a 'kingdom of sin'[18]) within which all human beings live, in the course of living a seemingly straightforward, everyday, domestic life.

As a contribution to this present study, the exploration of *Breaking Bad* to follow lays out a contemporary exposition of a Western understanding of the ease with which evil is practised and can consume a person. In no way do the multiple plot lines or the overarching narrative of *Breaking Bad* offer anything like an explicit, or even an implicit theology.[19] I shall, however, demonstrate how the drama expounds in a stark manner the continuing contemporary engagement with what Christians have often called 'original sin'. It maps the human problem which attempts to expound salvation and redemption have sought to address. It creates an 'affective space' for viewers within which emotional engagement followed by cognitive work may take place. *Breaking Bad* provides an excellent example of a major challenge

---

[18] The notion of a 'kingdom of sin' derives from Kant, and is used in theology by Schleiermacher, and then more especially by Albrecht Ritschl (1822–89). For a summary and discussion of their insights, see Derek Nelson, *What's Wrong with Sin?: Sin in Individual and Social Perspective from Schleiermacher to Theologies of Liberation* (London and New York: T&T Clark, 2009), 15–48.

[19] Though theological discussion of the series has begun to appear online, as in Jackson Cuidon, 'Why We Need *Breaking Bad*', at www.christianitytoday.com/ct/2013/july-web-only/breaking-bad.html, and Jason Kerwick, 'The Philosophy, and Theology, of "Breaking Bad"', at www.beliefnet.com/columnists/attheintersection offaithandculture/2015/09/the-philosophy-and-theology-of-breaking-bad.html, both accessed 12 April 2016.

to the adequacy of any current effort to expound a doctrine of salvation. 'What sort of redemption, what kind of hope, if any, is possible here?' is a persistent thread running through the entire series.[20] It is a clear exposition of one version of what human beings need saving from.

Across sixty-two episodes, constituting over forty hours of TV viewing, *Breaking Bad* follows the story of Walter White, a high school (secondary school) chemistry teacher who responds to the news that he has cancer with the drive to 'provide for his family' in material terms before he dies. The manner in which he chooses to do this is to become a drug dealer, producing, on the basis of his knowledge of chemistry, fine-quality crystal methamphetamine which, in partnership with a former high school student, he distributes across the southern US states, into Mexico, and with a later outlet to the Czech Republic. He makes vast sums of money and yet spirals downward morally as he does so, disrupting and destroying relationships with family and friends, becoming indifferent to killing, and becoming a killer himself. The extent to which he lies and deceives all those around him extends the range, depth, and complexity of the web of wickedness created by his actions, and the actions undertaken by, and in some cases that he requires of, others.

A number of examples of relationships affected can be given. Walter deceives his wife, Skyler, initially keeping the other world of his drug production secret, before eventually implicating her in his activity through needing her to help him launder the money raised. He deceives his brother-in-law Hank, a Drug Enforcement Administration officer, throughout the majority of the series, his actions causing Hank to be badly injured and then later killed. He fluctuates in his relationship with his younger business partner, Jesse Pinkman, to whom he at times acts like a caring father, yet to whom at other times he shows disrespect and a ruthless selfishness, not least when he

---

[20] See, for example, Jami Anderson, 'A Life Not Worth Living', in David P. Pierson (ed.), *Breaking Bad: Critical Essays on the Contexts, Politics, Style, and Reception of the Television Series* (Lanham, MD: Lexington Books, 2014), 103–18, a discussion undertaken with reference to categories drawn from disability studies. In addition to the Pierson collection of essays on the series, see also David R. Koepsell, and Robert Arp (eds.), *Breaking Bad and Philosophy: Badder Living through Chemistry* (Chicago and LaSalle, IL: Open Court, 2012), Jacob Blevins and Dafydd Wood (eds.), *The Methods of Breaking Bad: Essays on Narrative, Character and Ethics* (Jefferson, NC: McFarland and Co., 2015), and Elliott Logan, *Breaking Bad and Dignity: Unity and Fragmentation in the Serial Television Drama* (New York: Palgrave Macmillan, 2016).

fails to save the life of Jesse's girlfriend Jane, when he has opportunity to do so.

As a compelling TV drama the series keeps viewers grippingly entertained. Beyond the original US TV broadcast of the five seasons (2008–13) *Breaking Bad* continues to have a viewing life through streamed services and the availability of the DVD box set. As well as being a gripping story, however, with multiple interwoven plot lines, clever construction of onscreen visual imagery, and beautiful cinematography, the series offers an example of a fictional narrative which encapsulates some of the key concerns, issues, and assumptions which dominate Western culture at the start of the twenty-first century. Both as a 'text' which embodies such concerns in story form and in its reception by viewers responding to it, the series thus provides a case study of Western cultural anxiety. *Breaking Bad* maps a range of issues, not least to do with material well-being and the significance of money, the extent of self-reliance within Western individualism, addiction as a feature of Western culture, the importance of social structures, and the current state of the family as a social unit.[21]

The Basics of 'Original Sin'

At its simplest, original sin is the term given by Christian theology to the state of being in which it is claimed that all human beings stand merely by virtue of being human. Without, it is claimed, being wholly evil—for human beings remain God's creatures and are made in God's image—there is nevertheless within each human being an inevitability that all will display evil in their lives. Such 'sin' should not be deemed to be merely a list of wrong moral actions or choices. Rather, such choices and actions are the symptom of a basic tendency which, without correction and readjustment, perpetuates a fundamental orientation away from God—understood as the source of all goodness—and into oneself. Sin is thus, at its most basic, the temptation to take the place of God. It is 'original' in the sense that nothing can be done about it by any human being prior to its manifestation. Even then, God has to deal with it for us, whether or not our own

---

[21] Alongside these more general Western cultural issues are others (e.g. masculinity) and also more localized concerns (US relations with Mexico, the place of Latino/Latina citizens in the US).

activity contributes to that readjustment.[22] The sin is 'original' in the sense that it is inherited, part of the structure of existence into which we are born, and applies to all.[23]

None of this is presented as explicit theology in *Breaking Bad*, of course. If, however, we were to ask in the present 'But what, then, does this "original sin" look like in practice?', then it pays to unpick the actions of Walter White, and their consequences, as a way of exploring how the theological concept of sin, when understood as a fundamental disorientation of the human being and spirit, takes effect. I shall take each of the issues listed at the end of the previous section in turn in order to demonstrate how a contemporary work of fiction, into which viewers are lured affectively as they engage with it for entertainment purposes, can present a contemporary version of an existential challenge which persistently requires attention.

Concern for material well-being reflects a basic human need. Food, shelter, safety, and good health are sought by all. Walter White's ostensible reason for his drug-production enterprise is to provide such things for his family, in the absence of his own good health and his impending death. In the episode 'I.F.T.' (3.3), the point at which Walter seeks to involve his wife in the money-laundering operation, he again declares this as his motive. His quest for this becomes clinically rational at times. In the opening episode of the second season, 'Seven Thirty-Seven', Walter repeats his target figure ($737,000), his calculation of what will be needed to leave his immediate family with enough to live on once he is gone. By the fifth season, however, he has more money than he can count. In a memorable scene in a storage unit, Walter and Skyler stare at a vast pile of dollar bills (in 'Gliding over All', 5.8). Greed had long since taken over from the need to provide. In the same way that, as will be explored in Chapter 6, no amount of money can buy happiness or contentment once a basic level of material well-being has been reached, so also no amount of money proves satisfactory for White. Other factors have come into play: above all his desire to control and to run a drugs empire. This first hallmark of sin, then, is the quest for material wealth in one's own self-interest, well

---

[22] The Augustine v. Pelagius debate surfaces here and will reverberate throughout this entire study.

[23] There is no space here to discuss the merits of arguments, traceable back to Augustine, about how and why such sin is inherited. For our purposes here we need simply note sin's universality.

beyond what one needs for the physical well-being of oneself and immediate kin.

The desire to look after his family was understandable. The desire did, however, become tangled up both with Walter's need to reassert himself and with a weakened sense of his masculinity, which he believed to have been weakened by his failure—and now his apparent inability, due to his illness—to be the provider.[24] Even without a focus on Walter's challenged masculinity there is a strong emphasis here on self-reliance. At a number of points Walter refuses help. He does not accept financial help for his medical bills when it transpires he has inadequate insurance. On the contrary, he lies to his wife that he *has* accepted such help, whilst wanting to be the provider in his own (illegal and immoral) way. Self-reliance is thus taken by Walter to a destructive degree. Such destructive self-reliance—destructive of others as well as himself—is the apotheosis of an individualism which sees interdependence, or any form of reliance on others, as a mark of weakness. Whilst Walter may relate the self-reliance to his need to provide, in the final episode he corrects the repeated claim that he acted for his family by recognizing that he really did it all for himself ('Felina', 5.16). No closer confirmation is needed of Walter embodying a sense of sinfulness understood as being *'incurvatus in se'* (turned in upon oneself) than this declaration.[25] Second, sin thus manifests itself here as a form of destructive self-reliance.

The third feature of *Breaking Bad* which assists a contemporary exposition of the nature of sin can be drawn out of the first two features. Patterns of addiction are prominent in *Breaking Bad*. The drug culture and industry to which the majority of plot lines relate

---

[24] On the place of masculinity in *Breaking Bad*, see Brian Faucette, 'Taking Control: Male Angst and the Re-Emergence of Hegemonic Masculinity in *Breaking Bad*' (in Pierson, *Breaking Bad: Critical Essays*, 73–86). Note also David P. Pierson's comment: 'Neo-liberalism's economic-rational individualism is conflated with aggressive, hyper-masculine behavior in the series', in 'Breaking Neoliberal?: Contemporary Neoliberal Discourses and Policies in AMC's Breaking Bad' in the same volume (26).

[25] Though the phrase may not originate with Martin Luther, it receives its quintessential definition in Luther's commentary on Paul's Letter to the Romans: 'our nature, by the corruption of the first sin, is so deeply curved in on itself that it not only bends the best gifts of God towards itself and enjoys them (as is plain in the works-righteous and hypocrites), or rather even uses God himself in order to attain these gifts, but it also fails to realize that it so wickedly, curvedly, and viciously seeks all things, even God, for its own sake' (cited in Carl E. Braaten and Robert W. Jenson (eds.), *The Catholicity of the Reformation* (Grand Rapids, MI, and Cambridge: Eerdmans, 1996), 19).

set the basic context for the drama. Walter's business is successful because of the addictive culture off which it feeds. He himself becomes addicted to drug production and the accumulation of wealth. Jesse Pinkman, his collaborator, inhabits a world of drug addiction, moving in and out of the world of addicts as a drug user himself.[26] The climate of addiction is both the concrete context for the basic plot of *Breaking Bad* and a symbolic central motif of the culture within which the drama is set. The seeming domestic bliss of calm, comfortable suburban Albuquerque becomes the nodal point of a web of addictions. In exploring them, the series suggests that such loss of control, driven by distorted desire, is more typical of the culture in which the various plot lines play out than may first be supposed.

Disordered desire has become a commonplace definition of sin throughout Christian history since Augustine.[27] As with the first feature—the greed for wealth—it is not the fact of desire that in itself is wrong. Human beings have needs. The notion of disordered desire notes how easily the understandable thirst for what is needed or pleasurable (drink, food, sex, emotional satisfaction, physical exhilaration) can become uncontrollable. Highlighting the addictive patterns of behaviour prevalent in *Breaking Bad* should not be understood wholly to define the nature of sin as it is portrayed in the drama. In his study of the nature of addiction in its relation to Christian understanding of personhood, Christopher Cook shows that whilst addiction may not be qualitatively different from what occurs within the divided self of any human being, sin is not to be identified with addiction.[28] It might thus be better to say that the forms of addiction *Breaking Bad* portrays are simply the most striking manifestations in the West at present of the way in which sin takes shape. They are symptomatic of particular contemporary forms of the divided self. People may not want to do the things that they do. But they are

[26] It must surely be noted that there is a lack of realism about the ease with which he is able to free himself from that culture at different points throughout the series. Those who suffer from addictions and those who treat them will be able to report how much more entrenched and difficult to shift addictions are.

[27] This is a preoccupation of Augustine's *Confessions* (Harmondsworth: Penguin Books, 1961). For a recent exposition of this topic, see Anthony N. S. Lane, 'Lust: The Human Person as Affected by Disordered Desires' *Evangelical Quarterly* 78 (2006), 21–35.

[28] Christopher C. H. Cook, *Alcohol, Addiction and Christian Ethics* (Cambridge and New York: Cambridge University Press, 2006), 146–9.

compelled to do so by a potentially complex range of factors (e.g. internal drives or psychosocial factors), thus challenging the notion that addictive behaviour is an issue of individual will alone.[29] In Walter White's case, it might be argued that he is a 'willing addict', at least initially.[30] He is then bound by his initial choices so much so that he cannot stop his drive to create wealth, and to keep control of the means of production by which his wealth increases. Though there is some evidence he becomes an 'unwilling addict' in so far as he resolves many times to stop, and there is some sense that he struggles with an internal conflict, he is mostly bound by his desire to control.[31]

A fourth feature of *Breaking Bad* which helps us map the contemporary contours of sin concerns sin's social dimensions, and yet alongside this, paradoxically, the antisocial nature of sin. Building on the second and third features of sin already noted, Walter White's self-reliance is a key hallmark of the individualized, antisocial nature of sin, whilst also being a direct expression of the socio-economic context of the drive for personal wealth and the need to 'look after oneself and one's own' which shape Walter's behaviour. Walter is thus caught within a culture which encourages him to hide his material lack and initially pretend that things are better than they are, at the same time as believing that it is he, and only he, who can and should be the provider. Save for the structure of the family and the drug business empire he creates, Walter has little time or respect for the social structures to which he relates and within which he moves. He becomes disparaging to those he teaches, and 'loses it' with those who manage him in the school where he works, despite their pastoral care of him, and their gratitude for his efforts on the school's behalf.[32] Though dependent to a considerable degree on healthcare provision, yet initially prevaricating about whether to take up

---

[29] Cook, *Alcohol*, 149.

[30] A 'willing' addict as distinct from a 'wanton' or 'unwilling' addict (Cook, *Alcohol*, 156–7).

[31] One intriguing, though potentially also disturbing aspect of a drama about addiction being viewed in the present, when patterns of TV watching are changing rapidly, is that the watching itself becomes a form of addiction. Gone are the days when mass audiences viewed programmes synchronously. Such occasions now largely happen only for major sporting occasions. Otherwise, streaming services and box sets cultivate binge watching and addictive viewing. Whilst deeply pleasurable when well-managed, unhealthy behaviour patterns can also be cultivated.

[32] 'No Más' (3.1). See also 'A No-Rough-Stuff-Type Deal' (1.7).

treatment, he fails to respect those who value the care they receive.[33] As a criminal, he is consistently seeking to outwit and deceive those who seek to enforce the law, in particular the Drug Enforcement Administration, for which his brother-in-law Hank works. Thus, whilst on the surface presenting himself as a model citizen, a civil human being, his illegal and greedily acquisitive activity undermines his respect for others and both reflects and shapes the self-interest and self-absorption which drive him. He is respectful only of social structures which he can control, and this includes the family to which he belongs.

His kinship relationships are, however, significant for Walter. His desire to undertake actions 'for the family' as the only social unit outside his business empire which he deems important reveals aspects of his character and values which inform us about both Walter himself and the priorities of the culture in which he operates. Walter wishes to be provider for his family, even beyond his death. This is the reason he presents for his drug production. As noted already, this enables him to assert the kind of masculinity he believes he should demonstrate within the family unit. 'Family' appears, however, to be the only social unit in which he believes. At many points he assumes and seeks to assert patriarchal leadership within his family, although throughout the series he and Skyler are engaged in a power struggle, particularly with respect to decisions relating to the raising of their children, Walter Jr and Holly.[34]

The family unit functions in *Breaking Bad*, however, in a striking way as the primary social unit. Contained within Walter's declared purpose as provider is the assumption that this unit—the immediate, small-scale family—is what has to be preserved and fostered at all costs. Even if this declared intent is compromised by Walter's ultimate declaration of setting up his drug business *for himself*, I do not think this undermines a general point about the culture within which he lives. He believes that to strive to be the (male) provider for his immediate kin group has the best chance of proving a socially and

---

[33] 'Crazy Handful of Nothin'' (1.6), and also later, when he is pessimistic in the company of another patient ('Hermanos', 4.8). The question arises whether or not he is really in control.

[34] Some commentators on the series suggest that Walter is browbeaten, and subject to an overbearing wife in the early stage of the series. Whether or not this is an accurate reading, quite normal marital tensions exist between Walter and Skyler before the complexity of Walter's illegal activities take full effect on their relationship.

politically acceptable aspiration even in the face of illegal and destructive activity. It may not make the latter excusable, but it makes it comprehensible. In this respect, Walter reveals the extent to which, as a quite typical Western citizen, he prioritizes the immediate small family unit over all other forms of social living. It may even be possible to declare that he idolizes the family.[35]

Taking together these final two aspects of Walter's activity, we can note not only how little Walter respects social structures outside the family, but also the limited number of such structures and groupings which surface in the series. Religion, for example, plays little role, the only explicit appearance being the morbid fear of Heisenberg (Walter's alter ego once he develops a reputation for ruthlessness within the drug world) displayed by worshippers at a shrine for Santa Muerte, a saint of death (in 'No Más', 3.1), on which a drawing of Walter as Heisenberg has been placed. At the same time as being expressive of local fear of the mysterious drug lord, it could equally be seen as a parody of folk religion. It is nevertheless clear that such religion—and potentially all religion—has no place in Walter's own world, or the world of those immediately around him. For Walter at least it would clearly be the preserve of the less rational. Other forms of social structure are notable by their near total absence: sport, music, cinema, political groups, for example. The main spheres of activity are work, education, home/family. These are the contexts which have shaped Walter, his world, and his system of values, and which are the preoccupying structures of those to whom he relates. Of these, the most significant—and the one to which all other social groups are subservient—is family.

If this fivefold characterization of Walter's world—greed, self-reliance, addiction, disrespect of social structures, idolization of family—may be seen as presenting in sharp relief a dangerous underside of Western cultural life, then it is a characterization too of features from which Western culture needs saving. In this sense, it is accurate to call Walter's weaknesses a mapping of sin in its most basic form. What can be done about it we shall need to explore further in due course.

---

[35] I raise this both to point out the particular Western emphasis on the nuclear family, but also to begin to ask the question about what other forms of social unit might be considered as 'primary communities'. What shapes of social living, in other words, are we aspiring to create through the way we act? What are the limits of remaining tied primarily to kinship relationships in shaping just and flourishing communities?

At this stage we need simply acknowledge that *Breaking Bad* functions as a fictional drama which, whilst also providing compelling entertaining viewing, identifies features of Western society and of Western understanding of what it means to be human which merit close attention. There are features here which Western culture needs saving *from*. There is, for sure, no redemption for Walter White in *Breaking Bad*. There may be little present for any character in the drama. Whether this should be understood as suggesting that Western culture is beyond redemption in the eyes of Vince Gilligan, creator of *Breaking Bad*, and its team of screenplay writers is a moot point. But if the quest for a cultural theology of salvation is going to be successful, then it needs to take account of why dramas such as *Breaking Bad* and crime dramas such as *The Killing* and *The Bridge* prove so popular.[36] 'Scandinavian noir' may be merely the latest phase of a long tradition of crime fiction. But its stark and brutal realism and the way in which it presents challenging plots emerging from mundane daily life mesh with the popularity of *Breaking Bad*. They are all 'quality TV', and also belie the common misconception that popular culture is sugary and escapist. On the contrary, it is through such materials, in the course of daily life, within the world of entertainment, that 'the banality of evil' is being faced.[37] If, in theological terms, the identification and handling of sin are also to take place, then it is to such materials, too, that theology as a discipline needs to turn.

The two cases considered in this chapter enable us to look at what shape and content a contemporary soteriology must have. Whilst not offered as contributions to Christian theology, they are examples of Western cultural engagement with the theme of salvation from the perspectives of redemption and sin. Unlike the examples of Grünewald and Handel from Chapter 3, they do not work explicitly with theological subject matter. Yet they engage receivers (film and TV audiences) in ways similar to past and present viewers of the altarpiece and listeners to *Messiah* by creating an affective space within which constructive cognitive engagement can occur as a result of the

---

[36] *The Killing* ran for three series in its Danish original (2007, 2009, and 2012). *The Bridge* ran for three series 2011–15, and the fourth and final series aired in Scandinavia from January 2018, and began in the UK in May of the same year.

[37] The phrase 'banality of evil' was used by Hannah Arendt with reference to Adolf Eichmann (Hannah Arendt, *Eichmann in Jerusalem: A Report on the Banality of Evil*, Harmondsworth: Penguin Books, 1977).

works' emotional impact. Features of theological import now need to be noted.

Addiction is common to both examples considered. As noted, it may not be appropriate to equate sin and addiction. As well as being a concrete form of destructive behaviour, addiction is, however, also a particularly pertinent symbol of negative aspects of life from which salvation is needed: the uncontrolled need to acquire, or to believe that one would be satisfied with continual provision of some specific material or physical resource, or through some particular practice (be it money, drugs, alcohol, sex). One clear form of what contemporary Western people need saving *from*, then, is plainly presented: the thirst for ever more of something. Salvation is needed from an intense form of psychological enslavement, an inability to balance, control, or temper one's need for something. Acceptance of oneself as one is seems far away. It is implied that Blake—in film form at least—does find some form of resolution to his alcohol addiction. But, aside from the loss of the religious framework out of which his search for redemption emerges, it is not clear what he is saved *for*, or *into*, in terms of how his recovered life might be sustainable.

Second, common to both cases is what we may term a thin sociality. Blake resists his addiction through the help of another, and rediscovers friendships to some degree. But the future is not clear. White is the epitome of self-reliance and is overdependent on family, constructed, he hopes, in a manner of his own choosing. These contemporary encounters with forms of addiction thus disclose the way in which acute self-preoccupation and neglect of the full significance of others constitute a key element of what human beings need saving from.

Third, it would be inaccurate to claim that we have here unambiguous expositions of flourishing. In the case of *Crazy Heart* we may legitimately speak of recovery. In *Breaking Bad* there is either no redemption or, if there is, it is not of Walter White, but of his younger associate Jesse Pinkman. Even here it is an attenuated sense of redemption and may be more akin to survival and the possibility of later flourishing, rather than any current, life-enhancing emotional state or sense of well-being.

We are, then, far from any simple sense of happiness in either of these contemporary dramas. If these can be argued as typical of contemporary engagements with the reality of human wickedness, of sin and evil, or at least negative aspects of human living, then they may be deemed to offer a case study of the acknowledged current difficulty of securing redemption. This may be considered true to life. Theologically, it could be argued that the examples underplay the radical possibilities inherent in redemption, where human activity is considered insufficient to turn around a negative situation, and the experience of release from whatever enslaves may prove liberating to an extent not imagined. Highlighting the difficulty, unlikelihood, or apparent impossibility of redemption or rescue may, though, merely accentuate human activity occurring in isolation. It invites the question what *divine* activity could possibly mean in such a situation—for Blake, for White, for Pinkman. Neither example, however, suggests at this stage that happiness would be an accurate term for any positive result from, or response to, the struggles these key characters face.

A final twist in what these contemporary examples supply as an agenda for a theology of salvation, however, relates to the sin of self-reliance. The temptation to be self-reliant in the securing of redemption *from* self-reliance is great. Such a temptation merely compounds the sin of self-reliance. 'Working out one's own salvation' (with fear and trembling) can never mean being wholly responsible for one's ultimate well-being. Such would be a distortion of the Apostle Paul's words (Phil 2.12). We shall need in due course to return to the question of what it *does* mean, in the process of defining how much or how little human activity contributes to whatever liberative, salvific, redemptive activity is undertaken (and by whom) to promote happiness, flourishing, and well-being.

To conclude, a methodological observation relating to both Chapters 3 and 4 is needed. Isenheim, *Messiah, Crazy Heart*, and *Breaking Bad* constitute together a collection of resources combining high and popular culture, in different artistic media, with different levels of explicit engagement with the Christian tradition. They are not to be seen as definitive or in any way unique in their juxtaposition. They are simply examples, individually and together, of the ways in which cultural consumption evokes aesthetic and affective response and thereby prepares the ground for explicit theological engagement. The purpose of these two chapters has been simply to demonstrate that theological engagement occurs, still, in Western culture in many ways, with materials past and present, and not always directly in an ecclesiastical context. Such engagement is more than merely cognitive even if, in order to be articulated explicitly in theological terms, cognitive reflection is required, and will be developed further in due course. We are reminded that, by being evoked aesthetically and affectively, theology is a multidimensional, experiential matter. It could not be otherwise.

5

Salvation in Counselling and Comedy

I once asked a counselling training colleague whether she deemed that her work was intended to make people happy. She thought for a short time—though did not need long—before responding. 'Not directly', she said. 'If happiness results, then that's fine. But my job is to enable people to acknowledge and face the situation they are in, understand themselves better, and to find ways of handling what they are having to deal with.' I took that to be more of a 'no' than a 'yes' as a reply to my initial question.

This may already provide a major clue as to where we are likely to end up in a theological exploration of salvation, and in addressing the question whether salvation connects with happiness. If happiness is to feature, then there will be lots else going on around it in a person's life and self-understanding if they are to recognize that they are also 'saved' in some way.

But that would be to jump the gun. Not for nothing is it often remarked that counselling is a secular form of religion and of the ritual practices of penance and forgiveness in particular. As we noted in Chapter 4, popular culture reminds us forcefully of the challenges faced in the task of living. Addiction and a propensity towards wickedness remain as prominent as ever. These and many other life challenges have to be faced, and some people will use formal counselling to address these. But the majority will not. Salvation, redemption, liberation, forgiveness, release, joy, happiness, contentment, exhilaration, euphoria feature in mundane ways in the midst of friendships, in family relationships, and in religious and other social groups.

This reminds us that daily practices—whether religiously labelled or not—are contributing to what I am in this chapter acknowledging is a 'therapeutic' approach to salvation. Hence, whilst counselling may serve as a loose overall heading for the first part of this chapter,

I am not here exploring simply or primarily highly professional approaches and insights to the challenges and realities which make up the concept, practice, and processes of salvation. Undoubtedly, though, the work and insights of the caring professions, and the more informal practices which relate to that work, all overlap with what salvation is about.

Counselling practice in this general sense reminds us too that people's sense of unworthiness, failure, or despair may not be about their own failings but of handling feelings which result from being 'sinned against' (abuse of them by others), a feature of life which the history of Christianity's practical handling of salvation has been slow to recognize fully.[1] Only in the most general sense that the whole world (whole of creation), whilst 'good', is also caught up in a web of wickedness—and thus all are, in some way, 'sinned against'—has Christianity acknowledged this. There is, then, the danger that there may be less of a willingness to accept responsibility for one's own complicity. For the most part, though, Christianity has perhaps been more prone to make people feel bad about their own sins, and more inclined to accentuate people's carrying of guilt or shame for things for which they may not have been responsible.[2]

Paying attention to counselling, to the psychological theories and understandings on which its various forms are based, and to more directly therapeutic forms of Christianity will provide insight into important dimensions of how salvation works in practice for the recipient, or at least the one who seeks it. Whether or not all forms of counselling and counselling-related practice prove to be correlates of salvation, their dynamics help us approach salvation's therapeutic dimension.[3] There can be little doubt that salvation is received

---

[1] I mean this in two senses. Christianity has been less quick to pay attention to what it means to be 'sinned against' and more inclined only to address what it means to be a sinner (as an individual). Social and structural sin have been under-examined in much of Christian history. Related to that, the church's own role in structural forms of sin (e.g. covering up abuse) has only been slowly revealed and faced.

[2] For studies which focus directly on 'shame' as a theological topic or draw out the significance of shame within theology see Stephen Pattison, *Shame: Theory, Therapy, Theology*, (Cambridge: Cambridge University Press, 2000) and Alan Mann, *Atonement for a Sinless Society* (2nd edn, Eugene, OR: Cascade Books, 2015).

[3] By 'prove to be correlates' I mean whether or not it can be argued that counselling, however secular some of its forms may be, is in fact a means by which God acts to move people towards wholeness. Such a question lies beyond the immediate scope of this present study.

therapeutically by recipients in a great many ways. Only by examining current examples of where such therapeutic explorations and practices occur in the midst of everyday Western life will there be a chance to explore whether salvation and happiness may connect with what is being sought or experienced.

In this chapter, then, we take a slightly different point of departure from Chapters 3 and 4 in focusing less on cultural references to redemption and salvation, or on characterizations of human frailty or wickedness, and start at the other end of the soteriological dynamic: on possibilities of flourishing. Implicit within any examples which might be chosen lurk assumptions about what one needs to overcome (be 'saved from') to be able to flourish. Whether or not these are made explicit is not significant. My job is to identify and articulate them, not by suggesting that these are always 'implicit theologies' but by pointing out the structural similarity between what is happening and how a doctrine of salvation understands human life to work.

To begin with I focus on examples of the current popularity of positive psychology, and the forms of counselling, coaching, and mentoring which flow from it. References to 'flourishing' appear, as we shall see, prominently in the literature and practices of the move-ment. There are also explicitly Christian versions of positive psycho-logical practices, and I shall make reference to some of these. The main concerns in this inquiry will be, with respect to either secular or Christian versions: whether the language or conceptuality of salvation or redemp-tion is evident at any point; if it is, how this takes shape; if it is not, whether or how the language or practices of positive psychology are pertinent to contemporary discussions of salvation; whether 'flourishing' is helpful vocabulary for Christian theology to use with respect to salvation and, if so, at what points and in what ways.

From there I move on to a second example of flourishing, switch-ing back to a case study from popular culture to do so. Comedy—as live stand-up, film comedy, TV sitcom, TV panel show—is prominent as a form of art or entertainment in the West. It is easy to call it a form of therapy, as people readily recognize how positive, liberating, relaxing, cathartic, and pleasurable laughter can be.[4] It can be

---

[4] Freud cannot be allowed to have the last word on laughter or religion. Studies of the theological importance of humour include Karl-Josef Kuschel, *Laughter: A Theological Reflection* (London: SCM Press, 1994), Donald Capps, *A Time to*

escapism of the right kind—movement into a space which is not avoidance, but a place in which to be re-energized to be enabled to face the rest of life, having had things put into perspective. In this respect it can, whilst remaining entertainment, be a powerful coping mechanism. It can also be politically informative and values-shaping. But let us also be quite clear: all forms of comedy, whatever their other purposes or results, have one primary purpose: to make people laugh. That is how forms of comedy enable people to flour-ish. This means that all manner of distractions and red herrings will be present for an interpreter (not merely a theological interpreter) seeking to articulate what a form of comedy, as a genre, is 'saying', 'achieving', or 'doing to/for' the recipient. For, in truth, a form of comedy may not be 'saying' any single thing at all.[5] The content is driven by where the laughter is to come from, even when, in the case of stand-up, a comedian may well have particular (political or ethical) values she or he wishes to promote. This does not mean, though, that tough and valuable things are avoided. Political com-edy has specific, often biting purposes. In the case of the TV comedy I shall consider, important ethical considerations appear even alongside a whole range of plot lines which seem to pay lip service to ethical matters. That is how comedy works. It is, though, import-ant to use an example of comedy in this study to show how an area of life in which it may naturally be accepted that flourishing is prominent ('It is good to have a laugh,' 'If I couldn't laugh, then I don't know how I'd be'), may also connect not just with what salvation achieves, but also with how it is to be understood. In turn, such a reading of a feature of theology may offer in due course a contribution to understanding how comedy works and to noting its important function in the contemporary West.

Laugh: The Religion of Humor (London and New York: Continuum, 2005), and David Fergusson, 'Theology and Laughter', in Paul Middleton (ed.), *The God of Love and Human Dignity: Festschrift for George Newlands* (London and New York: T&T Clark, 2007), 107–16.

[5] This point also links with recognition of different models of communication which exist: the 'transmission' model (according to which a meaning is conveyed from one person to another) and a 'participative' model (where meaning is discovered or created between people). See, for example, James W. Carey, *Communication as Culture: Essays on Media and Society* (rev. edn, Abingdon and New York: Routledge, 2009).

POSITIVE PSYCHOLOGY AND HUMAN FLOURISHING

Writers and readers of theology books may need reminding that, for most of the world's population, formal counselling to support the practice of 'just getting on with life', coping, or even dealing with crises either is not on offer or would not be considered a realistic option (especially when needing to be paid for). Thankfully, counselling is now much more an accepted part of public life in the West. Helpline telephone numbers given after demanding TV dramas, references in news broadcasts to counselling being provided after major incidents (shootings, bombings, natural disasters), or mentions by celebrities or high-profile public figures of counselling they have received in their own struggles in life all enable the accessing of counselling to be recognized as quite normal. But taking advantage of professional counselling services may still not be regarded as an everyday practice by all, even whilst its concerns very much relate to daily life. Long waiting lists for counselling appointments are part of the experience of those who use the National Health Service (NHS) in the UK. Paying for counselling services may not be a financial option for many. It is therefore inevitable that a range of other, less professional, more informal forms of care tap into the same therapeutic stream.

Outside the world of formal counselling people have to get on with life. Informal counselling of all kinds occurs, even if not named as such. Listening and reflecting and, more directively and less related to counselling, tip- and advice-giving go on in abundance. In the field of employment, coaching, mentoring, and supervision of varying levels of formality occur, within which, at their best, strategies to encourage personal development and human flourishing occur. In spirituality, self-help strategies abound. The range of such practices can be deemed supportive or developmental with respect to human growth, or even therapeutic when there is a healing element involved: when something tough, problematic, or damaging is being faced, or when a difficult memory or experience is being processed. Where flourishing is blocked for any reason, then action of some kind is needed to clear the blockage. At this point, therapeutic activity of some sort begins to look like what salvation achieves in and for a human individual. Whether or not a wide variety of therapeutic practices may be able to be incorporated within a Christian understanding of salvation (on the grounds that all healing is ultimately of God) need not yet be the immediate focus of our attention. In accordance with the methodology being followed we do, though, need to take a critical look at where, in the current cultural climate, we find key examples of practices promoted to enable human flourishing. We need to see how, if at all, these may fit in with, inform, or critique Christian approaches to salvation which may themselves be deemed therapeutic.

PERMA and Flow in Theological Perspective

The positive psychology movement has been extremely influential across the world of psychology and beyond over the past three decades. Though it has its roots in the work of earlier humanistic psychologists such as Abraham Maslow and Carl Rogers, its recent resurgence comes through the research and writings of Martin E. P. Seligman and Mihaly Csikszentmihalyi in particular.[6] Succinctly expressed, positive psychology shifts the focus away from understanding the work of psychology, when made use of in therapy and counselling, as the relief of misery and more on the potential for human growth. Theory and practice thus become future-oriented rather than dwelling on the past. In Seligman's words: 'That we are drawn by the future rather than just driven by the past is extremely important and directly contrary to the heritage of social science and the history of psychology. It is, nevertheless, a basic and implicit premise of positive psychology.'[7] He recognizes the scale of the challenge that positive psychology issues to much therapeutic practice, especially psychotherapy, which, he suggests, 'is not designed to produce well-being, it is designed just to curtail misery', whilst also acknowledging that that 'is itself no small task'.[8]

Positive mental health, by contrast, 'is a presence... of positive emotion, the presence of engagement, the presence of meaning, the presence of good relationships, and the presence of accomplishment. Being in a state of mental health is not merely being disorder free; rather it is the presence of flourishing.'[9] This summary brings together

---

[6] Seligman's works include *Authentic Happiness: Using the New Positive Psychology to Realize your Potential for Lasting Fulfilment* (New York: Simon & Schuster, 2002) and *Flourish: A Visionary New Understanding of Happiness and Well-Being* (New York: Atria, 2013). Csikszentmihalyi's most well-known work is *Flow: The Psychology of Happiness: The Classic Work on How to Achieve Happiness* (London: Rider, 2002).

[7] Seligman, *Flourish*, 106.   [8] Seligman, *Flourish*, 183.

[9] Seligman, *Flourish*, 183.

the five elements which Seligman deems make up 'well-being', the term he prefers over 'happiness' in his more recent work, and which produce the mnemonic 'PERMA': Positive Emotion, Engagement, Relationships, Meaning, and Accomplishment.[10] It is worth looking at each of these briefly in turn.

Positive emotion is also termed by Seligman the 'pleasant life', and comprises 'pleasure, rapture, ecstasy, warmth, comfort, and the like'.[11] Positive emotion is subjectively measured—only I can tell you whether or not I feel happy—but it is vital as an element in well-being. Moving on from his earlier work, Seligman stresses the difficulty when the whole of well-being (or flourishing) is identified too closely with only this first element.[12] This explains why he has become irritated by the overemphasis on happiness, which he deems to denote only a mood (life satisfaction).[13] Nevertheless, to be well, it is understandable that one would expect also to be able to say one feels well (and is happy, content, satisfied).

Positive emotion is, however, inadequate when taken in isolation. Already at this early stage it may be possible to see how psychological insight contributes to a contemporary exploration of a theological understanding of well-being. *Engagement* is also crucial. Also to be measured subjectively, it denotes the thrill of being absorbed within and by an activity in which one is engaged, being 'lost' in a pleasurable way, even if this judgement is only made retrospectively.[14] This could, of course, be an activity of work or leisure. To live a life without a number of such (even regular) activities would be a gloomy existence.

Third, well-being presupposes one enjoys a network of positive *relationships*. 'Very little that is positive is solitary.'[15] Not only is no one an island, but interactions with others contribute to—even generate—'the pleasure, ecstasy, comfort, warmth, and the like' which are experienced subjectively.

Engaged activities and the intensity of one's experience of them may contribute to a fourth element of well-being: *meaning*. Meaning comprises, however, more than a merely subjective response to an

---

[10] Seligman, *Flourish*, 16–20.   [11] Seligman, *Flourish*, 11.

[12] Seligman, *Flourish*, 16.

[13] Seligman, *Flourish*, 14; 'I actually detest the word *happiness*, which is so overused that it has become almost meaningless. It is an unworkable term for science, or for any practical goal such as education, therapy, public policy, or just changing your personal life' (Seligman, *Flourish*, 9).

[14] Seligman, *Flourish*, 17.   [15] Seligman, *Flourish*, 20.

event or activity. Something 'counts' if it has meaning. Something is meaningful if it connects us with others and takes us beyond ourselves. There is no necessity of a transcendent reference here. There could be one, but it is not required. It is necessary, though, for others to recognize the meaningfulness of what is claimed to have meaning.[16]

Finally, note must be taken of what one achieves: one's *accomplishments*. Interestingly, Seligman was initially reluctant to make too much of this, disputing that accomplishments might be undertaken for their own sake, arguing that there was always something further in view (e.g. winning, mastery). It is, however, possible to undertake a task for the pleasure of the doing, and to see it through to completion. This need not be undertaken in a competitive, achievement-driven context. For an accomplishment to contribute to well-being, it is to be undertaken for the pleasure of the doing, and to be freely chosen.

When these five elements are supplemented by a key insight from Csikszentmihalyi, just how fulfilling human life can be becomes clear. 'Flow' is seen by Seligman as an aspect of Engagement.[17] But it accentuates that element, stressing that it must be distinguished from happiness, as flow may not necessarily be experienced at the time as a positive state. Flow is the exhilaration of experience one has when one performs something well or is caught up in a process of reception of an overwhelming work of art or sporting performance. Even if resulting from an act of exertion, and the product of a performance which derives from extensive practice, it still has the quality of a gift. One cannot summon flow in any guaranteed way. It is simply to be enjoyed when it comes.

What is to be made of this summary of positive psychology's key elements? It is striking that whilst none of the six features just described inevitably requires any level of material comfort in itself (save perhaps for the first: positive emotions of any kind arguably require a basic level of material well-being), there is an assumption that one has a context in which one can choose tasks freely (things to accomplish, in which one may 'lose' oneself, and experience flow). Flourishing may be less possible when—whether employed or not—such freedom is not obvious. Childcare, for example, can produce all such experiences but more readily presents a series of demands.

---

[16] Seligman, *Flourish*, 17–18.   [17] Seligman, *Flourish*, 11 and 273–4.

Thus, whilst this list of elements of well-being is sure to prove helpful in the longer term when this study seeks to clarify what one is 'saved for', and what such salvation amounts to in terms of flourishing human experience, for the moment it needs to be accepted that its job has been to question the overemphasis, even in secular experience, on what one needs to be 'saved from'. In the same way, in other words, as positive psychology challenged psychotherapy for its focus on release from misery and underemphasis on personal growth, so we may be helped in due course to see more sharply the limitations of focusing theologically on what one needs to be 'saved from'. Sin, guilt, and shame—as Christian tradition tellingly reminds us—all have to be addressed. But how these are to be understood and characterized, and what addressing them will mean, can be informed by what positive psychology presents to us.

A Gospel of Happiness

Positive psychology has, though, surfaced in Christian forms in recent years, and so it is important to take a look at some examples of these forms. When viewed in relation to the caring professions, religious forms of flourishing may seem questionable, even dangerous, by comparison: religious practice has perhaps become 'a poor person's counselling', insufficiently informed by psychological research. Inevitably, from the perspective of attention to millennia of Christian and even longer religious thought and practice, such a view is short-sighted. The wheat and chaff of religious belief and practice still have to be sifted— and this itself is not always easy to do—but religious activity at its best does more than just help people 'get through life'. It is life-enhancing and life-shaping. To claim this is not to deny that there are dangerous forms of religion around. Critics of what I shall go on to consider in this section would regard all forms of prosperity theology to be dangerous, for example.[18] And as I know from my participation in secular academic life, there are plenty around who would deem all forms of religious thought and practice dangerous!

That said, there are examples of forms of contemporary Christianity which tap directly into positive psychology. I use two, one Protestant,

---

[18] A very helpful recent study of prosperity theology is Kate Bowler, *Blessed: A History of the American Prosperity Gospel* (New York: Oxford University Press, 2013).

one Roman Catholic, to explore the forms that such use takes, before offering a brief evaluation.

Joel Osteen: *Your Best Life Now*

Joel Osteen (b. 1963) is pastor of Lakewood Church in Houston, Texas. Having begun as producer of his father's televised local ministry, Osteen became pastor himself after his father's death in 1999. Though without formal training and with minimal experience of leading worship and preaching himself, Osteen took over as head of the Lakewood Church.[19] In his own view, his editing and production of his father's work over the seventeen-year period he was producer of the TV side of the church's ministry enabled him to explore and learn about the content of the faith he professed.[20]

The basic version of the message Osteen now presents and seeks to embody is a firm call to, and affirmation of, human growth and potential. Whilst it may be considered a variant of a 'self-help' strategy, and it is true that there is a persistent thread on what a person must *do* to enable God to do what God would like to do for a person, it is clear that Osteen believes it is the action of God which brings human fulfilment about. The seven steps to a fulfilled life are clear: enlarge your vision, develop a healthy self-image, discover the power of your thoughts and words, let go of the past, find strength through adversity, live to give, and choose to be happy.[21] A person can help themselves towards this fulfilled life by taking the necessary actions implied and explored within Osteen's presentation of these seven steps. His exposition is replete with practical examples (anecdotes and stories) of how these steps come to life.[22]

Parts 4 and 5 (let go of the past, find strength through adversity) of this sevenfold strategy are clearly the points at which this journey of

---

[19] The fullest account to date of Osteen's ministry is Phillip Luke Sinitiere, *Salvation with a Smile: Joel Osteen, Lakewood Church, and American Christianity* (New York: New York University Press, 2015). See also the helpful studies of specific aspects of Osteen's ministry: Helje Kringlebotn Sødal, '"Victor, not Victim": Joel Osteen's Rhetoric of Hope', *Journal of Contemporary Religion*, 25 (2010), 37–50 and Luke A. Winslow, 'The Imaged Other: Style and Substance in the Rhetoric of Joel Osteen', *Southern Communication Journal*, 79 (2014), 250–71.

[20] Sinitiere, *Salvation with a Smile*, 113–17.

[21] These are the titles of the seven main parts of Osteen's *Your Best Life Now* (London: Hodder, 2008).

[22] On the skill of Osteen's rhetoric, see Sødal, '"Victor, not Victim"'.

living to one's full potential is to be seen also a salvific journey. In the midst of the positive approach to life which Osteen promotes it is recognized that there are likely to be things which have to be overcome. Indeed, Osteen seems to accept that this is universal: 'We've all had negative things happen to us.'[23] This is not, though, some inner turmoil or state of anxiety which bedevils the human condition.[24] Furthermore, Osteen talks little about sin. But whatever has befallen us, the impact of such negative events upon us can be overcome. Indeed, we have the power to turn things around, because it is we who are allowing things to remain that way.[25]

Osteen is far from explicit about his tapping into theories derived from positive psychology.[26] He plays down any reference to academic authorities, if he is even aware of them, in both psychology and theology.[27] Indeed, whilst he is an explicitly Christian evangelist and clear about the extent to which the turnaround of our human experience is God-dependent, Osteen's message is surprisingly light on biblical material and theological concepts. The Bible is used mostly for useful stories about characters (a 'like you and me' approach) than for theological themes. In his key work, *Your Best Life Now*, as Sødal notes, Jesus is referred to less than are Old Testament characters.[28] Sin and salvation are not prominent as themes, even though it could be argued that such a theological framework does provide Osteen with the basic shape of his message. There is a constant forward thrust in what he presents such that people are encouraged to be in continual development: becoming nicer, kinder people, giving more, loving more, caring more. This will both help them as people and be better for their communities.

---

[23] Osteen, *Your Best Life Now*, 191.

[24] Interestingly, though, there is a demonology of sorts within Osteen's theology. Whilst he does not speak of the devil, he does refer to 'the enemy'.

[25] Osteen, *Your Best Life Now*, 191.

[26] Though Barbara Ehrenreich includes Osteen within her negatively critical look at the positive thinking movement in *Smile or Die: How Positive Thinking Fooled America and the World* (London: Granta, 2009), 125–33.

[27] It would not be right to say that Osteen 'wears his learning lightly', for he makes no claims to scholarship. Whether or not there is much substance to academic inquiry behind what he presents would not, in any case, be deemed all that important for him. His job is to communicate, and to communicate as effectively as he can with as wide an audience as possible.

[28] Sødal, '"Victor, not Victim"', 45.

The eschatological framework within which this activity is taking place is unclear. The fulfilled life is certainly to be enjoyed *now*—the very focus of Osteen's basic message. Even if an afterlife is assumed, this is far from the key to Osteen's message. Osteen offers no reflection on this present life being made 'like heaven' (heaven and hell simply do not appear). God wants us to enjoy the now, so our task is how we go about fitting into that joy which God wants. That said, Osteen does not use the language of flourishing. We are, instead, to strive for *excellence*. Osteen seems to have a particular aversion to 'mediocrity', something which we are invited not to settle for on many occasions as we read his main text.[29]

Whether or not what Osteen offers here is, in fact, simply a thinly Christianized form of the (secular) American dream, there can be little doubt that Osteen is sincere in his message and practices. He is no charlatan and his church is clearly doing good work.[30] His message proves helpful for people in great numbers. As an example of how a form of positive psychology can function in a Christian form, it is clearly a valuable version of Christian faith for many people. Yet Osteen antici-pates opposition to what he says even in his own work. 'But Joel . . . ' objections are inserted into, and responded to, throughout his text, thereby recognizing that some objectors will claim he is dodging life's tough aspects, living a charmed life himself, and underestimating the extent to which those with deep problems (emotional, financial, phys-ical) cannot adopt his positive message. Osteen's message is credible as identifiably Christian but does not offer as full or as deep a version of Christianity as its theology of salvation is capable of supplying. In short, Osteen fails the test of doing justice to Isenheim and those who—as contemporary viewers—are able to get inside the experience of Isenheim viewers in the present.

Christopher Kaczor: *The Gospel of Happiness*

A second example of positive psychology's presence within contem-porary Christian circles is the work of Christopher Kaczor. Kaczor is a

---

[29] Osteen, *Your Best Life Now*, 10, 17, 35–6, 43, 96, 117, 202, 255, 377, 386, 395, 404, and 411.

[30] Whilst this book was in the final stages of preparation Osteen received criticism for not opening the doors of his church immediately at the time of the Houston floods in September 2017. It was some days before the Lakewood Church premises were made fully accessible. Osteen went public about the reasons for this, offering a full explanation, and faced direct questioning on TV.

professor of Philosophy and a Roman Catholic. He writes both academic and popular works. His *The Gospel of Happiness* is quite different in content, style, and tone from Osteen's work, and yet he is seeking a similar readership: the 'ordinary person', even if Kaczor may have practising Catholics in mind.[31]

Unlike Osteen, as an academic Kaczor 'shows his working'. He engages openly with past and present thinkers (there are nineteen pages of footnotes and explicit mentions of conversation partners within the text). He is much more concerned than Osteen to ground his presentation in external sources and defend his position, rather than invite the reader simply to adopt a particular positive lifestyle and see what happens. Kaczor's presentation is much more an invitation to a set of spiritual practices which clearly slot into an identifiable Christian tradition.

Pertinent to our current discussion is the fact that, in addition to presenting what he recommends in terms of Christian tradition and spirituality, Kaczor locates his exposition of the 'Gospel of happiness' directly in relation to Seligman's understanding of well-being. PERMA features explicitly as a contemporary backcloth against which the 'Gospel of happiness' becomes comprehensible. Even if not presented as a perfect fit—PERMA is not identical with the Gospel, and there are clearly things that Kaczor believes positive psychology cannot achieve—Kaczor has no doubt that the overlap of intentions and concerns between PERMA and the Gospel are important to spell out.

How, then, does Kaczor proceed? After a lengthy scene-setting opening chapter ('The Ways to Happiness'), in which connections to the five elements of PERMA are made explicit, Kaczor offers six steps to happiness: the ways of (1) faith, hope, and love, (2) prayer, (3) gratitude, (4) forgiveness, (5) virtue, and (6) willpower.[32] The book is therefore offered explicitly as a Christian take on PERMA. The five elements are appreciatively received and interpreted, and will become touchstones and conversation partners in what will later be expounded (across chapters 2–7 of Kaczor's study) in terms of the six 'ways'. Prior to that, however, Kaczor suggests six ways in which 'Christian

---

[31] Christopher Kaczor, *The Gospel of Happiness: Rediscover your Faith through Spiritual Practice and Positive Psychology* (New York: Image, 2015).

[32] Seligman's *Flourish* is introduced in the opening line of chapter 1 (Kaczor, *Gospel of Happiness*, 21). The five elements of PERMA are then treated in turn: positive emotion (22–7), engagement (28–9), relationships (30–2), meaning (32–5) and achievement [*sic*] (35–8).

happiness' differs from the happiness sought by and expounded within positive psychology. These merit scrutiny.

First, Kaczor suggests, 'positive psychology has no answer to the problem of death'.[33] Kaczor deals with this quite swiftly, however. 'Death destroys positive emotion, engagement, relationships, meaning and achievement, but not the Christian conception of happiness, because Christianity offers the hope of heaven.'[34] Whilst such a response is understandable, the danger of such a response, of course, is that this can lead to Christian relative lack of interest in this present life, a criticism often made of Christian belief. It is necessary neither to have a conclusive, clear eschatology nor to collapse all Christian interest into current living (heaven now) to accept that positive psychology and Christianity can do business with each other in relation to contemporary, everyday living (as indeed Kaczor goes on to do). Positive psychology may thus have little to offer in the face of the fact of death. Who has? It seems fairer to accept that positive psychology makes no claim to be dodging the reality of biological death and that, within the terms of its limited brief, it is nevertheless potentially of use to Christian thought and practice.

Second, Kaczor is critical of positive psychology for having no 'ordering of the elements'. It does not, in other words, rank them in importance or take note of the fact that we may only draw on some of the five in particular instances. By contrast, Kaczor says, Christianity will always put relationships (with God and others) first.[35] This does seem a slightly harsh criticism of the PERMA approach. It could be argued that flourishing will obviously result from the interplay of all five elements. It could also be said that a person may connect more readily with one of the five first in their search for contentment. On the other hand, because it provides Kaczor with the opportunity to accentuate this particular theological take on the five elements, and in a way which looks ahead to the social aspect of salvation that this study will be required to address in due course, then it is a useful insight.

Third, Kaczor opposes positive psychology's neutrality with respect to God's existence. Again, this is rather harsh. As Kaczor admits, an academic discipline which seeks to deal only with the empirically viable is not going to be able to deal with God. Psychology can only handle what people do and say in response to their beliefs

---

[33] Kaczor, *Gospel of Happiness*, 41.   [34] Kaczor, *Gospel of Happiness*, 41.
[35] Kaczor, *Gospel of Happiness*, 42.

and convictions about God. Both this and the fourth objection—that positive psychology cannot actually deal with people's feelings of guilt—are predicated on the assumption that only theology can account for what is 'really' going on and can actually happen through the working of God.

Kaczor's comments that: 'While psychological practices can help relieve people's feelings of guilt, they cannot relieve guilt itself . . . No psychologist can forgive sins, nor can any psychological practice.'[36] This is bound to be the conclusion of a theologian who is convinced that wherever forgiveness and the relief of guilt occur, then God is the author. But it underplays the role which may be played in the process by a variety of psychological and counselling approaches of which positive psychology is one. The contrast drawn is rather stark. It is reasonable to claim that God is at work in the midst of human psychological processes and practices.

Fifth, Kaczor notes that Christian faith supplies knowledge about love, on the basis of which loving becomes more possible. The love which God brings, says Kaczor, will inevitably be more profound than any approach to love based on human knowledge alone. Again, in theological perspective this is difficult to dispute. Once more, however, lived realities suggest a more complex picture than Kaczor's objection can account for. Human love, both the search for it and the discovery of it (the 'being found by it', we may say) interweaves so directly with divine love that such a sharp disjuncture as Kaczor presents is difficult to sustain. To claim that divine love is the deepest of all need not counter the possibility that human experience of love may be the means through which that divine love is discovered. The experience of human love can itself be the imparting of information about divine love to those involved. Theology's role is then a hermeneutical one: to enable the disclosure of what it means for the deepest love to be seen as 'of God' and 'in Christ'.

Finally, Kaczor suggests that 'psychology . . . cannot adequately satisfy the human desire for truth'.[37] Again this is a variant on his third objection. Where there is no conviction about God's reality, then aspirations towards transcendence are but that: aspirations. Empirical approaches to understanding human reality are insufficient. If it is held that the truth of reality requires a theological

---

[36] Kaczor, *Gospel of Happiness*, 44–5.   [37] Kaczor, *Gospel of Happiness*, 46.

interpretation, then this will indeed take us beyond empirical findings (not just in psychology). We will, though, still have to argue a case for the wisdom of using such interpretation of human experience. Ultimately, though, from a theological perspective Kaczor is quite correct to say that 'A Christian account of a fully flourishing human life includes elements that are not subject to scientific verification.'[38] The challenge will be to demonstrate the plausibility of a Christian account in relation to aspects of life which *are* subject to empirical testing. Our discussion of Kazcor's book has at least sharpened that point.

Positive Psychology in Salvific Perspective

What, then, can be said in summary by way of assessment and appreciation of these encounters with Seligman, Osteen, and Kaczor? How, if at all, do these presentations of, and engagement with, positive psychology assist the contemporary task of noting the relationship between a doctrine of salvation and belief in, and enjoyment of, human flourishing? Three important insights emerge.

First, all of these manifestations of the potentially helpful role to be played by positive psychology in developing a doctrine of salvation highlight the damage of focusing upon the negative.[39] Whilst it can be argued that a doctrine of salvation only exists because sin exists, and therefore attention to the negative is inevitable, it must equally be recognized that sin can only be named because a way of salvation is available. Only in theological perspective is sin 'good news'. But it is 'good news' because of what is on offer. In much of Christian thought and practice, however, one would not be able clearly to see the extent to which the doctrine of salvation is good news. What one is 'saved from', in all the different dimensions in which sin takes shape, cannot (must not) be underplayed. But to overemphasize sin leads to the difficulties which, in practice, positive psychology seeks to address.

Second, the evident tension between the value and importance of human agency and the theological conviction of human fallibility must be acknowledged. The strong sense that it is God who saves, and that there is something both cognitively and affectively vital

---

[38] Kaczor, *Gospel of Happiness*, 47.
[39] '(T)he best argument against Christianity is unhappy Christians' (Kaczor, *Gospel of Happiness*, 48). He refers to Chesterton here, though he could equally have drawn on Nietzsche.

in recognizing that human beings do not save themselves, stands opposed to the emphasis on what human beings need to do in order to be more positive about themselves and their future. This will become a key feature in later chapters of how a contemporary doctrine of salvation unfolds.

Third, positive psychology reveals a tendency to aim for the *most* that can be achieved. Human flourishing comes to mean that one should always seek to maximize one's potential. Osteen's campaign against 'mediocrity' was striking here. This is, of course, helpful as a counter to any sense of merely 'making do'.[40] Where it may prove unhelpful is in the way such an approach to human fulfilment depends on constant improvement and continuous striving. Though it need not do so, this sits easily alongside a competitive approach to life.[41]

Overall, though, the approach to living which positive psychology promotes is a helpful way to enable contemporary theology to examine the points at which an exposition of a doctrine of salvation undertaken from the perspective of human flourishing may have a chance of being comprehensible. The critical comparison—between doctrinal emphases and current cultural understandings of flourishing—is not simply about accessibility, however. The interaction enables ongoing tensions in doctrine (e.g. between the forms of divine and human agency) to be addressed afresh. The theological import (*Gehalt*) of positive psychology could, then, be said to be a form of 'living from the future' which enables people to be hopeful and constructively positive. It will, however, also become apparent that the social dimension of flourishing (respect for the concept and practice of the Kingdom of

---

[40] The tendency towards quietism ('putting up with' rather than seeking to change) shown within some branches of Christianity is also pertinent here.

[41] I have been taking note over many years now of the way in which the 'quest for excellence' in professional life appears to mask a thirst for perfection. This simply unrealistic form of perfectionism ends up making impossible demands on employees, whose job roles are structured in such a way that whilst they may not 'fail', they will never be able to feel wholly satisfied, because their posts will not allow them to. They must 'continuously improve' and there are even 'Continual Improvement Officer' posts emerging in large organizations. Even accepting that monitoring of efficiency is always necessary, I think there is a deficient anthropology at work here, as it leaves no real room for human frailty and limitation. Religions have, of course, contributed to the 'thirst for perfection', Christianity included ('Be perfect...as your heavenly Father is perfect', Matt. 5.48). More needs to made here, though, of the fact that religions wrestle with the *distinction* between humanity and God (the latter alone being perfect) and what it means to live within that distinction, and with frailty.

God) and the continued need to acknowledge human failings will have to be addressed.

THE BIG BANG THEORY: THE RECEPTION OF A TV COMEDY

If the examples of popular culture chosen for consideration in Chapter 4 seemed either sentimental (*Crazy Heart*), pessimistic (*Breaking Bad*), or non-theological (both), then, the selection in this section is markedly different. *The Big Bang Theory* is light, episodic, hit-and-miss, laugh-aloud funny, ephemeral, and, as I write, still incomplete. 'Classic' comedy takes time to prove itself, so it is too early to say whether *The Big Bang Theory* will become part of a comedy canon. I engage with it in this theological discussion for a number of reasons. First, I want to explore resources that evidently have an impact upon people; *The Big Bang Theory* has a huge following.[42] Even if, as with any comedy, it will have a limited appeal, it is at least accessible and appears to attract a wide cross section of viewers.[43] Second, it is important for my method that I interact with an example of cultural life which promotes, and seeks to promote, well-being, happiness, a feel-good response, flourishing, even if this may only be, or seem to be, in a superficial way. If it can be shown, for example, that 'happiness' pertains mostly to ephemeral cultural products, and is appropriate as a description of what such comedies bring about, then this could be seen as a counterargument to the notion that happiness be seen as one legitimate reading of what salvation produces. If, on the other hand, this further example of 'quality TV' fulfils a broader cultural function than the short-lived emotional highs which comedies clearly achieve, then explorations of salvation in contemporary culture would do well to interpret such shows. Third, in digging around for appropriate

[42] The viewing figures for US airings of the show have, for example, been consistently above 18 million from the sixth to the tenth series. The eleventh series (current at the time of writing) is commanding viewing figures of 13–14 million (https://en.wikipedia.org/wiki/The_Big_Bang_Theory_(season_11), accessed 20 December 2017).

[43] Viewer demographics show a spread of viewers across the 18–45+ age-range, with a majority being male, though female viewers rate it more highly than males. See http://z2solutions.com/demographics/big-bang-theory-audience-demographics/, accessed 25 September 2017.

resources to work with in order to undertake my cultural theological investigation, I came across a number of online groups and websites which interact with *The Big Bang Theory* because of its positive presentation of a leading fictional character (Dr Sheldon Cooper) who seems to be on the autism spectrum. Without explicitly declaring this to be the case, and whilst not wholly consistently presenting the character as such, the show has nevertheless slotted an 'on the spectrum' character into a mainstream comedy show. 'Dealing with Sheldon' is undoubtedly a clear motif in the series—his quirks are demanding. But the series does more than this. Putting four male 'geeks' together, initially with just one more worldly-wise female character, and then alongside two further intellectually bright (female) scientists, creates a group of strong characters whose abilities are all, in their different ways, exaggerated, and yet whose inadequacies and foibles are allowed for and accommodated within supportive friendships.[44] In such a mix, Sheldon Cooper is different in kind not in degree. It is this feature of the series which has endeared it to, and made it practically helpful for, viewers with Asperger's syndrome, and parents and carers of anyone on the autism spectrum.

The fourth reason for choosing *The Big Bang Theory* as a case study is that religion is not ignored as a theme in the life of its main characters. Though handled relatively superficially, easily caricatured, and often parodied, different types of religious commitment and conviction appear in the series: evangelical Christianity, Judaism, Hinduism, and atheism appear explicitly, particularly in so far as they interact with the majority of the lead characters' scientific rationalism in their work, and as it affects their customs and moral assumptions (and conflicts) as they set about forming relationships, including making decisions about their sex lives.

In short, the series offers an excellent basis through which to read and critique *from the positive end* of popular cultural life—where human well-being is sought and celebrated affectively—prevalent Western insights about what it means to flourish as a human being.

---

[44] I was once challenged for using the terms 'geeks' and 'nerds' in a discussion about the programme. It should be explained that these are self-descriptions of the lead scientific characters in the show, and much of the humour trades off their self-awareness in this regard—their detailed knowledge and enthusiasm for their subjects, alongside their social awkwardness.

Friends beyond *Friends*: Theological Aspects
of *The Big Bang Theory*

If TV functions now as Bibles have in the past, as I suggested in Chapter 4, then as well as mapping cultural assumptions about human evil, TV also provides materials with which people think through their approaches to how to live, and the values by which they are shaped and choose to conduct themselves. The phrase 'think through' admittedly implies a more conscious, cognitively controlled way in which this happens than is likely to be the case, of course.[45] And because such resources as TV can function in this way for viewers, this does not mean that they always do so, or that there is much of an interactive or reflective process which occurs even when viewers may be watching for *more* than entertainment.

TV comedy, though, is clearly a channel through which much reflection on contemporary cultural values is prompted. Despite their distance from the cultural context out of which they come, US comedy programmes (such as *Cheers* (1982–3), *Roseanne* (1988–97), *Seinfeld* (1989–98), *Friends* (1994–2004), and *30 Rock* (2006–13)) have set the standard and provided the tone for a brash but punchy and thoughtful style of comedy which reflects back to its viewers features of contemporary Western living. Transported and transmitted throughout the world, such comedy thus parades the preoccupations of (usually relatively affluent and relatively young) Western citizens.[46] The issues explored are thus a partial exploration of what is deemed significant. By virtue of their appeal and the demands of commercial interest, however, the human-interest dimension—and the need to address 'perennial issues' of life—is inevitably uppermost. Despite the specifics of its theme—clever scientists, social awkwardness—*The Big Bang Theory*, which first aired in 2007, is no exception here. Issues of

---

[45] Once more, I note that it is within '*affective* space', where the emotions and senses are first aroused, that cognitive activity may then go on to happen, though even then it is not a clearly sequential matter, i.e. cognition is always already tangled up with the emotional response. See also on this now Kutter Callaway and Dean Batali, *Watching TV Religiously: Television and Theology in Dialogue* (Grand Rapids, MI: Baker Academic, 2016).

[46] *Roseanne* is something of an exception here, being one of the few US TV shows, let alone comedies, to offer a sympathetic presentation of working-class life. In the UK there have been more examples, though they have not always escaped the charge of caricature (*Steptoe and Son* (1962–5 and 1970–4), *Till Death Us Do Part* (1965–75), and *Only Fools and Horses* (1981–2003)).

forming friendships, dating and mating, personal identity, challenges of domestic life, job dilemmas, developing confidence, relating to parents and siblings are all prominent in the series. It is precisely for this reason that such comedies sometimes work within and across cultures, allowing for adjustments made by viewers. When perennial concerns are identified, cultural equivalents can often be found.

I begin, then, from the premise that, whilst functioning as entertainment, *The Big Bang Theory* also addresses a persistent set of questions about what constitutes human flourishing. This being so, for the purposes of this present inquiry I shall ask what—in the course of handling relationships, establishing themselves in jobs and incomes, getting on in life, and, above all, dealing with their own foibles, inadequacies, and grounds for lack of self-confidence—is also being implied about what human beings need saving *from* and *for* as they seek to fashion meaningful lives. And in the midst of their self-interest, how do they relate to others? What are seen as obstacles to flourishing, and how are these faced? Who is included in, and excluded from, their world? What values are they living by? In the process of interpreting the series as a 'text', exactly as was the case with *Crazy Heart* and *Breaking Bad*, we attend too to what is happening at the point of reception, between the series and the viewer.

I begin by highlighting three features of *The Big Bang Theory* which pertain to human flourishing. As prominent, positive features, these merit careful scrutiny from the perspective of salvation simply because they entail the handling of obstacles in life or of negative experiences. In so far as the comedy series continually shows how such features are embodied within daily living, it functions constructively and therapeutically for viewers interacting with it as they face the challenges addressed.

First, the series confronts the issue of what it means to accept, and befriend, people *as they are*. The humour derives largely from the accentuated quirks and habits of four unconfident men who are nevertheless highly talented in their own individual ways. Penny, the new neighbour of Sheldon and Leonard, is actually less confident than she appears—and thus has more similarities with the men than initially expected—but represents a more 'ordinary' world out of which she is able to inform, instruct, and challenge the overachievers about aspects of social life. There are plot lines which find characters trying to change others (e.g. Leonard's struggle with Penny's low level of formal education, Amy's teaching Sheldon how to read signs and cues of people's emotions). But these are to be understood more as supportive, developmental aspects of friendship than conditions of acceptance. The series is a striking study of what it means to build relationships whilst letting people discover and express who they are.

In terms of the theological discussion being engaged in in this book, when starting from the end of flourishing, the comedy invites viewers to witness, within the drama itself, how people accept and interact with each other, whilst inviting them then to reflect on their own relationships and whether they make demands and enforce conditions prior to seeking to be friends. We seem at this point to be very distant from anything that one is to be 'saved from'. Yet what we are doing is entering the salvation template at the points of what one is saved for and into, i.e. *for* a flourishing life and *into* a supportive community. Only from the security of such a safe position might one then be able to see what one has been saved *from*.

Second, the series provides a wonderful example of where, in the midst of social awkwardness and lack of confidence, these friends can nevertheless, at their best, supply support and deep affirmation of each other's gifts and skills, and of the very fact of friendship. Despite much overt disparaging—Sheldon Cooper in particular needs to be challenged about his demeaning of people, of Howard Wolowitz especially—the love and respect they all have for each other, beyond the banter, creates a group within which they can each be themselves, be assertive about their successes, be uplifted when they are down, and be congratulated when they do well. And as they get to know more about each other, about their social and educational backgrounds, their past relationships (family, romantic, and sexual), their capacity to be able to affirm each other—and to enable each other to flourish—becomes more marked.

The third striking element of the friendship is the way that the characters, in their differences, cross a number of ethnic, religious, and social boundaries. Granted, the diversity is limited and trades off caricature at times in the way it is handled. Furthermore, the basic trajectory and plot developments in the series do depend largely on the intellectual similarity of most of the main characters. Yet there are also important aspects where difference surfaces and becomes both the focus of humour as well as a key point for insights to occur to the characters, and to viewers too.

For example, the ignorance demonstrated by the hyper-intelligent about aspects of ordinary living is accentuated throughout. Whilst the correlation of low socio-economic background and limited formal educational achievement is understandable, if uncomfortable, the challenge of Penny to all other main characters is considerable. Furthermore, *the viewer* is invited to respect, even admire, the 'homespun wisdom' which Penny often shows despite Sheldon's satire. Ethnicity and religion interweave in other facets of the relationships between the friends. Whilst not a dominant feature of the series, the religion-related motifs are far from insignificant. Howard Wolowitz's Jewish heritage is especially notable, the voice of his unseen, but highly influential mother being prominent in the early series. Rajesh Koothrappali's Indian Hinduism is presented appropriately in ways which sometimes do not distinguish ethnic heritage and religiosity (thus allowing for the fact that Hinduism can be seen as a Western construct). Sheldon's cynical atheism plays off against his Christian evangelical mother's faith. Yet the latter is not wholly negatively viewed. Here, again, practical wisdom challenges the harder edges of Sheldon's constant recourse to objective, evidence-based support for his life choices. Bernadette Rostenkowski's Polish Roman Catholicism is largely hidden, though it does surface at some points.

The key point here, however, is that their differences, including their different religious heritages and the current influence of those upbringings on their lives, are made apparent and woven into the plot. The impact, positive and negative, of their formation as people is seen as part of life and informs the ways in which they handle each other's strengths and weaknesses.[47]

The series stands, then, as a contemporary snapshot of some of the key features of how Western citizens are shaped, form relationships, and get through life. It is, of course, a very limited and particular example. It is not, though, wholly dependent on viewers being wholly up to date with higher education. University life is but the context in which some of the main assumptions are revealed about Western patterns of human relating. Being a comedy, the series is, however, an

---

[47] Two other prominent features of the series, which reflect the wider demographic and interweave further with the three themes highlighted are the handling of relationships with (often very demanding!) parents and the complexities of seeking a sexual partner. The latter issue causes some Christians particular vexation, as evidenced in such comments as: 'while *The Big Bang Theory* may be relatively better than it used to be . . . the series is still predicated on low humor—sex, swearing, bodily functions and sometimes squalid stereotyping (racially, religiously)', Bob Hoose and Paul Asay, www.pluggedin.com/tv-reviews/bigbangtheory/, accessed 17 April 2016.

uplifting take on the possibilities of human flourishing through relationships. Its main value for the purposes of this inquiry is that it accepts
that religion is part of the mix, and it confronts directly the huge
significance of human limitation and lack of confidence as a major
aspect of the search for satisfactory relating. Even accepting the place of
evil—so often an element in TV and film drama—and recognizing that
this has to be faced, it is through other, ostensibly lighter entertainment
that more mundane, though equally significant aspects of human frailty
are addressed. *The Big Bang Theory* is one such resource and, as such,
offers itself as a contribution to human flourishing.

The Big Bang Theory as Theological Resource

What, though, has any of this to do with understanding salvation?
From one perspective there is a simple response: anything to do with
human flourishing is also to do with salvation. So long as it is accepted
that a major purpose of articulating a doctrine of salvation is not to be
hung up on the negative aspects of the doctrine (what one is 'saved
from') but to articulate also the joyful results of God's activity (what
one is 'saved for'), then human flourishing is of theological interest.
Placing attention to examples of human flourishing within the framework of salvation, however, means identifying what one has needed
'saving from' for the flourishing to occur. Even in such a lightweight
comedy, then, the features we have identified become significant both
for understanding the various characters and for grasping the reson-
ances which are found by viewers. Hence, Sheldon does not need
'saving' from any autistic tendencies he may have. That is who he is.
But he does need saving from not realizing the impact he has on others,
which is complicated because of the entanglement of his lack of
empathy with his personality. Howard needs saving from his early
leery, predatory behaviour towards women in order to have a chance of
finding a stable partner. At root, however, is the communal setting
within which all their self-discovery and character development occurs.
It is wrong to call this a church. It is not wrong to call it a manifestation
of the Body of Christ.[48] In Richard Rohr's words:

---

[48] As I sought to show in *Christ in Practice: A Christology of Everyday Life* (London:
Darton Longman and Todd, 2006), where I argue that Christ's contemporary presence
needs to be seen as taking multiple communal forms, which have clearly identifiable
Christologically shaped hallmarks.

God's basic method of communicating God's self is not the 'saved' individual, the rightly informed believer, or even personal careers in ministry, but the journey and bonding process that God initiates in community: in marriages, families, tribes, nations, events, scientists, and churches who are seeking to participate in God's love, maybe without even consciously knowing it.[49]

It could be argued that the characters in *The Big Bang Theory*, and the fan communities formed amongst its viewers, are not 'seeking to participate in God's love'. I dispute this. Rohr's phrase 'without even consciously knowing it' is, admittedly, a rich and expansive get-out clause, for it can be claimed that all human beings are 'seeking to participate in God's love'. I think it is indeed true that most are in so far as they seek love and seek to be loved. What is added to the search for, and giving of, love by locating such a quest for flourishing within a doctrine of salvation is the dimension of sin. But rather than being a debilitating concept, sin becomes helpful when placed within a hopeful framework. And rather than always beginning with sin and the negative aspects of creaturely living, as so much Christian preaching often has, it is wise only to present an exposition of sin in the context of salvation's full rich template. Overemphasis upon what one needs to be saved *from* obscures what one is saved *for* and *into*, and *by* whom (always) one is being saved.[50]

Hence, it is wholly appropriate, and in keeping with Grace Jantzen's challenge to Christian understandings of salvation, sometimes to begin with flourishing and work back. I am even suggesting here beginning with a seemingly lightweight example of human flourishing—within a TV drama, and in the context of its reception—so that the possibility of flourishing is presented, on the basis of which the elements which make for flourishing can be expounded and disclosed. *The Big Bang Theory* has enabled us to do precisely that. Rather than simply illustrate a Christian understanding of salvation, however, it highlights some key

[49] Adapted from Richard Rohr, *Near Occasions of Grace* (Maryknoll, NY: Orbis Books, 1993), 49–51, and featured in this form in Richard Rohr's daily meditation, '"The Body of Christ", Sunday, April 17, 2016' (email to subscribers, accessed 17 April 2016).

[50] There are helpful insights on this issue in Deborah van Deusen Hunsinger, 'Forgiving Abusing Parents: Psychological and Theological Considerations', in Alistair McFadyen and Marcel Sarot (eds.), *Forgiveness and Truth: Explorations in Contemporary Theology* (Edinburgh and New York: T&T Clark, 2001), 71–98, especially 92–3, 96.

features and invites further Christian reflection on contemporary challenges, not least those of the limits of ecclesial life. Human flourishing has to occur, be explored, and encouraged in a context where those of many faiths and none seek together to create thriving human communities and a sustainable and healthy relationship with the non-human world. But days of Christian dominance have gone. Furthermore, a practical, embodied form of saved/salvific living occurs in the midst of participation of multiple communities. If this is less apparent from the diegesis of *The Big Bang Theory* itself, where the main plot moves between home, work, and leisure (meals in the Cheesecake Factory), it would be an essential component of any exposition of the lives of viewers interacting (as people of faith) with the TV series. Christian viewers, for example, may watch for 'pure pleasure' or 'mere enjoyment' and not intend in any way for it to inform their faith. And yet they may watch 'religiously' in the sense of never missing an episode or undertake some devoted viewing (of the streamed version or the box set), and it becomes part both of their general life satisfaction and a kind of discipline which helps them stop doing other things, in a positive way. The TV viewing becomes either itself a spiritual practice or part of their chosen Christian lifestyle. It might not even feel qualitatively different from some aspects of direct participation in Christian activities if it became true that watching the series proved uplifting and thought-provoking *even whilst* being watched primarily for 'pure pleasure'. Being a member of *The Big Bang Theory* fan community is then one of the communities to which a Christian may 'belong'.

As Western citizens live their lives within multiple communities, however, it should be noted how the explicitly Christian community to which any Christian belongs (church, whatever form that may take) features inevitably alongside a great many other groups to which a person belongs. It has always been so. In a digital age these groups are greater in number and more diverse (embodied and virtual). Whilst it must always be theologically necessary to suggest that in some sense 'church' must always be the primary community to which a Christian belongs (the primary community out of which a person receives and continually 'works with' their value system), the lived reality of life relativizes that primacy. Work, friendships, education, leisure (sport, media, arts), online activity, family, political life all create groups which feed us as people and to which we devote time. They make us who we are. In theological terms, they all contribute to the flourishing life the doctrine of salvation seeks to describe and commend. Participation in them will not, however, always be as positive and enjoyable as sustained viewing of *The Big Bang Theory*. This is why therapeutic TV viewing must be seen as one small part of the many dimensions of salvation as a lived experience, and also why a richer theological template is needed to encompass the many different contexts in which salvation is discovered and worked out.

In this chapter, then, we have looked at a disparate range of examples of where positive emotions are aroused and focused upon within Western life. Though the examples chosen (positive psychology and secular TV) are neither specifically Christian nor even directly religious, it has been shown how in practice all of the examples interweave with religious belief and practice in explicit ways. As such they contribute explicitly to contemporary understanding and exploration of the themes with which religion is preoccupied. In the specific terms of this present study, they offer clear examples of ways in which the positive outcomes of salvation may be identified as a living experience, in relation to which theological background work appropriate for present times can be undertaken. It is yet to be determined whether happiness is a legitimate way of grasping salvation and whether what has been explored in this chapter really does amount to a form of salvation, but it has been necessary to make such explorations to have any sort of chance of grasping and explicating the doctrine of salvation in current Western culture.

6

Salvation in Capital and Money

Whilst completing the final drafts of this book, Western European news broadcasts have been dominated by stories of migration. Often tragic, due to overloaded boats from Syria or Libya capsizing at sea, sometimes hopeful, but always challenging, due to the sheer numbers of desperate people taking risks in seeking a better life, the stories of migration from North Africa and the eastern Mediterranean to southern Europe are a striking contemporary example of the fact that explorations of salvation cannot neglect the material dimension of human life. Whether refugees or economic migrants, people seek rescue from harm and strive for well-being for their loved ones and themselves. In the light of such present realities, however focused much of Christian belief and practice may have been on the inner life, the concrete aspects of everyday life—the need for food, shelter, and physical safety—have to be acknowledged and addressed.[1] If Christianity has in practice throughout much of its history focused on well-being *beyond* this life, this is no longer possible in isolation. Even if Christians may themselves disagree about whether there is a life beyond this life, and about what form such a life might take, they must now accept that a sole focus upon salvation in an afterlife is misplaced. There is so much of everyday life's experience *now* to be taken account of (in terms of expected lifespan). The tendency towards the over-spiritual also has to be counterbalanced to correct the relative neglect of what happens now, materially, *before* biological death.

---

[1] This is not to say that material issues are wholly new for Christians, as such concerns have inevitably been ever-present throughout history. What is new is the consequences of greater life expectancy for many people around the world (and thus closer attention in religion to this life, and less so to what lies beyond this life) and the linking of material concerns with salvation.

Offering such a counterbalance will require care not to create a new imbalance, so that material concerns wholly envelope attention to the inner life.[2] No amount of material comfort necessarily produces or guarantees salvation and its benefits. But this chapter will enable us to address the issue that absence of a basic minimum of the securities and necessities for a healthy life can damage the possibility of perceiving and enjoying 'life in all its fullness'.

The chapter will look at the issue of material well-being and its potential relationship to salvation in two respects. First, it will examine the importance of the concept of 'capital' for understanding what salvation does to and for a person. Though in many ways itself a metaphor—when used in such expressions as 'social capital' or 'cultural capital'—it provides a helpful bridge for the more direct engagement with money and possessions which forms the second part of the chapter. It is also arguable that in a world dominated by capitalism it is a prime way of communicating what salvation entails. In the process, the limits of attention solely to economic capital can also be exposed and explored. *Being saved does mean 'having' certain things,* even if what one has is pure gift. This applies even if what is acquired is an internal possession. In this sense, then, it proves helpful to consider such ownership through the lens of the concept of capital. Drawing especially on John Field's *Social Capital,* I shall show that a crucial issue for understanding salvation today is the recognition of how one gains what one acquires, to what extent what one has is given, to what degree it is shared with others, and how it sometimes has to be accepted that ownership of intangible goods is simply 'held' across and amongst groups.[3] Although not at all a work of theology or religious studies, Field's mapping of the meanings and significance of the concept of social capital are extremely helpful for the task of addressing the embodied, material aspects of salvation, and as preparation for considering social, as opposed simply to individual(istic), interpretations of the doctrine.

On the basis of that discussion I shall then go on to be more concrete and talk about money. Whilst this study is limited in the extent to which it can enter in any depth into a discussion of the economics of salvation—and my own competence is lacking anyway—it is vital not to dodge blunt and realistic questions about what one needs in bodily terms to be human, and thus what it means to be 'saved' as an

---

[2] A charge often wrongly made of liberation theologies.
[3] John Field, *Social Capital* (2nd edn, Abingdon and New York: Routledge, 2008).

embodied human being. There have been strands of this concern already present throughout this book—physical ailment and disfigurement appeared in Chapter 3, embodied (aesthetic and affective) experience featured in Chapters 3 and 4, concern about addictive behaviour haunted Chapter 4. Here the concern for embodied aspects of human existence is even more basic and everyday. In what sense do *all* human beings have to be freed from poverty and undue concerns for the basic needs of life if salvation is to make much sense? To what degree is it almost immoral and unjust to be speaking of salvation for *anyone* so long as many people go without? The second part of the chapter picks up, in a theological key, the telling quip of German dramatist Bertolt Brecht (possibly even borrowing from Martin Luther): '*Erst kommt das Fressen, dann kommt die Moral*' ('Let's eat first; then we can talk of morals').[4] At the very least, then, the chapter is acknowledging that a lack in the realm of material well-being distorts human life and limits the possibility of participating in redeemed existence (full human flourishing), whether in this life or beyond.

FORMS OF CAPITAL

It may sound odd to be discussing 'capital' in relation to the concept of salvation. 'Capital' is a collection of possessions: 'anything that an individual or social entity has that generates something of value for that individual or social entity'.[5] It exists in at least three forms: economic, social, and cultural capital, each of which merits consideration in turn.[6]

---

[4] The quote is from Brecht's play *The Threepenny Opera* (1928). 'Fressen' is the term used for eating done by animals, hence denoting the desperate way in which hunger needs to be satiated by those short of food. Luther's remark, in commenting on the Gospel of Luke (14.15), that to 'eat bread in the Kingdom of God means to partake of blessedness' is telling here ('"Das Brot im Gottesreich essen" heißt, an der Seligkeit teilnehmen'; cited in Johannes Ringleben, *Das philosophische Evangelium: Theologische Auslegung des Johannesevangeliums im Horizont des Sprachdenkens* (Tübingen: Mohr Siebeck, 2014), 459 n. 27.

[5] Arjo Klammer, 'Property and Possession: The Moral Economy of Ownership', in William Schweiker and Charles Mathewes (eds.), *Having: Property and Possession in Religious and Social Life* (Grand Rapids, MI: Eerdmans, 2004), 337–52, here 343. I am indebted to Klammer's essay in the paragraphs to follow.

[6] There is merit here in noting the link between attention to multiple forms of capital and Robert Bellah's insight into the way in which religious, cultural, scientific, and economic worlds all overlap in relation to 'the world of daily life' (cited in John

Economic capital has to do with hardware and cash, possession of means by which one can generate income and acquire even greater means. Often also called 'human capital' (as opposed to 'natural capital', which denotes the earth's natural resources), it is in and through the use of humanly produced resources that it is commonly assumed in the West that one may be able to live a satisfied life.[7] Without some money, its plastic equivalent, or (increasingly) its contactless on-screen replacement, and some possessions, it is not possible to get by in the West today. It is therefore no accident that economic capital is likely to be the definition which most readily comes to mind when 'capital' is mentioned.[8]

There are, however, at least two other forms of capital which have featured prominently in academic discussion in recent decades: social and cultural capital. 'Social capital' denotes a range of groups, activities, and practices which highlight the positive aspects of human relationships of all kinds. Denoting elements of human life which are more difficult to measure than economic capital, social capital points, structurally speaking, to friendships, family life, associations, and social, religious, and political interest groups. It accentuates the quality of relationships which can result from participation in such structures: responsibility, trust, reciprocity, respect, colleagueship, affection.

Social capital can in turn be seen to exist in two forms: bonding capital and bridging capital.[9] Bonding capital refers to the quality of ties which bind people together *within* a group. Hence, this form of social capital notes that people of like mind, interest, or background are likely to benefit from groups and contexts in which 'people like them' come together. This is two-edged, of course. Forms of bonding capital can be supportive of people of like mind, but then potentially demonize an Other for being different. Political or ethnic differences

Atherton, *Challenging Religious Studies: The Wealth, Wellbeing and the Inequalities of Nations* (London: SCM Press, 2014), 14.

[7] Human capital could also be divided further into 'human resources' and 'plant or finance', but such distinctions need not detain us here (Atherton, *Challenging Religious Studies*, 190).

[8] Atherton, *Challenging Religious Studies*, 32.

[9] Field, *Social Capital*, 36 and 73. I do not add here a third type of social capital suggested by Ann Morisy ('brave capital') in *Journeying Out: A New Approach to Christian Mission* (London and New York: Continuum, 2006). Though helpful as part of her discussion, it is a *qualitative type* of bridging or bonding capital and does not, therefore, add anything significant to the basic two types identified here.

can be accentuated and become divisive even whilst supporting positively the identity of those who bond within a group. Positively understood, though, bonding capital is vital for identity formation and confidence building. We discover or construct who we are through those with whom we bond.

Bridging capital, by contrast, denotes a form of social capital which forms as people make links *across* and *between* groups. Hence, as a form of social capital which may enable people to cross social strata or ethnic differences, risking potential difficulties and tensions as they do so, society may be made stronger when new combinations and relationships form. The potentially negative aspects of bonding capital are overcome when the quality of bonding relationships is carried forward into new forms of bridging capital.

The third form of capital, cultural capital, denotes a wide range of practices and resources which enhance the quality of life. Arjo Klammer suggests that cultural capital 'is, in short, the capacity to inspire and be inspired'.[10] Though a little elusive as a definition, it is an understandable attempt to express the way in which cultural activity takes many forms (he suggests 'a walk in the woods, a visit to a museum, or a church service').[11] Such breadth has often not been respected in discussions of 'culture', and thus is not always present in explorations of cultural capital and its significance.[12] Defining cultural capital more precisely and seeing it as often related to social status or economic means have been an emphasis in the work of the French sociologist Pierre Bourdieu. In *Distinction*, his classic exploration of the class-related aspects of culture, Bourdieu shows how participation in particular forms of cultural life correlate with the cultivation and development of capital in social and economic forms.[13] Although, as Field notes, 'Bourdieu emphasized repeatedly, people's ownership of cultural capital did not just mirror their resources of financial capital', the links which do exist need noting and examining.[14] Within the complex mix of cultural activity, certain forms of high culture then become privileged and allied with power and influence because of the cultural interests and activities of those who participate in them.

---

[10] Klammer, 'Property and Possession', 344.
[11] Klammer, 'Property and Possession', 344.
[12] I refer to the discussion on Matthew Arnold in Chapter 2.
[13] Pierre Bourdieu, *Distinction: A Social Critique of the Judgement of Taste* (New York and London: Routledge, 1986).
[14] Field, *Social Capital*, 16.

As has been emphasized throughout this book, however, and in keeping with the aspirations of Klammer's definition of cultural capital, attention to the breadth of what constitutes cultural capital is vital. Otherwise, definition of the term and the range of practices to which it refers are too easily tied to one social group. Too narrow a definition of cultural capital, we might say, ends up mirroring a restrictive, exclusive form of bonding capital in that it allows the cultural concerns of the few to control how cultural capital is defined and what it achieves. Only by attending to a radically wide range of culturally different forms of cultural capital can a form of *bridging* cultural capital come fully into play.

Cultural capital needs to be understood in the broadest possible terms. To the discussion already entered into in Chapter 2 with respect to the so-called 'high arts' and popular culture, we can add adult and continuing education (lifelong learning) of both informal and formal kinds, sporting activity, family get-togethers, meetings with friends, craft groups, political associations, music associations, and campaigning organizations. All of these, and more, merge social and cultural groups in enabling a quality of relational (and, crucially, sometimes intergenerational, interethnic) life to develop as cultural activities are engaged in. I have been involved in lifelong learning for nearly thirty years, and at a time when the existence of departments and organizations in the field is under constant threat, it is perhaps especially poignant to highlight this aspect of communal life. At its best, lifelong learning is an arena where personhood, identity, cultural and social background, and ethnicity are explored *whatever* one is studying in academic disciplinary terms merely by virtue of who one studies with.[15] I consider the acquisition of such cultural capital to be an intrinsic element in the identification of what salvation is and does to and for people whether or not the origins or intentions of such activity are explicitly religious.[16]

---

[15] I have explored this in 'The Feeling of Engagement: Lifelong Learning about Religion in Part-Time, Secular Higher Education as a Private and Public Good', in *Widening Participation and Lifelong Learning* 19 (2017), 8–32.

[16] In my experience, those who study at 'departments of the second chance' (Continuing Education, Lifelong Learning) are more likely to use the terminology of salvation than those who begin to study in higher education as 18-year-olds simply because they discover more about why they want to study and to recognize what education can do to and for them. They are open to personal change, to being 'liberated', to having their thinking 'transformed'. Without wanting to underestimate

Religious activity and practice should, of course, be considered a form of cultural capital and are sometimes highlighted as 'religious capital'.[17] More precisely, religious practice and participation in a religious community could be considered a form of social capital through which cultural capital (religious knowledge or belief, faith) is then acquired. In this way it could be said that social and cultural capital absorb the religious dimension of life. This may be satisfactory as a sociological or psychological account of religious practice. It is, however, a reductionist account of what occurs. For this reason some scholars of religion wish to speak of 'spiritual capital' as a distinct, fourth, form of capital. Even if clearly overlapping with the other forms of capital already considered—social and cultural capital especially—spiritual capital seeks to identify a slightly different dimension from what is secured through participation in social and cultural life.[18]

the transforming power of higher education for the young, it is valuable to note that theological education in particular may actually prove especially beneficial for people in later life (when built on greater life experience). Theological concepts may begin to make more sense. This is telling, given how readily it is assumed that the religious education of the young should be of paramount importance. Whilst understandable, the developmental, social, and political importance of religious education (both religious literacy and theological insight) into adulthood must not be overlooked. See now my article 'Theology's Part-Time Future: A Fresh Initiative in Theological Education and Religious Literacy?', *Theology* 121(2018), 171–9. The notion that central government resources should always be targeted at the education of the (very) young is questioned by former UK Cabinet Minister and Minister for Universities David Willetts in *A University Education* (Oxford: Oxford University Press, 2017), 152–63. In the same work Willetts also offers this telling confession (87):

> one of the courses hardest hit [by the UK government's decision not to provide loans to people wanting to study a different subject, but at the same level as any earlier study they had undertaken] was theology... When eventually we once again provide loans to mature theology students a historic mistake will finally have been reversed.

[17] See Chris Baker on Bourdieu's usage in 'Exploring Spiritual Capital: Resource for an Unknown Future?', in Michael O'Sullivan and Bernadette Flanagan (eds.), *Spiritual Capital: Spirituality in Practice in Christian Perspective* (Farnham and Burlington, VT: Ashgate, 2012), 12–13. Also useful is Robert Furbey et al., *Faith as Social Capital* (Bristol: The Policy Press, 2006).

[18] Spiritual capital has also appeared as a term used in organizational psychology (e.g. Danah Zohar and Ian Marshall (*Spiritual Capital: Wealth We Can Live By* (London: Bloomsbury, 2004))). Whilst clearly related to my concerns here—Zohar and Marshall are keen to transform capitalism and call for attention to the inner aspects of people who work, and they do not neglect religion—it is not possible to do justice to those discussions here.

When 'religious capital' is highlighted within social or cultural capital, the specificity of religious practice is being noted.[19] When it is characterized as 'spiritual capital', particular hallmarks of social or cultural capital are thus being drawn out. In words used by the Templeton Foundation, spiritual capital can be defined as the 'effects of spiritual and religious practices, beliefs, networks and institutions that have a measurable impact on individuals, communities and societies'.[20] Now whether or not 'religious' or 'spiritual' capital does merit siphoning off from, or subdividing within, identified forms of social and cultural capital, what matters here is that there is a particular set of *effects*, and a recognizable *impact* of religious beliefs and practices upon people. If any reference to 'capital' refers to 'acquisition' or 'ownership', even if of non-tangible goods, then what the term 'spiritual capital' denotes is acquisitions deriving specifically from religious insights, beliefs, or activities. It will therefore be in this realm that what may be termed the 'benefits' of salvation may be sought.

There are, then, three or four forms of capital which can be evoked in a discussion of salvation. Contemporary theological exposition of the doctrine requires some exploring, sifting, and sorting of the import and meaning of these various forms both for the sake of comprehensibility and to acknowledge what the experience of salvation brings, and is connected to, in daily living.

THE BENEFITS OF SALVATION

Why, though, does this have anything to do with salvation? For Protestant readers especially the discussion will seem highly suspicious, as the notion of any form of acquisition implies that one may seek salvation and contribute, as a human agent, to its acquisition.[21] Far from it being pure gift, and a thing of grace, discussion of capital may begin to suggest that human beings *earn* their salvation. Even if

---

[19] As 'the practical contribution to local and national life made by faith groups', a definition coined by Chris Baker and Hannah Skinner, cited in Baker, 'Exploring Spiritual Capital', 11.

[20] Cited in Baker, 'Exploring Spiritual Capital', 12.

[21] I do not, of course, mean thereby to imply that Roman Catholic thought and practice are not also about unmerited grace! I merely note the extent of this Protestant emphasis.

salvation is not bought—via some contemporary equivalent of the Reformation era purchase of indulgences—the discussion so far may suggest that one earns salvation through acquisition of social capital (through active participation in a faith community) and of cultural capital (by means of building up religious knowledge or profession of belief). Churchgoing is being rewarded and becomes the means of earning God's favour. Attendance at training courses, learning a catechism, knowing the creeds by rote are what matters. The notion of salvation as gift has gone.

These challenges are important. But they are not sufficient to derail the inquiry in which I am engaged. As I shall show, attention to the various forms of capital identified proves instructive in enabling a better, practical understanding of salvation to be gained. Such analysis will then, in turn, prove informative in the specifically theological task of clarifying, in and for the present, what salvation is and how it works. To anticipate at this stage, in highly compressed form, where I shall end up: God is discovered transformatively at work amongst people in a range of social settings, and by many cultural means, building them up as people, whatever their material circumstances. It is, however, vital also to attend to the material circumstances in which people find themselves, as these may obstruct and obscure the possibility of the social, cultural, and spiritual capital which salvation brings of even being recognized, let alone acquired and enjoyed.

How, then, does salvation relate to the forms of capital identified? A 'capital' approach to salvation cannot and must not be taken to mean that 'being saved' will lead to, or is a direct consequence of, material prosperity. There are many forms of the so-called Prosperity Gospel around, according to which it is held that God will bless materially those who turn to God, are generous in their own financial giving, or make good use of their material wealth. It is sometimes argued that there is biblical warrant for such views (e.g. Matthew 25.14–30, Mark 10.29–30, John 14.14). Whatever salvation may mean, however, it cannot mean simply or primarily that one is saved *from* material poverty *for* a life of material riches. Christians are not always wealthy and very often do not even try to be. On the contrary, a great many see that their calling is to a frugal life, or one in which they give away, or use in the service of others, the material wealth that they acquire. Even if some account will need to be given in due course of how the doctrine of salvation relates to material wealth (money in particular), it is more with respect to the other three forms of capital—social, cultural, spiritual—that salvation and its benefits are more helpfully articulated. So let us look at each in turn.

Attention to *social capital* raises the question of how individualistic a doctrine of salvation can be. In Protestantism, and Pentecostalism in particular, the notion that it is the individual sinner who stands in need of salvation is especially strong. All forms of Christianity, however, have some sense that in being saved or redeemed an individual person comes into a community of faith (a church). The degree to which active participation in the Church is deemed essential to salvation differs across traditions. Protestantism's individualistic tendencies often in practice imply that individuals have no need of the church, despite the many creedal, catechetical, and doctrinal statements which would suggest otherwise.[22] 'Church' is, though, necessary for all forms of Christianity, both as the carrier of the tradition of belief in which Christians are rooted and as the term for the concrete form of practical, spiritual support which any Christian needs. Though every believer must, in some way, attest to their belief of belonging to God in a Christian way for themselves, if they wish to call themselves Christian, there is ultimately no such thing as a solitary believer. Hence, even if, in Part III of this work, we shall need to articulate the sense in which an individual receives the benefits of, or commits to, a saved life, there will equally need to be clarity about how participation in the social capital of salvation takes shape. Where and how does the bonding capital of the saved/redeemed occur? Is it only in the form of church? However this will be expressed, attention to social capital reminds us of the concreteness of the relationships within which the saved life is enjoyed. Real people engage with real others in the experience of salvation.[23]

Attention to *cultural capital* forces us to address the many and varied forms of whatever cognitive content is imbibed or appropriated, consciously or unconsciously, in the course of living and participating in media-saturated Western culture. All theologies take shape within complex media worlds and their exponents seek to articulate a viable, living, usable theology in and out of such complexity. Why, though, characterize the process of engagement, sifting, listening, and dialogue

---

[22] 'We believe in one, holy, catholic, apostolic Church' is embedded in the Nicene Creed, repeated in many other Confessions of Faith (e.g. in the *Service Book* of the United Reformed Church in the United Kingdom (Oxford: Oxford University Press, 1989)) and its sentiments and content echoed across all Christian traditions across the world.

[23] Atherton, *Challenging Religious Studies*, 80.

as 'cultural capital'? Why might it help to speak of the articulation of a doctrine of salvation as the acquisition of any form of capital?

Such a step is necessary because wherever the benefits of salvation are deemed to come from—whether generated by human agency, by divine activity, or both—they add something to human experience. Indeed, if a doctrine of salvation describes in practice an understanding of human existence and experience (as the object of divine action) in the manner which Christianity proposes, then it will prove decisive and transformative for the shaping (formation) of a human life. A viable, contemporary doctrine of salvation will thus have to map out an understanding of what one is saved/redeemed from, for, by, and into as a (the?) crucial piece of cultural capital by which a person lives, even if this is received or expressed in the midst of much other cultural capital. To put this differently: salvation understood as flourishing, of the individual and communities/society under God, will be understood as the central *Gehalt* of whatever cultural products (whether Christian, religious, or not) contribute to the Christian task of articulating a viable, truthful doctrine of salvation. It is Christian theology's task to identify, highlight, and expound fresh cultural capital to be added to the cultural (spiritual) capital which the Christian Church already carries with it. *Christians do not gain salvific capital solely from Christian products or practices.* This is also why, in due course, we shall need to conclude that all cultural theology is 'interstitial', that is, happening in the spaces and cracks between the communities and activities which people participate in merely by engaging in everyday life.[24]

We shall also see, though, that this will not be a comfortable task. If salvation/redemption is from sin, then sin has to be named. It also has to be articulated in forms which are comprehensible in any particular age.[25] Flourishing is not possible without confrontation with all that is negative and destructive. This observation serves as an important

---

[24] The term 'interstitial' has been worked with in sociological discussion by Homi Bhaba in particular, and in religious studies by Tinu Ruparell, in 'The Dialogue Party: Dialogue, Hybridity, and the Reluctant Other', in Viggo Mortensen (ed.), *Theology and the Religions: A Dialogue* (Grand Rapids, MI, and Cambridge, UK: Eerdmans, 2003), 235–48 and 'Inter-Religious Dialogue and Interstitial Theology', in Catherine Cornille (ed.), *The Wiley-Blackwell Companion to Inter-Religious Dialogue* (Oxford: Wiley, 2013), 117–32.

[25] This is the particular reason for exploring *Breaking Bad* in Chapter 4 of this study.

reminder—obvious though it may seem—that not all participation in every daily practice and not all consumption of cultural material are necessarily constructive or conducive to flourishing. Salvation—as doctrine and experience—has to acknowledge this. Yet the fact that the gift of salvation is available in the midst of such negativity and destructiveness is what makes it a hopeful doctrine.

Third, salvation pertains to *spiritual capital*. As already noted, spiritual capital overlaps with both social and cultural forms of capital. One might therefore well ask what further dimension is added to an understanding of salvation by reference to capital in this final form. Indeed, the potential detachment of the spiritual from the other forms of capital could be deemed to perpetuate a common criticism of Christianity (and most religious practice), namely that to switch attention away from economic capital to other forms of capital means ignoring the real material inequalities which exist in society. It leaves people in poverty and asks them to make do with non-material benefits as a substitute for material well-being.[26] Though it is a common critique and one which undoubtedly carries weight, I do not accept that it always applies to the way in which salvation has been, and now needs to be, understood. There are two main reasons for this.

First, the process of unpicking salvation in the manner I am suggesting becomes a way of identifying a material component *at all*. Far from neglecting or devaluing a material, economic dimension, the strategy ensures that salvation is not spiritualized. It enables us to perceive how the material takes shape alongside other forms of capital. Second, the approach I am adopting prevents attention to the economic, material dimension of salvation dominating. Whilst on the one hand it is very easy to exclude material concerns in Christian faith and practice (implying it is only the wealthy who have time for reflection), it is also easy to permit material concerns to control processes of reflection. This is quite understandable. When the stomach is empty, it is difficult not to think of food. When there is no money and there are bills to pay, it is hard to think of anything else. But even in the midst of material lack, and without ignoring the importance of material lack, other forms of capital are vital and

---

[26] This is, for example, a key thread in the argument of E. P. Thompson's influential reading of religion's influence in society in *The Making of the English Working Class* (London: Victor Gollancz, 1963).

need to be respected.[27] Attention to the other three forms of capital, then, ultimately enables us better to see how salvation can be participated in and effected economically and materially, i.e. in a way which respects people's embodied selves, and how all four dimensions of salvation interrelate.

The point of referring to the concept of capital with respect to the doctrine of salvation, then, is that it enables us to channel the aesthetic, affective, and therapeutic concerns considered in Chapters 3–5 towards real-life concerns without reducing them to material matters. The aesthetic, affective, and therapeutic dimensions of salvation cut across social, cultural, and spiritual forms of capital, whilst at the same time requiring us to say how, and how much, salvation is about the body and its material needs. In the second part of the chapter I shall develop this concern for the material by exploring how salvation relates to money.

THE COST OF SALVATION

A great many of the stories in the canonical Gospels of the New Testament are to do with money. For a while some years ago it seemed as if every Sunday I was in church, the Gospel reading began something like 'the kingdom of heaven may be compared to a king who wished to settle accounts with his slaves' (Matt 18.23) or 'he sat down opposite the treasury, and watched the crowd putting money into the treasury. Many rich people put in large sums' (Mark 12.41). Jesus did not dodge the task of addressing very concrete, everyday matters to do with money, and of using powerful stories about and illustrations to do with money in his teaching. The Apostle Paul, too, takes money issues seriously. Whether raising money for emerging congregations (1 Cor. 16.1–4), being concerned about payments for his co-workers (Rom.

---

[27] Atherton, *Challenging Religious Studies*, 60. Here there is a link with counselling's approach and role, with respect to flourishing: enabling people to take a step back, to 'reframe' their experience, and to re-evaluate what is happening to them. Such a process may not lead to material improvement, but may help create a more constructive way of handling the context and conditions in which a person finds him-/herself. Again, I am not arguing here that counselling is simply a different form of (secular) spirituality, thereby reducing theology to human processes alone, but merely noting a parallel.

16.1–2), grateful for gifts received (2 Cor. 11.7–9; Phil. 4.15–18), or conscious of the ways in which he himself must make ends meet (1 Cor. 9.6), Paul does not shirk his responsibility to talk about finance. Both of these first-century Jews are building upon a rich prophetic tradition within Judaism of being upfront about the just use of wealth and possessions.

None of these examples may be considered at first to relate directly to salvation.[28] They do, though, highlight the fact that both Judaism and Christianity face squarely the practicalities of daily human existence. Both these religious traditions in their own different ways engage issues of materiality in their practice.[29] Judaism's structure as a form of spirituality is shaped around domestic practices, particularly relating to food. Christianity's central symbolic meal celebrates incarnation in flesh and blood. Respect for and attention to such materiality are key to both traditions. In this respect, if we try to deny that each tradition's approach to wealth and possession has little or nothing to do with salvation, then we confront once more the dangerous tendency to spiritualize salvation so that it becomes solely an inner experience or an other-worldly phenomenon. This will not do.

Alongside these concrete examples of concern for money and possessions, there is also no escaping the prominence of imagery within Christian theology drawn from the world of finance. Here, the link with salvation is clear. Redemption itself means 'buying back'. Paul regularly reminds his readers of the cost of that redemption (they were 'bought with a price': 1 Cor. 6.20, 7.23).

To use financial imagery is one thing, however. The question arises as to whether the language of redemption, and associated terminology, is anything more than that. Even if we accept that early Christians were embedded within the commercial world of the first century and had to earn money to buy food and to trade as best they could, this does not mean that imagery relating to such practices carried any particular significance. Language of debt repayment may simply be an accessible way of offering a reminder of how human relationships work—forgiveness will inevitably have to feature if they

---

[28] Accepting that such a statement itself betrays a starting point within a Christianity which does not begin from economic or material concerns. Liberation theologies of many kinds have, of course, been at the forefront of challenging this neglect.

[29] Whether or not he was correct, Archbishop William Temple's claim that Christianity is 'the most avowedly materialist of all the great religions' (*Nature, Man and God* (London: Macmillan & Co., 1935), 478) remains telling.

are to be successful and flourish (and it is 'costly'—emotionally draining, even). Understanding this to be the case, how much more, then, the emerging Christian tradition was suggesting, must this be true of God. A variety of images would need to be found—perhaps none ever wholly adequate (but they would need to be expressive and powerful)—to articulate the scale of God's 'self-expenditure' in and through the person of Jesus Christ. Images of cost and expense (and thus of ransom and redemption) would inevitably be grasped. But how are we now to understand the relationship, if indeed there is one, between salvation and money?

Salvation, of course, costs both nothing and everything. In Christian understanding it costs nothing because it is a gift (Is. 52.3). It costs everything in the sense that to understand the drama of what is involved in salvation being available in the first place, Christian theology places the self-giving of God in the person of Christ at the centre of its exposition of who God is and what God does. Salvation does not, therefore, cost *us* everything. But by relating salvation's availability to a death—that of Jesus of Nazareth—we get the picture of just how costly salvation is *for God*. We are invited to take it all the more seriously precisely because of that.

It is, though, striking that despite any talk of 'costliness' there is very little reference to money or wealth in Christian discussion about salvation. Here is not the place for detailed exploration of atonement theories, and about whether God or Satan is 'paid off' in any way by the death of Christ. If we are indeed to be said to be 'bought with a price' (1 Cor. 6.20, 7.23), then this is a powerful metaphor, but the question of whether 'money changes hands' is not relevant to the issue of how the narrative of salvation works.

Relevant, though, is how the experience of salvation in the present is related to material well-being from the perspective of the ownership of material wealth, including money, by the saved person. It is easy to claim, on theological grounds, that salvation costs nothing. But as we have begun to see throughout this second part of the book, the dimensions of the experience of salvation are multiple. There may well be a relationship between the aesthetic, affective, and therapeutic aspects of salvation with how much one owns, materially. Salvation may cost nothing, but the kind of aesthetic and affective experiences one can buy (which in turn enable salvation as free gift to be glimpsed or experienced) may be very different depending on one's level of income. Hence, whilst salvation may well be free, how one understands and accesses the various therapeutic dimensions of that free gift may differ depending on the availability of, and access to, medical and pastoral care. If physical healing is not possible, or medical care could help but is not forthcoming, then salvation may inevitably take on a less tangible meaning.[30]

The issue can be expressed sharply in this way: how materially well off does one need to be to be open to the offer of salvation's free gift? Can one truly flourish as a human being with *nothing*? Perhaps salvation is free, but flourishing costs. Yet if so, is this merely another way in which salvation is spiritualized and becomes the preserve of the prosperous? The words of a well-known Christian hymn, 'Nothing in my hand I bring, / Simply to thy cross I cling', can be taken to mean that there is no prerequisite (material or otherwise) for salvation. But it is not clear how much one might need to live and flourish as a saved person. 'Naked come to thee for dress', the line which follows in the same hymn, invites the simple question where the real, actual clothing will come from lest any metaphorical meaning of 'dress' not protect a person from the cold.[31]

God, then, demands nothing in the sense of needing no payment for salvation to come about. God cannot even demand love, for love cannot be demanded or earned. It can only be offered or accepted. God hopes for a response, in love, to the free, gracious offer of salvation. But God is the one who pays, in love, to enable the free gift to be available.

Such divine self-expenditure is difficult, even dangerous, for human beings to try and imitate. We cannot cope with the cost of such self-giving. We also cannot cope with the lavish generosity of the salvation made available to us. 'There is no such thing as a free gift' is an everyday saying which reveals the lack of trust that anyone can give freely, without strings. It is precisely such lack of trust which confounds human understanding of salvation as a free gift and has led, in Christian history, to the many different attempts to work out what payment can be made, and how salvation may be earned.[32]

---

[30] This is in large part the reason why understandings of salvation amongst the materially poor sometimes tend to look into the 'world beyond' (in an afterlife) for their fulfilment. Or, when the notion of any afterlife is rejected, it becomes an explanation of why it can be hard to accept that salvation can have any real, practical meaning, except for the already materially comfortable.

[31] The hymn is 'Rock of Ages, cleft for me', written by Augustus M. Toplady (1740–78).

[32] Notoriously, Johann Tetzel at the time of the Reformation. Perhaps, though, the entire history of the doctrine of the atonement can be included within the attempt to

That said, human frailty and fallibility demand that money come into play in our exploration of salvation in two important respects. First, the use of monetary metaphors, for all their inadequacy, at least enables us to appreciate real cost, and that a real transaction—of sorts—occurs. Second, if we talk figures, then despite the disappearing solidity of money (as cash, as coins, as banknotes) in times of plastic and electronic trading, we are nevertheless compelled to become attentive to the material conditions of life in a direct way. A wholly non-material spirituality and theology are inadequate.

To consider first the importance of monetary metaphors, it is vital to note that the all too human assumption that a transaction *does* occur when a person is saved or redeemed by God taps into a basic human refusal to receive a free gift, or to the notion that free gifts simply do not exist.[33] These assumptions are wholly undermined by the generosity of God. Theologically, however, as we shall see later in this study, the inability to accept a free gift, or even to acknowledge that a gift can be freely given, relates to a fundamental tension and trajectory through the history of Christian thought: the question whether humans are free enough to contribute to their own salvation in any way (Pelagius) or whether, being so bound to sin, there really is nothing they can do (Augustine).

There is, though, one sense in which concern for capital and for money has to become very concrete, which brings us to the second way in which talk of the 'cost' of salvation may be explored. Salvation's material dimensions have to be recognized. Whilst salvation may always have a spiritual focus, *the incarnational emphasis of Christian faith will never permit salvation to be a merely spiritual matter.* Yet in acknowledging salvation's material dimensions, the way in which material aspects are to be addressed has to be detached from the

explain how salvation can be bought. Human beings cannot but see such a transaction in commercial terms. Even divine love is being commodified.

[33] This question has been much explored in recent theology, stimulated by Marcel Mauss's *The Gift: The Form and Reason for Exchange in Archaic Societies* (London: Routledge, 1990; French original, 1950). Major contributions to theological discussion include John Milbank, 'Can A Gift Be Given?: Prolegomena to a Future Trinitarian Metaphysic', *Modern Theology* 11 (1995), 119–61 and Miroslav Volf, *Free of Charge: Giving and Forgiving in a Culture Stripped of Grace* (Grand Rapids, MI: Zondervan, 2006). Recent valuable studies which re-evaluate biblical and historical contributions to contemporary debate include J. Todd Billings, *Calvin, Participation, and the Gift: The Activity of Believers in Union with Christ* (Oxford and New York: Oxford University Press, 2007) and John Barclay, *Paul and the Gift* (Grand Rapids, MI: Eerdmans, 2015).

means by which salvation is gained. No money may change hands, but at a more fundamental level it is essential to ask the question about the material conditions under which people may even be able to entertain the prospect of salvation *at all*. To put that differently: material conditions do not of themselves effect salvation, but it is easy to see how a person with few possessions might hope and expect that salvation may include an improvement in their material well-being. To express it differently again: money does not make people happy but it is understandable to assume that a basic level of material well-being needs to be presupposed for openness to salvation to be made possible.

It is at this point that the extensive interdisciplinary work undertaken with respect to happiness and well-being becomes relevant to theology once more.[34] With reference to such research it can be stated: salvation is not to be bought, but everyone—to use financial imagery—needs some kind of deposit, or 'float', to have the chance to flourish. Whether or not such a deposit has any direct monetary content, it will have material value, be it in terms of food, shelter, clothing, a safe place or space in which to live. Salvation, when understood as human flourishing, may only prove possible when basic, minimum conditions for human well-being are met. The question then becomes how such minimum conditions can be made available to all (the whole of humanity) lest salvation be available only to some, or even to a few.

Let us consider, then, some of the findings of research into human happiness from the perspective of the potential material and economic aspects of salvation. If salvation—as doctrine and lived reality—may not instantly put bread on the table for those who are hungry, it is important for us nevertheless to ask how material salvation must be.

Starting from the question of what human beings need saving *from* is not likely, given the history of Christian spirituality and theology, to issue in an immediate response to do with the material dimension of life. But the matter is now pressing. And if one were to start at the other end of the salvation template—what is salvation *for*—and the answer is 'for flourishing', beginning *now*, then salvation has to be seen as release from poverty, deliverance from material lack, provision of safety and adequate shelter. Concluding that such practical material concerns are directly related to salvation does not, of course, mean that salvation is then reduced to such concerns. Nor will their

---

[34] See the works of Paul Dolan, Carol Graham, Daniel Haybron, Richard Layard, and Martin Seligman cited in the Resources Used at the end of this book.

provision mean that salvation (and life *in all its fullness*) has arrived. It may not even mean that interpreting the lack of such necessities as an aspect of salvation carries great weight, especially for those who experience such a need, often in desperate circumstances. Doctrinal reflection can, once more, seem the preserve of the wealthy, or at least of those who are already in possession of the means for living. But what, then, *does* the location of material need within the framework of the doctrine of salvation amount to in practice?

First, it means that a doctrinal emphasis which has so often ended up rather individualistically conceived (Am I saved? Will I be saved?) shifts its focus elsewhere (How can all be saved?). One is not to think only of one's own well-being—inner or otherwise—whilst others suffer. Attention to salvation's material dimension cannot, in other words, leave salvation pertaining solely to the inner life of individuals, even whilst all dimensions have an individual element to them. In the case of the material dimension, interpreting it too individualistically means turning it into the kind of prosperity theology which, as noted in Chapter 5, can be easily criticized. Salvation's material dimension is thus a further reminder of the corporate dimension to the doctrine. The whole of humanity's well-being is at stake here.

Second, addressing the material dimension of salvation entails asking the question of how much—or, more appropriately, how little—one needs materially to enable it to be possible to live life in all its fullness. This is a demanding question, capable of being answered differently in different countries and cultures because of the diverse economic conditions which pertain and the related levels of aspiration.[35] To compress the consequences of a considerable amount of research into a few sentences, however, it is clear that whilst a minimum level of material resources is needed for general well-being, increases in income (for example) do not then correspond to commensurate increases in human happiness.[36] There is also the phenomenon of the 'happy peasant and the frustrated achiever', identified by Graham and Pettinato, which recognizes that, because all assessments of well-being are relative, it is possible to be satisfied

[35] There are many studies of relevant data. I have found Carol Graham, *Happiness around the World: The Paradox of Happy Peasants and Miserable Millionaires* (Oxford and New York: Oxford University Press, 2009) and Richard Wilkinson and Kate Pickett, *The Spirit Level: Why Equality is Better for Everyone* (London: Penguin Books, 2010) especially helpful.
[36] Graham, *Happiness*, 25–6, 123; Wilkinson and Pickett, *Spirit Level*, 6, 8.

with less in the same context than others with greater mobility and higher aspirations who are deeply unsatisfied because they cannot fulfil their ambitions.[37]

Similar research also shows that religious people tend to be happier people, on the whole.[38] This leads, though, to the possible supposition—as voiced by Marx—that religion makes people happier with less, and less willing to challenge inequality. Religion may thus encourage people to be the happy peasants and to stifle their aspirations.

This is, of course, possible and undoubtedly does occur in some settings, for some people. Yet such an all-encompassing reductionist verdict should not be allowed to hold total sway when applying it to understanding how religious faith, and the Christian doctrine of salvation in particular, is informed by, and informs, material concerns. Being able to be content with relatively little need not be equated with stifling aspirations. At issue is how aspirations and ambitions take shape, whether these may be in favour of others (and not just oneself), and how they relate to the political views that one holds.

Whatever country or culture one is in, then, entails recognizing that, when understood as 'flourishing', salvation commits individuals and communities to work for the well-being of *all*. This commitment will then also entail accepting constraints on one's own need for ever-increasing material wealth and possessions. As soon as salvation is understood as a doctrine which comprises a concern for the well-being of all people (and all creation), then the sense of well-being one already has (as a God-given gift) enables one more easily to be content with what one has, knowing that self-restraint can assist the well-being of the other.

There is a third aspect to this material dimension of salvation, one which pertains to the negative aspects caused by lack of, or desire for, wealth and possessions. In parallel to the way in which no amount of material wealth necessarily leads to salvation, lack of the basics for material well-being can prove an obstacle to hearing and receiving God's offer of salvation. When the search for food, shelter, or safety is all-consuming, then nothing else may matter. Whilst it is not impossible to recognize that they alone do not produce a wholly fulfilled life ('One does not live by bread alone', Matt. 4.4 = Luke 4.4), their absence may hinder the very possibility of seeing that a framework of salvation can enhance how one best participates in a fully human life.

---

[37] Graham, *Happiness*, 151–2.   [38] Graham, *Happiness*, 19, 61–2, 190–2.

Material concerns which hinder the possibility of perceiving the value of salvation also apply at the opposite pole. Those who have, materially speaking, may be prevented by their wealth from seeing that they lack anything at all ('Those who are well have no need of a physician, but those who are sick', Mark 2.17). Ownership may thus hinder openness to salvation's gift. Indeed, 'the paradox of unhappy growth', according to which 'individuals in countries with positive growth rates have lower happiness levels', and the possibility that individuals themselves may be on some kind of 'hedonic treadmill' or caught up in the consequences of a country's continual quest for economic growth, could lead to profound unhappiness. It could obscure all opportunity to recognize the potential benefits of a gift which is not related directly to possessions and material wealth at all.[39]

SALVATION AS FREE GIFT

We have come full circle here. We reach a conclusion that salvation is, unsurprisingly, not to do primarily with material well-being. But we do this by taking material well-being seriously within an overarching approach to human living which puts material well-being and economics in their appropriate place, noting their necessity, whilst relativizing their importance in relation to other dimensions of daily living and spiritual practice. We could say that an appropriate approach to economic capital is best shaped by the benefits of salvation articulated through the other three dimensions of the doctrine (aesthetic, affective, therapeutic). In truth, though, the four dimensions are best not ranked, any more than the four 'moments' on the template of salvation (from, for, by, into) are to be seen only in linear or temporal fashion. All four dimensions and all four moments are, if not equal in importance, then at least essential to salvation's make-up. There may be different reasons why individuals or spiritual or theological traditions might emphasize one dimension or moment over the others. But it would be wasted effort to spend time on such a debate. All dimensions and moments command respect, whatever their relative weight.

[39] Graham, *Happiness*, 146, 15, 18.

That said, that I have here considered salvation's economic dimension *at all* in such a project as this is unusual. We may at this point seem at some stage removed from most of the mainstream Christian (perhaps especially Protestant) debates about salvation across the centuries. Though Luther may have been more materialistic in some of his concerns than is often recognized, his understanding of God's redemptive work was not primarily about anyone's income levels. And, ultimately, his theological outlook did not extend to siding with the peasants.[40] Various forms of liberation theology—Latin American forms in particular—have, however, now been challenging individualistic and inner life-only approaches to salvation for more than fifty years. Including attention to the basic practicalities of human living within an exploration of the doctrine of salvation is therefore but acknowledgement of the importance of that challenge, and a recognition of the adjustments needed to much of Christian doctrinal history.[41]

At the conclusion of his study of 'the happiness industry', William Davies remarks: 'As a point of principle, we might state that the pursuit of health and the pursuit of money should remain in entirely separate evaluative spheres.'[42] For 'health' we may here read 'salvation'. Perhaps the pursuit of salvation and the pursuit of money—and all that is related to it—should be kept quite separate. Perhaps I have muddied the doctrinal waters by including this entire chapter in my exploration. From another angle, the language of 'pursuit' may not be at all appropriate. For salvation, it can be argued, is not to be pursued, but received with gratitude with open hands. The only sense in which 'pursuit' may in any way apply is when, in desperation—over recognition of one's plight, be that material, existential, spiritual, psychological—one looks outward and begs for help.

Yet, as I have shown in this chapter, whilst it is understandable why any quest for health, happiness, or salvation should be sharply distinguished from the quest for material wealth, there are points of connection at least. What are material concerns but a recognition that

---

[40] On this see, for example, Lyndal Roper, *Martin Luther: Renegade and Prophet* (London: Bodley Head, 2016), 259–72.

[41] Atherton, *Challenging Religious Studies*, Chapters 1 and 3.

[42] William Davies *The Happiness Industry: How the Government and Big Business Sold Us Well-Being* (London and New York: Verso, 2015), 274.

we are flesh and blood? In theological terms, belief in an incarnate God requires us to take flesh and blood seriously whilst, in keeping with the Apostle Paul, not allowing the concerns of the flesh to control all of our thinking and acting ('flesh and blood cannot inherit the kingdom of God', 1 Cor. 15.50). Hence, Davies is only partly correct when his insight is applied to the kind of cultural theology I am seeking to construct here. Distinguish indeed; but if we wholly separate health (or salvation) and money, then we would be guilty of what Christian theology and spirituality have long done: insufficiently address material matters whilst attending to the spiritual. Belief in an incarnate God cannot permit this.

Better, then, to adapt a further insight from happiness studies for theological ends. In his extensive study of the psychology of happiness, Daniel Haybron remarks: 'human well-being mostly depends not on what people have but, among other things, on what they do with what they've got'.[43] This coheres to some degree with Davies's conclusion, undercuts any reductionist tendency when taking material matters seriously in theology, and yet respects that 'having' does matter. With Haybron we can say that salvation comes more easily, because there is time and space to reflect on what it might be when the basics of life are met. Beyond that, however, it is very much a spiritual affair. It then needs subdividing and clarifying in terms of different kinds of capital (social and cultural), which can in turn be expounded along aesthetic, affective, and therapeutic lines: hence the categories of this present study. All forms of capital are a gift (for all is from God). All we do is decide what to use within the parameters of what we are given. Taking too much is sinful, as is refusing to share, and as is refusing to enjoy and celebrate the gifts we have been given. The notion of 'taking too much' makes most sense to us when we consider material things, which is why this chapter's subject matter is important when considering salvation. 'Taking too much' may, though, feel inappropriate when applied to the riches of media, the arts, or culture, unless these too have become so highly consumerized that our focus is less on the quality and significance of our responses and more on the scale of what we consume.

The insights of this present chapter can be applied in a further way to what we have considered thus far in this part of the book. In the

---

[43] Daniel M. Haybron, *The Pursuit of Unhappiness: The Elusive Psychology of Well-Being* (Oxford: Oxford University Press, 2008), 27.

same way as the accumulation of capital (literal and metaphorical) can be an addictively acquisitive pursuit—as if happiness, well-being, fulfilment, or flourishing can simply be bought—so also the tendency toward self-absorption may need to be kept in check. The concern for one's own riches (or happiness or flourishing) at the expense of other people is more starkly evident when material wealth is being considered. It is less evident when qualitative aspects of life are in view. Yet the Christian history of salvation, especially in its post-Reformation form, has been preoccupied with the salvation of the individual believer. As such, it has been less open to communal notions of salvation (and social understandings of sin) and prone to overlook the way in which it has fostered individual self-interest, even whilst inviting people to respond to God's generosity.

Attending to capital and cash has, then, enabled us to ensure that we remain grounded as we consider the doctrine of salvation. Furthermore, looking at salvation's material aspects has provided a fresh lens through which to look back on the less tangible, but traditionally more dominant ways of approaching salvation's spiritual content. Now it is time to move on to ask what all of these inquiries—into the aesthetic, affective, therapeutic, and economic dimensions of salvation—amount to in practical, theological terms. That will be the substance of Part III of the book.

Part III

Salvation Reworked

7

The Shape of Soteriology

There are two kinds of fools: one says, 'This is old, therefore it is good'; the other says, 'This is new, therefore it is better.'

William Ralph Inge, *More Lay Thoughts of a Dean*, 200

Doing cultural theology is very much like walking a tightrope. On the one side is the need to respect a particular theological tradition in relation to which a theology is being articulated. In this regard I seek to stand in continuity with the Christian tradition in undertaking constructive theological work. On the other side is a huge mass of material which characterizes the context in which theology is done and yet also provides—directly and indirectly—resources with which theology works. Some of this material has similar, overlapping concerns to what the various loci (or themes) of theology are seeking to express. It may therefore add something to theology's content. Other material may challenge it, actively seek to debunk it, or just seem plain irrelevant to what theology tries to do.

The previous four chapters have been an attempt to provide a composite but not comprehensive picture of that messy, complex context. I took up eight case studies of cultural products, concepts, or practices as a way of characterizing contemporary everyday Western life within which any doctrine has to be reworked. Together, such case studies offer a worked example of how, specifically, an exercise in *navigation and negotiation* has to take place in order for a compelling contemporary, connected, comprehensible doctrine of salvation to be expounded. In the same way as it would have been wrong simply to present Christian resources, so also it would have been wrong to neglect them. Christian material is all the time entangled with the products which citizens in Western culture use to find a way through life. Theology's job, as I have been emphasizing from the start, is not

simply a matter of extracting from cultural products what it is already
known beforehand will prove identifiably Christian. Its task is to work
with the tradition it carries with it in specifying, under the guidance of
the reality of the God that Christian theology believes accompanies
human beings towards a new and more hopeful future, what forms
of human life will shape that future.[1] Only as that critical creative work
is done can fresh, living formulations of Christian theology's key
themes emerge.

I must reiterate that whilst the eight examples chosen were not
random, they were not meant to be the 'best' examples in some way of
what will deliver a neatly packaged soteriology for today. I did not set
out with a doctrine of salvation which I wanted to articulate and then
search for materials which would readily enable me to present that
understanding. It was important to offer a *selection* of examples,
Christian and not, of how salvation/redemption and forms of
human flourishing take root and are understood in the West. Some
of the examples appeared and have been wrestled with simply on the
basis of how they are being handled and presented in broader culture
(*Crazy Heart* being 'about' redemption, for example). On that basis, an
exploration of how Christian insights do and do not interweave with
(and inform, and are informed by) such expressions becomes possible.

In the process of walking the tightrope, the suspicion is always
present, of course, that a Christian framework and Christian content
are simply being imposed upon daily life, and upon the interpretations
of that life which are contained within the case studies presented. In
this chapter I shall show that whilst a framework is indeed being
offered by Christian theology as a way of 'reading' human experience
and that this framework can be regarded as shaping the experiences
being interpreted, such a process does not distort those experiences. On
the contrary, through the way in which I reflect on the case studies
in moving towards the constructive theological work of Chapter 8,
I contend that the theological insights which are brought to bear
both disclose important dimensions of what is being interpreted and

---

[1] The church—which only ever exists in concrete form as a vast and varied
collection of churches—is responsible for holding and carrying that tradition, in all
its own diversity. Church and theological (doctrinal) tradition thus always belong
together, with the possibility that the church/churches, in recognizing their responsibility for carrying the tradition, will always be prone to seek to control what can be
said of God. But because God is always bigger and more creative than the church,
theology always has to respect the church's limits in the theological task.

offer crucial imaginative insights for practical action. Through further critical reflection on the case studies presented in Part II, I shall demonstrate the practical usefulness of what I have called the Christian template of salvation (being saved 'from, for, by, and into'). Use of this template enables honest, critical, constructive engagement with life experience as mediated through the various artistic and cultural forms and concepts presented in Part II. In this process of critical interaction Christian meanings critique and are critiqued by the resources which are being studied and permitted to 'do their work' (as art, film, music, TV, psychology, forms of capital). In this way the truthfulness of what the template contains—in both form and content—can function as an interpretative channel of what is believed by Christians to be the presence and action of God in the present and immediate future.

A CHRISTIAN TEMPLATE OF SALVATION

I suggested near the start of this study that a template of salvation which seeks to identify what a person or people needs saving *from*, is saved *for*, the means *by which* that salvation happens, and the communal context *into* which a person or people is saved offers a helpful way of understanding the shape of soteriology. Such a template need not be seen as exclusively Christian. In its shape it could equally, for example, be presented in a Jewish or Islamic form.[2] There is nevertheless a specifically Christian version of this template which I shall eventually make use of in the next chapter. But in formal terms, what the template offers is more than just a framework for presenting particular religious concepts; *it suggests a way of understanding the structure of human life*. The shape of soteriology is, in short, a helpful way of looking at how human life can be well lived. That negativity in life (one's own proneness to wickedness or the impact of evil actions in society) has to be overcome, that it is wise to have a vision of what a fruitful, flourishing human life can be, that some grasp on how this might be achieved is needed, and that a social (rather than just an individualistic) goal is to be sought constitute together a rich super-structure for the mapping of hopeful human living. The shape of

---

[2] On the theme of salvation in world religions, see Harold Coward, *Sin and Salvation in the World Religions: A Short Introduction* (Oxford: Oneworld, 2003).

such a template can, admittedly, be regarded as heavily influenced by Abrahamic traditions. But even though those in the Abrahamic traditions may find it easier than those in other religious traditions (or none) to make use of this 'shape of soteriology' as a framework for life, I contend that it need not be seen as exclusively Abrahamic. It is more flexible and adaptable than may first appear, even if in this present study it is a Christian version of the template which is being discussed and developed. 'From, for, by, into' creates, then, a soteriological shape for understanding and exploring human life.

It would be possible to accept this template and expound a Christian form of it for the present solely with recourse to biblical and doctrinal traditions. In keeping with the cultural-theological methodology of this study, however, it is essential that such a procedure is resisted. Whilst biblical and doctrinal traditions will be used, we must first distil from the conversations with culture insights into what it is possible to hear about what contemporary Western citizens are already aware they need saving from, for, by, and into. In addition it is important to identify what can be discerned from the cultural readings of human life offered in Part II about what fits, or does not fit, the template. Only in this way will it be possible to articulate a truthful Christian soteriology which resonates with contemporary experience.

Such a process is not a simple *application* of the Christian template to contemporary experience. It entails the placing of the conversations conducted in Part II within the framework which the template presents so that it is possible better to grasp aspects of contemporary life (What do we fear? What are we wrestling with? What are we living for? What kinds of community are hoped for?) and to become clear about what is likely to be comprehensible theologically.

FROM GRÜNEWALD TO MONEY

The case studies offered in Part II of this book were but snapshots of aspects of contemporary Western life which pertain to the doctrine of salvation. Wherever elements of life appear which block human flourishing, then the question of salvation arises. Hence, illness, disease, addictions of many kinds, wickedness, inner turmoil, social exclusion, loneliness, poverty all feature amongst many negative aspects of life to which the doctrine of salvation pays attention. Conversely, wherever manifestations of human prospering and flourishing occur, then it is of interest to the doctrine of salvation to identify what has been overcome to enable such fulfilment to occur. It may not always be immediately apparent that adversity has been present. It may indeed prove that there is no specific adversity that has been overcome in a given case. Use of the template of salvation nevertheless offers an overarching framework within which the causes and content of the experience of flourishing are better understood. Human experience as a whole is not capable of being addressed fruitfully without a constructive means of encountering and handling adversity, negativity, and evil. A reflective response to the collective impact of the Part II case studies which uses the template of salvation thus provides a creative way of mapping the means by which Western citizens consume culture and respond to the challenges of life. Such a mapping exercise supplies a foundation on the basis of which a fresh revisiting of the known key themes of, and challenges for, the doctrine of salvation becomes possible. This will be the substance of Chapter 8.

The chart supplied in the Appendix to this book offers a summary of the issues and discussions which arose in considering the cases in Chapters 3–6.[3] At this stage, it matters less whether individual cases are Christian (e.g. Isenheim, *Messiah*) or not (*Breaking Bad*, capital) than that the composite picture shows how Christian themes appear in everyday and cultural life, and that Western citizens—Christian or not—interact with a range of resources and experiences simply by the fact of living. Placing such cultural consumption and life experience into an interpretative template enables the different dimensions of salvation (from, for, by, into) to be recognized and examined more easily.

Close observation of the summary of findings from Part II of this book allows a number of conclusions to be drawn about how contemporary 'salvific experience'—in the broadest sense of that term—is to be understood. In what follows I cannot explore every possible avenue suggested by the discussions of salvific themes which the case studies generated. I shall, however, explore seven conclusions which will, in turn, steer the next chapter's contemporary exposition of a doctrine of salvation.

[3] As I suggest in the Appendix, mapping the template in this kind of way assists those who learn best, or first, 'visually'. It also serves as a further reminder that the combination of case studies is but one of many possible ways of 'filling in the template'. Readers are invited to devise their own versions of the chart commensurate with resources they have found instructive and stimulating.

If What People Need to Be Saved *from* May Be Classed as 'Sin', then the Definition of Sin Needs to Be Broadly Defined.

Sin can be quickly defined in Christian theology as 'living against God's will' or living 'in a state that opposes God's will for our flourishing'.[4] It is 'a general all-encompassing condition, not individual acts', which is 'universal in scope . . . no one escapes it'.[5] The difficulty is that as a basic condition which can manifest itself concretely in many different ways, sin is most easily recognized and spoken of within the context of a community which recognizes sin's basic nature. It is in communities of people who recognize their need for release from this basic condition (for example, religious communities who know their need of salvation) where sin can be most readily identified, named, and faced. Otherwise, it is more commonly referred to in Western culture in the form of 'individual acts' which are but manifestations of the basic condition. Hence, talk of 'sins', understood as moral misdemeanours, is more prominent in wider cultural discourses outside specifically religious contexts. This has two consequences. First, it turns sin into only a moral rather than a theological term. This means that only moral issues are labelled sins, and there is then the implication that sin/s can somehow be dealt with via adjustments in human ethical activity alone.

A second consequence is that the broader range of aspects of human life which stand in the way of the fulfilment of God's will for the world—including those which are not simply the result of human moral indiscretion—may not be identified as sin which is in need of redemption. Thus, whilst the sin from which release is required includes actions for which forgiveness and amendment of life are needed, a contemporary exposition of the Christian doctrine of salvation will need careful theological handling and not be equated simply with a moral understanding of the sin and sins from which liberation needs to be sought. God's salvation is more flexible and adaptable than may often be thought, though also richer and more encompassing. It is here that the significance of Part II's case studies becomes clear.

---

[4] Serene Jones, 'What's Wrong with Us?', in William C. Placher (ed.), *Essentials of Christian Theology* (Louisville, KY, and London: Westminster John Knox Press, 2003), 148–9.

[5] Jones, 'What's Wrong with Us?', 149.

The case studies do not, of course, constitute or offer a uniform or coherent understanding of sin. As snapshots of cultural activity and concerns they expose Western society's preoccupations as well as providing some of the means by which those concerns are addressed—spiritually and materially. The composite picture of what contemporary Westerners need saving *from* can, however, be grouped under three headings: internal individual failings, social shortcomings, and material lack. In the first group appear gloom and despair, whether caused by disease, low self-esteem, addictive behaviour, or purposelessness. Self-reliance practised to a destructive degree, as embodied in the character of Walter White (*Breaking Bad*), could be regarded as a central hallmark of this grouping. Even if, as in the case of disease (Isenheim), an individual may not be to blame for their affliction, the refusal to be open to others, and through others to God, in the face of affliction is an indicator of a reluctance to receive from outside the self, thus accentuating an understanding of sin as being turned in upon oneself (*incurvatus in se*).[6]

Exaggerated self-reliance is itself an expression of a refusal to relate to others. Not all social forms of what requires redemption—the second grouping—result from wilful human action. Some forms of sin are the consequences of social, structural sin in the sense that individuals experience the results of what may actually be harmful but which is accepted as socially conventional. Addiction harms individuals but fractures many relationships—families and friendships. Patterns of addiction may, however, themselves emerge in social settings within which individuals find it very hard to counter what is regarded as a social norm ('Everyone gambles, don't they?'). Similarly, unless there is resistance to patterns of social exclusion—such as would occur for the character of Sheldon Cooper in *The Big Bang Theory* were it not for the acceptance of the friends around him—then exclusion and ridicule of anyone who is different, or other, become the norm. Openness to the possibility of salvation has to involve the identification of such social exclusion as social sin, and the quest for its overcoming.

Finally, attention needs to be paid to material lack as an aspect of sin. Here it would be easy to suppose that salvation entails the acquisition of material wealth, within some form of Prosperity Gospel, according to which individuals or groups experience redemption as a

---

[6] See Chapter 4 n. 25 for the key Luther quotation.

result of having a material lack met: money or goods are lacking, and their provision turns a person's life around. It became clear in Chapter 6, however, that whilst the absence of basic material needs can obstruct human flourishing, the provision of material need does not necessarily guarantee well-being, material or otherwise. This does not lead to the exclusion of material aspects from a doctrine of salvation, however. Material aspects of sin and salvation have to be considered from a social perspective. Here, the sin which needs overcoming, and needs understanding as such within a doctrine of salvation, is as much the presence of unjust economic structures which prevent people having access to a reasonable amount of material wealth to function and prosper as a human being as it is how individuals respond and act within such a structure.

'Material' aspects of sin and salvation are also, of course, not just to do with money and wealth. Money and material wealth are in many ways but symbols of *embodiment*. Wherever, then, aspects of physical well-being appear in the map of what people need saving from, material considerations are in view. This applies to any refusal to let the beauty of *Messiah* do its work on the emotions (as experienced in the body) in responding to Handel's music. It relates to failure to note embodied aspects of human relating in *Breaking Bad* (physical contact, for example, between Walter White and his son Walt Jr) or *The Big Bang Theory* (the running story line of Sheldon Cooper's difficulty in coping with physical contact).[7] It pertains, too, to the physical impact upon Blake's body of his alcohol addiction (*Crazy Heart*). In short, there are many examples within our case studies of the interplay between spiritual/mental/emotional/cognitive aspects of sin and physical aspects. They may be able to be distinguished, but they cannot be separated.

We can go further: the content of all of these three groupings (individual, social, material) interacts. Release from poverty stands to free people from being sinned against, a liberation which they would experience as individuals whatever forms of individual sin people may embody by virtue of being human. Such material lack is itself a social sin, having effects on individuals with and without wealth. Similarly, personal relationships can be sources of human

[7] An early example of this is found in 'The Bath Item Gift Hypothesis' (2.11), when, in response to Penny's thoughtful Christmas gift, Sheldon finds a way to give her a hug of gratitude.

flourishing and locations of sinfulness. Wilful hostility to or disparaging of others clearly obstructs the possibility of good relations. Individual psychological conditions or personalities and other circumstances which create complex social situations are, however, only sinful in so far as they are permitted to become obstructions to good relations. There is debate as to whether addictions are illnesses (and thus, in the case of our example, whether Blake in *Crazy Heart* is ultimately responsible for his actions).[8] Sheldon Cooper is irritating, insensitive, emotionally distant, and hard work for those around him. But his personality is not a sin. It is part of who he is. A social sinful context is, though, created where he is excluded because of his personality. As it is, the characters around Sheldon work hard, whilst also being themselves, to respect him as he is and work with him, challenging him where necessary, but building him up, as they are built up themselves, through the character-forming exchanges of everyday life. Collectively, they create a safe and constructive community (a foretaste of the Kingdom of God, as we shall explore in the next chapter) even whilst acknowledging, and at times participating in (when they do not respect him and make fun of him), the social sin of the tendency to exclude those who are different, a tendency which pervades the wider society of which they are a part.

Identification of these three groupings of aspects of sin as things with which salvation must deal, and which emerge from our varied collection of case studies, suggests that a broad definition of sin has to be ventured both to do justice to the forms which sin takes and to be able to be comprehensible for Western citizens today. It could, though, be deemed that such a broad-based understanding of sin is too vague and dilutes the full force of a definition of sin derived from the Christian biblical and doctrinal tradition. I dispute this. In following the method of cultural theology I have outlined, my contention is that the content of the doctrine of salvation being sought is not simply brought to life by such a procedure. The method invites (requires!) contemporary theology to dig deep into a range of contemporary human experiences where it is not only human subjectivity which is at work, but where also the God identified in Christian theology as creator, redeemer, and sustainer of life is entangled with the messy complexity of everyday living. An adequate understanding of salvation

[8] Christopher C. H. Cook, *Alcohol, Addiction and Christian Ethics* (Cambridge and New York: Cambridge University Press, 2006).

requires an adequate understanding of sin. An adequate understanding of sin requires in turn that it be an understanding which relates appropriately to the range of human experiences within which the will of God for the world is seen to be obstructed. It is this task which the theological methodology being followed achieves. Rather than perpetuate the Western tendency to reduce sin to a series of moral lapses, the composite, diverse picture of sin, made up of multiple elements which obstruct and prevent human flourishing, has more chance of being consistent with the very variegated tradition about sin which the biblical-doctrinal tradition at its best describes. It is more appropriate for the contemporary theological task than one which simply repeats an understanding of Bible and tradition without listening closely to the context in which an interpretation of Bible and tradition is located and is being reworked. Western understandings of sin have simply been truncated and narrowed too easily into inner psychological states *alone*.[9] It is inaccurate to exclude intrapersonal aspects of sin. It is also inaccurate to characterize sin solely in such terms. Hence, the broader understanding of sin suggested by the approach I have adopted sits well with the wide-ranging interpretation needed to do justice to the Christian biblical-doctrinal tradition at its most expansive.

Salvation Is more than a Feeling, but Does Need to Be Felt: Healthy Human Flourishing Inevitably Involves Affective Experience.

It is commonly assumed that religion is primarily about belief. It may even be especially the case in the West, and particularly in northern Europe and North America, where bookish forms of Protestantism have often been culturally dominant. The more the Word and words (Bible as Scripture) are emphasized over ritual and practice, the more that cognitive aspects of believing are accentuated. Salvation, too, can be restricted to its cognitive dimensions. Where emphasis is placed on

---

[9] This was noted by Krister Stendahl in a very important and influential essay, 'The Apostle Paul and the Introspective Conscience of the West', *Harvard Theological Review* 56 (1963), 199–215 (repr. in *Paul among Jews and Gentiles* (Philadelphia, PA: Fortress Press, 1976; London: SCM Press, 1977)).

the declaration of faith one is to make, then as an act of conscious will the cognitive processing required is prominent.[10]

All forms of Christianity, however, contain both cognitive-mental and affective-sensual dimensions, no matter where emphasis is placed. Though some forms have accentuated aesthetic dimensions (one thinks of the attention to the visual and the promotion of high-quality music in Roman Catholicism and Anglicanism, or the interplay of visual imagery and chanting in Orthodox traditions), a cognitive element remains.[11] Few forms of Christianity have paid explicit attention to the affective dimension of faith. How it *feels* (now) to be saved or redeemed—even when understood as a foretaste of what can only be experienced fully post-mortem—has rarely been a prominent feature of most forms of Christianity. Where the affective has been evident and acknowledged (e.g. in forms of Pentecostalism, in Methodism, in charismatic Christianity or in other forms of evangelicalism), or where it is accentuated by scholars of religion in relation to many different forms of Christianity, the affective is too readily associated with those less well educated, or with religious practices identified as superstition.[12] The aesthetic is preferred to the affective, even though the latter

[10] For example, as expressed in the recitation of a creedal formula ('We believe . . . in one Lord Jesus Christ . . . who for us, and for our salvation, came down from heaven, and was incarnate by the Holy Ghost of the Virgin Mary, and was made man', *Nicene Creed*) or via the words of a catechism ('I believe that Jesus Christ, true God, begotten of the Father from eternity, and also true man, born of the Virgin Mary, is my Lord, who has redeemed me, a lost and condemned creature', Martin Luther, *The Small Catechism* (1529), http://bookofconcord.org/smallcatechism.php, accessed 23 August 2016).

[11] Some with mental disabilities may not be able to relate to cognitive elements of faith, and hence other dimensions prove crucial for participation in religious belief and practice. It is also important to note the many reassessments of visual dimensions of Protestantism which have occurred over the past few decades, e.g. within the work of David Morgan, *Visual Piety: A History and Theory of Popular Religious Images* (Berkeley and Los Angeles: University of California Press, 1998) and *Protestants and Pictures: Religion, Visual Culture, and the Age of American Mass Production* (New York: Oxford University Press, 1999); John Harvey, *Image of the Invisible: Visualization of Religion in the Welsh Nonconformist Tradition* (Cardiff: University of Wales Press, 1999); Paul Corby Finney (ed.), *Seeing beyond the Word: Visual Arts and Calvinist Tradition* (Grand Rapids, MI: Eerdmans, 1999); Christopher Richard Joby, *Calvinism and the Arts: A Re-Assessment* (Leuven: Peeters, 2007).

[12] Whilst anthropologists and sociologists may be able to be more dispassionate about 'popular religion', theology has been less sanguine about the value of popular religious practice. Frank Burch Brown is something of an exception in tackling the question head-on, and in including a discussion of art considered as 'kitsch' (*Good Taste, Bad Taste, Christian Taste: Aesthetics in Religious Life* (Oxford: Oxford

is invariably enmeshed with the former, because the affective is deemed too prone to sentiment, is less controllable, and is less serious.[13] This simply will not do. If the doctrine of salvation is to be given its full worth cognitively and is to feature as a key component within Christian life, then its content will also have a dramatic effect beyond what occurs in a person's head, and no matter what the social class or status, intellectual or educational background, ethnic origin, or sexual orientation of the one who experiences salvation. It could even be argued that the affective dimension of salvation has to have priority over the cognitive simply because not all can necessarily attain a particular level of cognitive ability, or are prevented through illness or being in possession of a particular condition, to grasp salvation mentally or intellectually, whilst nevertheless participating in a salvific community or enjoying salvation's benefits.[14] I note this point here without developing it further. For the purposes of this study, I need simply state that whilst salvation as a doctrine is a mindset, it is also a characterization of a religious framework for living and a state of being. These elements will be brought out more fully in the Conclusion to this book.

What, though, can we learn from the affective dimensions of redemption and flourishing which cut through the chapters from Part II, not only those dealing with religious subject matter, and not only in the chapter which highlighted affectivity? The first thing to say is that when we examine affective dimensions of salvation, we are not talking about *any* human feeling, even if experienced positively. Salvation is, for example, not the same as experiencing transcendence, even if closely related to it. A positive human experience of exhilaration may be an indicator of, or a precursor to, an experience of salvation but is not necessarily to be equated with it. And feelings are not always positive. A journey to salvation may be filled with

University Press, 2000)). More generally, it is practical theologians who pay more attention to lived experience and culture in its widest forms.

[13] Jeremy Begbie, 'Beauty, Sentimentality and the Arts', in Daniel J. Treier, Mark Husbands, and Roger Lundin (eds.), *The Beauty of God: Theology and the Arts* (Downers Grove, IL: IVP Academic, 2007), 45–69, is especially helpful on the question of sentiment. I have sought to rehabilitate it as an important theological category in *Cinema and Sentiment: Film's Challenge to Theology* (Carlisle: Paternoster Press, 2004). Whilst I accept Begbie's strictures, there is more to be said to break the easy associations made between the popular arts and sentimental affectivity and the 'higher' or 'fine' arts and aesthetic appreciation.

[14] John Gillibrand, *Disabled Church—Disabled Society: The Implications of Autism for Philosophy, Theology and Politics* (London: Jessica Kingsley, 2010) is important here.

many memories and evocations of negative experiences (sadness, guilt, worthlessness, shock, anxiety), even as a positive experience is moved towards. Indeed, salvation, whilst ultimately to be received and enjoyed positively, is unlikely to be experienced only as positive, and certainly not at first, given the range and depth of its impact upon the human life. Because sin is being addressed and dealt with within the salvation experience, there is inevitably a negative 'moment' or aspect to it.

All such considerations are apparent from the cases we looked at in Part II. Even as we move towards a feeling of comfort, reassurance, uplift (exhilaration, even) as we look at the range of images which makes up the Isenheim altarpiece, we are, at the same time, to be repulsed, as well as compelled, by the crucifixion image. But this is important, for it is how the altarpiece 'works' (and worked in the past) as a collection of images. In viewer response to *Breaking Bad*, as this is a piece of entertainment, then an abiding affective response is going to be *pleasure*. As with the horror genre, the viewer may wince or recoil in shock at some of the scenes, images, or plot lines in the drama, but because the TV-viewing experience is 'contained' within the comfort of a living room or some other viewing space, then the shock—whilst real—is not linked to real danger. The contribution to human flourishing may, of course, last only as long as the pleasure of watching the series. There being no obvious redemption for Walter White within the drama, and potentially no impact on the viewer outside it, the affective dimension of viewing is thus a short-lived, short-term matter.

Yet, whilst there is closure within the drama, in the response of viewers willing to permit the drama's affective impact to linger further upon them (or unable to prevent it doing so), the cognitive work stimulated by the viewing experience may go well beyond the viewing time. As with all such dramas, intensity of feeling does something to and for a person. Watching *Breaking Bad* is unlikely to lead a viewer directly, via an emotional viewing experience (however intense), to any clearly defined religious experience of salvation. It does, however, leave an emotional imprint, requiring a cognitive response, through its confrontation of the viewer with the depth, complexity, and ordinariness of evil. Because such resources are the ones in current use which address such issues in appropriate depth, they are more likely in the present—than, say, reading Augustine's *Confessions*—to invite Western citizens to consider what release is needed from and for.

The positive aspects of salvation—the affective dimension of the flourishing that one is saved *for*—appear in many forms (positive psychology, a pleasurable response to comedy, the impact of the acquisition of cultural capital). Care, though, needs to be taken not to identify such flourishing solely or even primarily within individual nice feelings. They are present and of huge importance. It is totally appropriate, in ways that Christians often overlook, to see feeling good *now* as a potential outcome of divine salvific activity. Salvation may not always be clearly *felt*, even by all Christians who name explicitly their participation in the action God has undertaken.[15] There are obstacles to the present enjoyment of the many dimensions of salvation (physical ailments, psychological blockages, material lack). Attention to the affective aspects of salvation is not meant to play down such real obstacles. Inquiring into what people may actually feel, as saved/being-saved/to-be-saved people, is, though, a legitimate and important theological—and not merely a physical or psychological—undertaking. It will not do to leave a contemporary theological exposition of salvation as a cognitive statement on the basis of which things *then* happen to and for a person. Salvation's affective elements are existentially bound up in the theological exposition. *Feeling* the need for salvation (as this takes shape in an awareness of one's own and humanity's shortcomings) and *feeling* the enrichment brought by divine action to effect release from the burdens of whatever oppressions enslave are intrinsic to any contemporary exploration of the doctrine. Whilst the feelings alone are not enough, theological assertions lacking existential correlation are of little value.[16]

The examples considered in Part II show that wherever deep feelings of belonging, transcendence, acceptance, or well-being occur, there exists a distinct possibility that such intensity is a signal of salvific activity. Likewise, wherever deep feelings of abandonment, loss, neglect, lack, or suffering are evident, then openness to a wide range of salvific action is called for. Salvific reflection can thus begin

---

[15] It is timely to recall here Jonathan Edwards's insistence (in *Religious Affections* (New Haven, CT: Yale University Press, 2009; first published, 1746)) that certain 'religious affections' *must* be felt. One need not share all Edwards's theological convictions to recognize the significance of what he is driving at here.

[16] This is not to say that theological statements only have meaning and value if human beings make them, because this would amount to a denial of God's aseity. God is God regardless of what humans make of God. The point here is that if human beings are to make statements about God, based on who God is, then they have an existential component: human beings are related to God, and depend on God for their very existence. Theological statements therefore cannot but have an existential dimension, with all the affective consequences which result from that.

from the affective wherever it occurs in life and move on from there. We are not to assume that clearly labelled religious experience alone is the starting point for reflection pertinent to a contemporary doctrine of salvation.

Accepting that the Positive Benefits of Salvation Are Experienced and Enjoyed in *this Life* Is Two-Edged.

For a variety of reasons it is understandable that an emphasis upon salvation in the present should be expected in a contemporary cultural theology. Greater life expectancy, uncertainty about the afterlife, preoccupation with experience, the search for happiness, living in the moment are all factors which lead to a major shift from thinking that salvation is something that relates to the future to focusing on what happens now. The exposition of the form such an emphasis will take will follow in the next chapter. For the moment we need simply note that an emphasis upon present salvation has risks and drawbacks.

Positively, looking at salvation's present aspects enables theological discussion to connect with live contemporary debate. The question whether happiness is or is not a helpful term to use as a synonym for salvation remains live. The dimensions of present salvation go further. Even if happiness may prove to be a useful term, it will require precision. In terms of our exploration in Part II we can see that the dimensions of salvation subdivide into a wide range of contemporary experiences: healthy human relationships, a strong sense of inner well-being, the joy of being in a group of supportive people, having the means and an appropriate context in which to face one's weaknesses and flaws, being stretched in one's thinking and believing, knowing how best to use the material wealth that one has, participating in rich aesthetic and affective events. All of these were features of what was examined and, it can be argued, should appear within a full exposition of what salvation entails. Theology's existential dimension becomes clear.

Such a composite picture may sound enticing. It may, though, produce difficulties in at least two respects. First, despite the social elements inherent in some of the features just described, a present emphasis on salvation can all too easily become individualistic. The more that present experience is accentuated, the more the concern can be about 'my' experience primarily. Second, more significantly, a focus on this life can lead to a devaluing of theological insights which may be contained in treatments of salvation which do clearly view salvation as more about a future event, or even about the end of time. In a climate when there is a lack of confidence about any form of afterlife, all references to final judgement or salvation beyond this present life could be excluded from view. That would be too harsh and hasty and fail to respect the figurative and poetic language and imagery which have, in any case, always been part of soteriological discourse. But even allowing for such linguistic considerations—and the fact that the imagination has had to come into play in handling salvation as a topic—too heavy an emphasis on the present could still lead to a stifling of what, theologically speaking, construals of salvation have been seeking to express.

In short, Roy Porter's suggestion that 'The Enlightenment... translated the ultimate question "How can I be saved?" into the pragmatic "How can I be happy?"', glossed by Darrin McMahon with the observation that the 'answers, eighteenth-century men and women increasingly believed, could be found through human effort and understanding alone', can quickly be linked with the potential truncation of attention to salvation's future dimension into a series of present human activities.[17] Attention to the potential, positive, present aspects of salvation could, in other words, simply be yet another way of resurrecting the ghost of Pelagius. Simply accepting what Christians may have said in the past about future salvation may not, of course, be the way forward. But doing justice to what they were trying to do and finding a contemporary way of understanding how the present–future dynamic (and tension) inherent in a doctrine of salvation will need to take shape will be essential.

A Broad Understanding of Salvation Implies that Human Beings Can Make a Huge Contribution to the Flourishing they May Experience by the Choices they Make and the Actions they Take.

As we shall see in the next chapter, there are a number of key debates in the history of Christian theology which qualify heavily any

---

[17] Darrin McMahon, *The Pursuit of Happiness: A History from the Greeks to the Present* (London: Penguin Books, 2007), 209.

suggestion that human action can contribute to the salvation which ultimately God alone brings about.[18] At its simplest, a Christian view of salvation suggests that all that human beings can do is participate in the plan of salvation for the created order which God has mapped out. What this means in practical terms, and why it may be such an important insight to hold onto, will need to be spelt out fully in due course. For the moment, having picked through the case studies, we must simply note the assumptions being made about the degree to which human activity is deemed capable of demonstrating salvific potential. To what extent can human beings in practice do anything about the negative aspects of living in which they find themselves—their own inner shortcomings, the consequences of past actions, the limitations of their environment, the impact of circumstances, or the actions of others upon them?

It is clear that human beings try to direct their lives, influence their surroundings, and act politically and effectively in an effort to shape society. Not to do so may suggest that life is ultimately meaningless, or that the course of life is so bound and predetermined that human actions have no effect. Christian theology has to wrestle with the strong tradition it carries with it that such actions are, however, worth little unless they are related to the will of God for the world: human effort of itself cannot transform the world. How human activity is therefore to be understood and what value it has need careful scrutiny.

There is little doubt that the composite picture of cases suggests that human beings are capable of much. It is human creativity which produces great art (visual and musical). It is human choice which enables us to benefit from such art, by opting to see and listen to it and to be affected by it. We exert ourselves to resist addiction, apply firm resolve to fight illness and disease, engage in psychological exercises better to structure our emotional lives, make choices about

---

[18] The two most prominent opponents are Augustine and Pelagius, though Luther and Erasmus and, slightly differently, John Calvin and Jacob Arminius (and then John Wesley) engaged in related disputes. More recently, most forms of liberation theology (e.g. Latin American, feminist, black, womanist, mujerista, Dalit, LGBT), as well as being positive about specific groups' identity, also contribute to those groups' empowerment. In so doing they highlight the significance of human action. This does not make them Pelagian, but it highlights the importance of any theology's clarifying how human action is to be understood with respect to God's saving action.

which friends to have, and work hard to acquire capital of all kinds. These are human efforts to make life meaningful and fulfilling.

In present times, it is common to assume that all such meaning is solely the result of human construction.[19] Salvation is therefore likely to be seen as the result of human work—both the salvation itself and the doctrines of salvation which describe and interpret such activity. The thought of such activity being a *participation* in something which is not simply human or a *response to* or *reflection of* a state of being which lies beyond the human realm will prove deeply unfashionable. We shall need in due course to explore what the merits might be of working in such unfashionable terrain.

Alongside this confidence in the value of human activity, however, there is a helplessness and unexpectedness too. Humans may work hard to overcome their faults or the obstacles they face. What can be characterized as 'sin' continues to intervene in the midst of the recognition of what humans can achieve. But there can still be little doubt of the emphasis placed upon the worth of human activity. In the face of such positivity it will be a challenge to work out how it is possible to retain a perspective on sin, on human limitation, on frailty, when so much is expected of, and claimed for, human action.

Respecting the Means by which, and Contexts in which, Salvation Occurs Leads to Accentuation of the InterPersonal Contexts in which Salvation Is Enjoyed.

Salvation is a process of being saved 'by' and 'into' (as well as 'from' and 'for'). If the 'by' aspect cannot in any unqualified sense be 'by human effort', then there is nevertheless a need to specify and explore how that 'by' process occurs. If, as I am arguing, salvation is to be seen as more than a merely hidden, inner, individual, mental, cognitive,

---

[19] However we characterize these 'present times' (e.g. whether as late modern, postmodern, post-religious, or post-secular), there is little doubt about the prominence of notions that it is up to human beings to structure life and create their own meanings as otherwise there is, or would be, none. Though the natural sciences might be able to note the presence of order in the cosmos, this does not necessarily present human beings with an understanding of the meaning of such order. A constructive human element is involved.

and emotional process—as it must, if social sin and social salvation are taken seriously—then exploration of the interpersonal dimension of salvation is crucial. How salvation occurs is decisive for understanding the nature of God's working in Christ in the present. The preposition 'by' will reveal itself to be ambiguous, in that a causal use ('by Christ', meaning that Christ enables salvation to happen) and what we may term a 'locative' use (meaning that Christ brings about salvation in and through personal relationships) both come into play.[20]

It is no accident that a wide range of interpersonal and social contexts needed to be explored in Part II to begin to unpack the many dimensions of salvation as a doctrine and as a theological experience. *Crazy Heart* found us looking at the way in which a key relationship proved transformative for an alcoholic. *Breaking Bad* showed how the refusal to work at relationships, or only using relationships with others for one's own ends, perpetuated a spiral of sin to a destructive degree. Attention to cultural, social, and spiritual capital, together with reminders of what music played, art shown, and television watched in social (and, in the case of Isenheim, therapeutic) contexts can achieve, showed how being with and learning from others can prove salvific in a variety of ways. Whilst the practice of Christian worship itself could be mined at great length in its own right as a context of the social experience of salvation, it was, of course, my aim to look beyond immediately obvious religious practices. Nevertheless, considering Joel Osteen's Lakewood Church under a therapeutic heading ensured that attention to flourishing in relation to the positive psychology movement accentuated the transformative, (inter)personal aspect of the church's work alongside its theological purpose.

The many interpersonal dimensions considered, then, identify the potential locations of divine salvific activity. In the case of works of art and media they are accounts of transformative occurrences, and become so also for recipients (watchers, hearers, viewers) in response to the works. Salvific activity thus occurs in the present as response, reaction, and participation. At the level of present experience, all such social contexts provide opportunities and locations in which people are

---

[20] Reference can here be made to the concept of 'double agency', the theological concept which acknowledges that God works through secondary agents. Hence, divine and human action are synchronized, though in truth the human action would not be possible without the divine initiative.

moved from discomfort or negativity to a more hopeful, constructive place as a result of their interactions with others.[21]

A number of objections arise, of course, to seeing such examples as 'salvific'. First is the obvious response that 'This is just life'—normal, everyday life: having setbacks, getting over things, dealing with tough stuff. Why start calling it salvation *at all*? Though true to some extent, it has to be asked where one might expect salvation to take root if not in the midst of ordinary life. However extraordinary and dramatic the sense of what salvation is, and how astonishingly transformative it could be, its drama may not be great for the majority of people. In the same way that not all people who come to faith experience dramatic conversions, so also it is a theological responsibility to show that the practice of faith—and thus the experiential dimension of each Christian doctrine—has to be understandable in a mundane way. God saves, in short, in the midst of everyday relationships.

Second, though, why introduce God-language at all? The more one stresses the mundaneness of the contexts in which salvation in the present occurs, the more it would seem to non-theological interpreters of human experience that it is unnecessary to offer a theological interpretation at all. Why bother reading *The Big Bang Theory* theologically or trying to understand economic inequality through a soteriological lens? The response needed here is straightforward. Whether or not God is (or 'exists'), it is necessary to work out what is going on within human relationships and societies, and to establish good ways of structuring human relationships and societies to enable them to flourish. Religions have always been part of those attempts, sometimes not positively, and yet it is clear that they are likely to remain involved. Despite the short-lived secularization thesis and the declining numbers of people who self-identify as religious in the West, religions persist and, at the very least, the question of whether theological interpretations of human reality may continue to prove beneficial for human well-being has to be posed.[22]

---

[21] Note may be taken here of the way, in common language used about death, the deceased may be spoken of as having 'gone to a better place'. In this case, somewhere beyond earthly life is being referred to. More recently, in reference to this life, and as a result of the popularizing of counselling language, it is quite common for people to refer to themselves as 'not being in a good place'. Salvation moves people to a better place whether in this life or beyond.

[22] I write this section on the day after hearing a report that for the first time ever in the UK the number of the population self-identifying as having no religion exceeds

A doctrine of salvation will, then, be incomplete if it addresses only what is deemed to occur within the life of the individual. As soon as a social understanding of sin is taken seriously, and thus a social grasp of salvation is recognized as a necessary counterpart to it (alongside addressing individual construals of both), then explorations of inter-personal relationships become prime material for theological—and here specifically soteriological—reflection. As we shall need to explore in the next chapter, the way in which such exploration overlaps with, but is also to be distinguished from, an understanding of 'church' (as a prime social form of Christianity) will become apparent. In add-ition, the Christological aspects of flourishing human relationships— what it means to be 'in Christ'—will be explored. And both of these facets of understanding human relationships theologically will in turn need to be considered within the main overarching framework for a theological approach to human social living: the Kingdom of God.

In Contemporary Understanding, the Forms of Social Life and the Communities which one Is Saved 'into' often Lack Robustness.

We now need to take the question of what kind of groups people may be 'saved into' a stage further. 'The church' is, of course, one of the

those who profess affiliation to a religious group. For supporters of the secularization thesis this would amount to confirmation that their thesis is far from misplaced. For others of us it is evidence of declining support for the major religious traditions and of a continuing shift (especially amongst the 18–30 age group) from religion to spiritu-ality. The situation was as follows in May 2017: 'The avowedly non-religious— sometimes known as "nones"—now make up 48.6% of the British population. Anglicans account for 17.1%, Catholics 8.7%, other Christian denominations 17.2% and non-Christian religions 8.4%', Harriet Sherwood, 'Nearly 50% are of no religion— but has UK hit "peak secular"?', *The Observer*, 14 May 2017, www.theguardian.com/ world/2017/may/13/uk-losing-faith-religion-young-reject-parents-beliefs, accessed 5 September 2017. Yet see '53% of Britons are Non-Religious, Says Latest British Social Attitudes Survey', Humanists UK website, 5 July 2017, https://humanism.org. uk/2017/07/05/53-of-britons-are-non-religious-says-latest-british-social-attitudes-sur vey/, accessed 5 Sept 2017:

The British Social Attitudes Survey is a robust national survey of British people's beliefs and attitudes published each year by NatCen. Its 34th edition, published in June 2017, found that 52.8% of the population were non-religious, while 15% identify as Anglican, 8.5% as Roman Catholic, and 17% as other sorts of Christian. Just 6.3% of of people in Britain belong to the smaller religions (Islam, Judaism, Hinduism, Sikhism and others grouped together).

answers (the key answer in so many ways) to the question of what, in Christian theological terms, a salvific community might look like. But it is wrong to be too sidetracked or preoccupied by church as either concept or living reality.[23] In any case, within and beyond churches themselves there are a great many other subgroups and para-groups in and through which Christians are formed and practise their spirituality: house groups, cell groups, special interest groups, support networks, study groups, prayer groups, mission organizations, online chatrooms, to name but a few. Within churches it is often the case that one of the smaller groups may prove the most formative and faith-enhancing for its members.[24] Regularity of meeting (whether real or virtual) and intensity of exchange, correlated with depth of friendship, prove key factors here.

Such intensity can also occur in groups which are not explicitly church-related or even religious. It is the *quality of experience* which is at issue here. What the composite picture of the examples considered across Chapters 3–6 shows is that it is in the midst of intense personal interactions, where people face themselves and each other honestly, and together with others face life's challenges directly, that the groundwork for God's saving action is prepared. Health, wealth, and happiness—and thus a transformative outcome in every case— are far from assured. The wicked will still prosper in many places (Psalm 73). And yet high-quality social interactions are both the potential ground for and the potential result of God's salvific activity.

That said, it is clear that many forms of constructive and formative social groups—precisely the contexts in which human beings may be enabled to flourish—are often weak in the West. Churches often struggle in numbers and in the quality of relationships they actually foster (evidenced in the loyalty of their members). The relative weakness of social groups is not, however, confined to church life. Robert Putnam's important work in the US has been much discussed and

---

[23] In *Christ in Focus: Radical Christocentrism in Christian Theology* (London: SCM Press, 2005) I identify ecclesiocentrism as one of the distortions of Christocentrism, 60–1.

[24] In the Christian tradition in which I have spent most of my adult life, Methodism, 'classes' and 'bands' were important in the origins of the movement, and wherever they can be sustained, house groups have remained significant. Churches always need, in other words, to find ways of enabling a Sunday (or midweek) congregation to be subdivided into smaller, more manageably sized groups within which deep, spiritually supportive relationships may form.

relates to one specific national context but has echoes elsewhere.[25] People belong to fewer organizations than in the past. We must, though, add two caveats to this. Failure to sign up may not necessarily mean that people do not have informal groups to which they attach huge significance. People do not, for example, formally join friendship groups or families. Second, the switch to virtual groups (which sometimes overlap with informal face-to-face groups) should also be noted. Intensity can often happen online more than in face-to-face encounters. Whilst virtual activity can indeed sometimes be avoidance of embodied contact, it can also at times enable a greater depth and intensity of engagement.[26] As is well-known, online activity can often lead to people revealing more of themselves than they may choose to do otherwise.

One of the difficulties, however, is that all such groups are too easily (and lazily) referred to as 'communities'. Community is an overused word. Its use assumes a positive connection between those who make up a group: communities are 'good things'. Beyond an aspiration to positivity, however, the term does not tell us much: church communities, fan communities, local communities, learning communities, communities of practice, embodied communities, music communities, virtual communities are all to be affirmed, and the quality of relationship between those who make up such groups will be deemed to be of help in helping members grow in some way. But whilst I shall also want to speak of 'salvific communities', meaning thereby any social context in which the features of salvation appear, I shall spell out in the next chapter the importance of stating that it is the *salvific* features which will describe why any such community (be it family, church, group of friends, learning group, work team, or whatever) qualifies as such. Then, truly, a community will be affirmed as having a particular quality and purpose because of the presence of these salvific features.

[25] Robert Putnam, *Bowling Alone: The Collapse and Revival of American Community* (New York: Simon and Schuster, 2001). His work has been widely discussed, not least in the writings of John Field, considered in Chapter 6.

[26] When contributions are made to online communities, authors are often less guarded in their contributions even in comparison with emails. This is a result of the expansion of multiple communication platforms created by social media. This can have negative repercussions but can also have the positive effect of opening up depth and frankness in online exchange. On this see Heidi A. Campbell and Stephen Garner, *Networked Theology: Negotiating Faith in Digital Culture* (Grand Rapids, MI: Baker Academic, 2016).

In the meantime we have to acknowledge that many uses of the term 'community', whilst descriptive in a limited way (people coming together in person or online) are often not very robust in practice. If we are to talk of 'salvific communities' and want to explore how a particular quality and intensity of interpersonal relationship evidences divine activity—a means by which God saves 'in Christ'—then it will be important to spell out, with reference to human groups in and beyond the life of the church, what exactly is happening in the experience of salvation.

The Action of God in Christ Is Frequently Inexplicit within Human Experience, even when one Is Handling Christian Resources.

As one final step in the sifting and narrowing-down process from the case studies of Part II through to the substantive theological chapter to come next it is important to accept that God's saving activity sometimes does not come clearly labelled. In exactly the same way as the motivation for, or outcome of, human actions do not come 'marked' in any way and may not even be known, let alone apparent, so it cannot be surprising that God's involvement in the midst of human activity is not always clear. God does not depend on conscious human actions in order to be gracious, for God's availability as a saving agent is a constant presence alongside what humans do. But human actions do influence whether or not the availability of God's gracious, saving activity is taken up. This is the price God has paid for being a loving God, letting creation be, and having taken the risk of grace being refused.

Even when the grace of God is given room to take salvific effect, however, it may often not be in an explicitly theologically informed way. The hundreds of acts of kindness and forgiveness which may occur within a single day within the life of a family or between friends, say, may not take place with any kind of theological preamble or commentary. But they are no less of God.

It may be thought that in Christian contexts or in relation to Christian resources the presence and action of God are always self-evident. Yet this is not so. The complexity of what occurred in the past, and occurs in the present, with respect to such Christian resources as *Messiah* and the Isenheim altarpiece demonstrates the multiple ways in which such resources are used and received. To use the language of communication theory, these resources do not simply 'transmit' a message to their receivers. As we saw in Chapter 3, those who interact with them (as hearers and viewers) 'participate' in their subject matter, responding to both their form and content in the way they respond aesthetically and affectively.[27] Again, such responses are not necessarily identified as explicitly theological, even whilst they may be uplifting, restorative, transformative, or inspirational. The experiences enjoyed may need a larger interpretative framework to be seen as salvific.

Here, though, we can see the point of theological interpretation of such cultural interactions. By going public with such interpretations— be it of explicitly Christian resources or more general products of media, arts, and culture—theology seeks to enhance human experience, and assist human flourishing. If the theological sense that what is happening here—that theological conclusions about background divine activity are being drawn out—is resisted then so be it. Non-theological interpretations of what is happening remain. If, however, theological interpretations not only enhance understanding of the human experiences under scrutiny, but also contribute to the practice of daily life (e.g. via a helpful framework for living such as the 'template of salvation' being examined in this book), then theology will have done the first stage of its work. If it then also invites people, in making use of the framework, to discern that divine reality, and not simply words about God, is at work, then it will also have fulfilled a missiological task. But the systematic task—to demonstrate how a doctrine works in practice and to elucidate its meaning—will only be missiological incidentally.

This process of interpretation could, of course, be seen as hermeneutical imperialism (only Christians know what is 'really' going on). More humbly and generously, it is a Christian way of offering, in the public realm, a reading of what is good and true about the present, with a view to shaping a more flourishing human future.

This chapter has brought together seven 'filtering insights' from the cases considered in Part II which have filled out in largely non-theological terms some of the key features which will need to be borne in mind as

---

[27] James W. Carey distinguishes between 'transmission' and 'ritual' approaches to communication, the latter presupposing a more participative role for the 'receiver' (*Communication as Culture: Essays on Media and Society*, rev. edn (New York: Routledge, 2009)).

we move on in the next chapter to become explicitly theological once more. What these seven insights have done, however, is provide markers for what to look for in life, and how to read daily experience so that one is attuned, ready to identify where and how God in Christ may be at work to salvific effect. What it means to be a person who is saved, being saved, or to be saved is, I submit, much more interesting and much more enriching than being terribly religious or seeing salvation as limited to inner activity alone or to something that happens in the future. That has been the underpinning thesis of the whole study. It will now need to be fleshed out more thoroughly in theological terms.

To conclude this bridge-forming chapter, though, one final thought: how might the features of the Christian template of salvation (being saved from, for, by, and into) be used beyond the kinds of examples studied in Part II of the book? Before we draw together the theological conclusions too tightly, it can be put this way. Where do you flourish? Where do you feel fully alive? Where do you feel accepted, but encouraged and corrected where necessary, i.e. without your flaws being overlooked? Amongst whom do you most connect at a deep level with other human beings? In what contexts and in response to what daily or other regular activities do such questions arise? Start there, but do not just stay there. For it is in identifying such experiences that the theological work of exploring a cultural theology of salvation may best begin.

8

Salvation in Contemporary Christian Understanding

'our belief systems are not just ideas we espouse but rather spaces in which we live and move'.

Serene Jones, 'What's Wrong with Us?', 142

What is a doctrine of salvation *for*? To some readers this may sound too pragmatic a question. It may imply that the practical implications of what is being sought control the content of the results: practical theology controls systematics, or—yet worse—usefulness trumps truth. I have endeavoured to resist this implication throughout this study. Now, though, is my opportunity to spell out where we have ended up *theologically* after the multidimensional foray undertaken into contemporary Western culture (Chapters 3–6) and the transitional critical reflection upon the content of the case studies (Chapter 7).

In this chapter I do not simply rework biblical, doctrinal, and historical-theological material. Nor do I attempt to be comprehensive in what I present. I rework past material taking into account the ways in which such material is internally self-critical (Scripture interpreting Scripture, doctrine interpreting Scripture, selected theologians interpreting doctrine, and so on) whilst respecting the experience and reflections which flow from the attention paid to patterns of redemption/salvation and flourishing in daily and cultural life. I am happy to take the risk of being charged with 'pragmatic relevance'. I must, though, make some clear assumptions and adopt certain positions and commitments without being able to argue for them extensively, in order to make my case.[1]

---

[1] In other words, much of the doctrinal interplay is left behind the scenes. I can only 'show my working' at significant points.

The theological discussions I shall enter into, however, are the ones which are necessary *now*, given the context of the moment.

Ultimately, a doctrine of salvation has to be *for living*. It has to give structure and meaning to life. Even if versions of that doctrine point to a life *beyond* this life, the doctrine affects *this* life. A Christian doctrine of any branch of systematics which did not have a shape and content which enabled people to live by it would be unsatisfying. It would also be disrespectful of the God it was seeking to interpret: a creating, incarnate, enlivening God who is deemed by Christians to be thoroughly involved in the present world.

This concluding main chapter, then, takes very seriously the emphases and insights drawn from Chapter 7. The chapter revisits versions of the doctrine of salvation that the church carries with it, keeping in mind classical expositions of such terms as sin, redemption, atonement, blessedness, forgiveness, and reconciliation whilst exploring how it is possible even to use such concepts, and what they might mean, in the present.[2] The chapter will inevitably be highly selective. Each background concept would ideally merit a book-length

---

[2] Here I must come clean about theologians and theological traditions and movements on whom/which I lean heavily. To be specific: I was raised in Calvinist evangelicalism, studied alongside Anglicans and Lutherans in my early twenties, and have since then been a Methodist for over thirty years. I am directly indebted to the writings of Luther, Schleiermacher, Ritschl, Troeltsch, Rauschenbusch, Bultmann, Bonhoeffer, and Tillich, most of whom I have written about in the past. Calvin, Wesley, and Barth have never been far away, and I owe a huge debt to James Cone, Karen Bloomquist, Albert 'Pete' Pero, Rosemary Radford Ruether, and Rita Nakashima Brock for giving some of my sometimes hidden (especially white, male) assumptions a good shake-up at various stages in my theological career. Especially helpful texts with which I have been working as I prepared this book include B.A. Gerrish, *Christian Faith: Dogmatics in Outline* (Louisville, KY: Westminster John Knox Press, 2015) and Cornelis van der Kooi and Gijsbert van den Brink, *Christian Dogmatics: An Introduction* (Grand Rapids, MI: Eerdmans, 2017). On the theologically specific topics I have been dealing with, I have made particular use of David H. Kelsey, *Imagining Redemption* (Louisville, KY: Westminster John Knox Press, 2005), Gerald O'Collins SJ, *Jesus Our Redeemer: A Christian Approach to Salvation* (Oxford: Oxford University Press, 2007), Derek R. Nelson, *What's Wrong with Sin?: Sin in Individual and Social Perspective from Schleiermacher to Theologies of Liberation* (London and New York: T&T Clark, 2009), Ivor J. Davidson and Murray A. Rae (eds.), *God of Salvation: Soteriology in Theological Perspective* (Farnham and Burlington, VT: Ashgate, 2011), Keith L. Johnson and David Lauber (eds.), *T&T Clark Companion to the Doctrine of Sin* (London and New York: Bloomsbury T&T Clark, 2016), and essays by Paul Fiddes and Ian McFarland in John Webster, Kathryn Tanner, and Iain Torrance (eds.), *The Oxford Handbook of Systematic Theology* (Oxford: Oxford University Press, 2007).

treatment. The selectiveness is *steered* by the insights of Chapter 7 without being *determined* by them. The questions and issues raised throughout Chapters 3–6 do, though, 'bite back' as a contemporary theological understanding of salvation is taking shape.

In proceeding, the chapter will address the challenge issued by one theologian who asked, on hearing a presentation I gave of some of the material from Part II: 'But what will this *add* to our theological knowledge?' My contention is that far from simply providing a contemporary contextual location for the theological insights to be expounded here, Chapters 3–7 help us see new things about Christian theological truth claims. As is often remarked, it will not do to 'say the same things in a new age'. Nor, though, are we simply to 'say (the same) things differently'. In some cases, we may have to say new things.[3]

WHAT *IS* WRONG WITH US?

> Estrangement from the Creator may, as mistrust, be guiltless; but as defiance to the Creator it is sin, which arises from inborn egocentrism and the collective pressures of society, infects a person's entire existence with self-interest, and makes the self powerless to achieve the purpose of its creation without redemption.
>
> Gerrish, *Christian Faith*, 77[4]

I have no idea whether Brian Gerrish is a *Breaking Bad* fan, but this statement could have been written for, and about, Walter White. White's 'entire existence' is indeed evidently 'infected' by his self-interest, whatever the spark of concern for others which may have set his corrupt actions in motion. We see that he needs rescuing from his downward spiral (some form of redemption or salvation is essential), though this does not come. 'Defiance' is certainly there, and it grows. He no longer wants to be or do good. His 'inborn egocentrism' is accentuated and insufficiently challenged. His conduct is not excused

---

[3] Even if there really is very rarely anything 'new under the sun' (Eccl. 1.9). The point is not to conclude that 'everything's already been said' but to note how what *has* been said—at different times, in different contexts, for different purposes—needs to be reminted for what has to be said now. This becomes a new thing out of old material.

[4] I shall from here on use Gerrish's formulations of doctrinal theses where appropriate as they are beautifully succinct summaries of complex doctrinal issues.

by the 'collective pressures of society', though their importance in explaining and amplifying how and why he acts as he does should be noted. Social sin is very real and extremely potent.

Breaking Bad sets up nicely, then, an exposition of the sin from which salvation is needed. But is it any more than a useful illustration? Gerrish's exposition of 'what's wrong with us' stands regardless of the supporting material. Through the interplay of Gerrish's exposition of the doctrine of sin, however, and the composite pressure of insights distilled from Chapters 3–7, particular theological considerations are sharpened in five ways.

First, the context of social sin is crucial in a contemporary exposition.[5] This occurs in two ways. 'What's wrong with us?' means that 'we' (in whatever society we are located) are enmeshed in corrupt systems. However well we may feel that the organizations and institutions within which we operate (businesses, schools, governments, charitable organizations, faith communities) are well-run and well-meaning, they are flawed. They are flawed not simply because sinful people operate within them. The composite sinfulness only compounds the sin of individuals. Seeing them as manifestations of social sin means accepting that human institutions cannot be perfect and have to be worked with, and worked within, despite their profound limitations. Acknowledging this does not mean that a bit of tinkering here, some management restructuring there, would solve things. Nor does it mean that improvements in institutional structure or culture should not be attempted. Accepting weakness does not then mean making do with the worst. Recognition of social sin entails honest acknowledgement of the way things are in all human structures. Being 'saved from' such social sin will not mean being taken out of structures but learning how to live within such sin.[6]

Social sin also takes effect in a tendency not to construct or develop institutions or structures which enable people to flourish. Objections to this claim are ready to hand: what about hospitals? What about

---

[5] Gerrish, *Christian Faith*, 87: 'To hold collective and individual responsibility together is not always easy, but it is nonetheless essential to a proper understanding of sin and redemption.' Here is where liberation theologies of many forms have proved hugely significant in the development of Christian theology. On social and structural sin, see, recently, Nelson, *What's Wrong with Sin?*, and Stephen Ray, 'Structural Sin', in Johnson and Lauber (eds.), *T&T Clark Companion to the Doctrine of Sin*.

[6] Luther's insight that a Christian remains *simul iustus et peccator* (justified and yet still a sinner) needs translating, in other words, into a social key.

schools? What about sports clubs? These are, of course, all good things and do have the opportunity to help people get well, grow, and develop. But despite their professed purpose even these precious institutions can fail to enable those who are active within them to feel fully alive. The sometimes oppressive regimes which those working in the fields of healthcare and education often report are evidence of this. As a further, profoundly ironical example of how social sin takes effect, I can report on a UK restaurant chain whose employees some years ago wore 'training for perfection' T-shirts whilst undertaking their work as serving staff. Though meant as an indicator of managerial intent to encourage employees constantly to improve their performance, the statement only highlighted the level of pressure placed upon the employees. They were invited (required?) to aspire to an unattainable goal. Whilst it might have improved efficiency in a limited way, it perpetuated a deficient anthropology with potentially damaging psychological repercussions. Demanding continuous staff improvement does not necessarily enable them to flourish as people.

One particular form of social sin provides the second aspect of the theological diagnosis ('What *is* wrong with us?') being expounded here: the fact that we do not share material wealth as fairly as would be good for all. As Chapter 6 made clear, salvation will not come about through wealth creation and wealth-sharing in itself, but the refusal to create economic and material conditions in which the human flourishing of all becomes possible is itself a social (as well as an individual) sin. It is then in turn a further dimension of sinfulness to make do with a state of affairs where rampant inequality is deemed acceptable. Working to counter such cultural acceptance of inequality amounts to more than alleviating poverty and is not itself to be understood as a 'work' contributing to salvation. The challenging of inequalities has to be undertaken within a sinful social culture.

A third aspect of 'what is wrong with us' is that despite the fact that we may be aware that salvation is a gift, we still try and earn it, and cultivate it, in a variety of new and creative ways. This is an especially significant insight, theologically speaking, and deeply indebted to Reformation traditions in particular.[7] It may, however, seem surprising

---

[7] Though this is in truth a general Christian conviction. That all is 'of grace' is standard Roman Catholic theology too. Reformation traditions are only known to place specific emphasis on human helplessness because of the Reformers' responses to the church of their day.

in the light of the trajectory followed in Part II of this book. For have I not been arguing that human cultural activity is highly important for theology? Have I not even been suggesting, if only by implication, that human cultural activity is necessary for the gathering of theological insight? Did Chapter 6 not even commend the acquisition of cultural, social, and spiritual capital as a theological task?

All of those rhetorical questions demand an affirmative response. But recognition of the importance of such activity does not alter the accuracy of the basic insight that none of this activity of itself contributes to the receipt of the gift of salvation. It would be wrong to suppose—and sinful to assume—that the amassing of any form or amount of cultural capital is a prerequisite for God to act salvifically. Attention to cultural, social, and spiritual capital serves as a reminder (to be adapted by readers to whatever cultural milieu is appropriate to them) that in the midst of whatever cultural world one inhabits, God can speak and act. If a person makes any implicit contribution to the working out of their own salvation in 'fear and trembling' (Phil 2.12), it is only by seeking to put themselves in a situation (e.g. by going to a concert, by participating in sport, by engaging in political activity, by involvement in a faith community) where God may choose to reveal Godself. It is, then, theologically essential to recognize that God offers salvation freely, and that salvation can be freely received. The mistake (the sin) would be to seek to manipulate God and to manufacture a particular optimum set of conditions or type of experience producing specific aesthetic or affective responses, such that it may be deemed that God will inevitably act.[8] It is, in short, sinful to seek to gather 'moments' or 'existential highs' if this is done with the intention of controlling God's activity and manufacturing transcendence.

One strikingly pertinent observation here in relation to *Breaking Bad* is the 'thinness', indeed the near total absence, of any sort of cultural life within which Walter White operates. There are no *Messiah*, Isenheim, *Crazy Heart*, or *The Big Bang Theory* equivalents for him to swim within, culturally speaking. Again, the suggestion here is not that such a life might have 'saved him'. Nor does it

---

[8] Lest there be any confusion here, whilst this may sound similar to the doctrine of *ex opere operato*, according to which Christian sacraments are deemed to be effective 'by the doing of the thing done', in the case of sacraments it is not the human performance which counts. The point is that the ritual practices work because of God's action regardless of the human agents.

necessarily imply that a life without an artistic element or environment is inevitably impoverished. How a person inhabits their particular form of cultural life does, however, provide an arena within which their 'inborn egocentrism' may be challenged and overcome. If there are no contexts within which stimulation, critique, inspiration, or challenge occur—precisely the kinds of things which deep friendships and cultural engagement offer—then self-absorption can result. The two further aspects of 'what's wrong with us' to be addressed relate to this point.

Fourth, the prevalence of individualism is to be noted. It is ironic that alongside the strong assertion of a social understanding of sin just made I also want to point to individualism. Individualism is, however, one of the legacies of the Reformation in Western culture.[9] The fact that social sin has had to be reasserted—even if in the modern period that reassertion goes back at least to Schleiermacher—is in large part because of the great emphasis upon the individual believer which the Reformation brought about. Many readers might have expected the therapeutic aspect of salvation (Chapter 5) to have been the main focus of this present work precisely because of the Reformation-driven emphasis upon the fallen state of the individual human being. That it is not so is because there is more than the therapeutic aspect to God's saving activity, and because those other dimensions require attention to more than the individual, especially the individual viewed in isolation.

Sinfulness entails egocentrism. Egocentrism is fostered by individualism (and vice versa). Whilst there is an appropriate level of personal (individual) responsibility to address the consequences of one's own sinfulness—i.e. to be open, individually, before God to find out what God can and is willing to do—the saving which leads to flourishing will inevitably cause the individual to look outwards and relate to others (to other human beings and to God). Individualism is harmful where it moves from appropriate self-knowledge and self-assertion to hubristic self-reliance. Churchgoing could, of course, be part of the remedy for the malaise, though would not be so where it became merely a gathering of souls seeking their own individual salvation. Ecclesiology at that point has something to gain from close

---

[9] See, for example, Brad S. Gregory, *The Unintended Reformation: How a Religious Revolution Secularized Society* (Cambridge, MA: Harvard University Press, 2012). It is striking that the Reformation features little in Larry Siedentop, *Inventing the Individual: The Origins of Western Liberalism* (London: Allen Lane, 2014), Siedentop's conviction being that the roots of liberal individualism can be located in pre-Reformation thought.

attention to *The Big Bang Theory*, as from any comedies about intense groups of friends in and through whom the quality of relationship—as always more than the sum of what individuals could achieve—counters the egocentrism of all its main characters.

Fifth, and finally, in this exposition of 'what's wrong with us?' we must attend to the refusal to accept difference. This is a vast and topical issue—variously addressed in the form of such discussions and actions as 'Equalities and Diversity' or 'Social Inclusion'—yet it must be faced as an aspect of sinfulness in so far as it represents a refusal to accept the God-givenness of the radical diversity inherent in creation. This applies not just to human diversity but also to the relationship between human beings and other creatures and, indeed, to the whole planet. Failure to acknowledge and respect difference is but a distortion of appropriate self-worth, allowing the 'inborn egocentrism' to turn respect for self into inflated importance about one's own kind (e.g. ethnic group, nation, sexual orientation, social class, religious affiliation, gender). Recognition that this is an aspect of sin anticipates that an articulation of salvation in the present will have to take seriously what it means that 'there is no longer Jew or Greek, ... slave or free, ... male and female; for all of you are one in Christ Jesus' (Gal. 3.28) without flattening or, in effect, disregarding the real differences which still exist within the oneness.

These five dimensions of sin—flawed social structures, material unfairness, seeking to earn salvation through cultural activity, individualism, and refusal to respect difference—are, I suggest, the main focal points about 'what is wrong with us' as we seek to articulate a contemporary understanding of salvation. They are not a rival picture to a basic sense of 'inborn egocentrism' as identified by Gerrish. Rather they are stark, contemporary manifestations of the estrangement he has defined. In and through attention to these five dimensions we are able to get at the way in which sin takes shape in the West today, both to expound it and the better to approach articulating God's salvific response.

HOW HELPLESS ARE WE?: AFFIRMING HUMANITY WITHOUT BEING PELAGIAN

A statement I have used often in teaching comes from the end of David F. Wright's article on 'Pelagianism' in the *New Dictionary of*

Theology. Wright remarks 'the Pelagian assessment of the effects of Adam's fall and understanding of grace cannot be squared with Scripture, although the church, in decisively rejecting Pelagian views, did not wholly endorse Augustine's refutations'.[10] I take this to mean that the Bible gives us a tough job in working out how to understand the value of human activity but that, when push comes to shove, Augustine is more right than Pelagius in his claim that human actions contribute nothing to salvation, salvation being a gracious action of God. Pelagius, though, even whilst being basically wrong and standing less in continuity with the Bible's general tenor of thinking on this question than Augustine, still nags away, even now, with an important insight for Christian theology in any age. Wright's pithy summary is well-put. Even as Augustinians—as all Christians have to be, to some degree—we need still to have a listen to Pelagius. Why is this?

First things first: there is no escaping the Augustinian emphasis upon the grace of God and humans' inability to save themselves, so firmly re-emphasized throughout the Reformation. This insight and commitment reverberate, for example, through the recent dogmatic work of van der Kooi and van den Brink: there is simply no place for salvation, justification, or sanctification 'by works'.[11] That said, for most theological thinkers and activists the recognition that human works contribute nothing to salvation has never meant either that human beings are of no value (in themselves or to God) or that seeking to do good is ill-advised. On the contrary, as even Luther—an especially trenchant critic of any hint of salvation by works—emphasized, it is assumed that good works follow the recognition that one is justified by grace through faith.[12]

So how is this long-standing and very significant tension to be understood and articulated now? I wish at this point to distinguish, but then also to connect, two important theological considerations, one to do with human worth, the other to do with the value of human actions. Reformation convictions that human activity contributes nothing to salvation, for all is of grace, relate to the second of those two points. But what about the first? However strong may be a sense

---

[10] David F. Wright, 'Pelagianism', in Sinclair B. Ferguson and David F. Wright (eds.), *New Dictionary of Theology* (Leicester and Downers Grove, IL: IVP, 1988), 501.

[11] See, for example, van der Kooi and van den Brink, *Christian Dogmatics*, 689.

[12] The clearest exposition is Luther's 1520 text 'A Treatise on Good Works', www.ccel.org/l/luther/good_works/cache/good_works.pdf, accessed 29 November 2017.

of sin, or the damage done to the human person by the reality of sin (universal, original, or otherwise), the knowledge that all human beings are made in God's image and likeness (Gen. 1.26–7; 5,1; 9.6) ensures that human beings are never without hope.[13] Even if we emphasize that all is of grace, and that therefore salvation is first of all received rather than earned, there still needs to be a capacity to be receptive to divine activity. This is not a human ability, however, but a reflection of the God who makes salvation available.

Whilst the retention of the divine image makes the reception of salvation possible, and human activity is well and truly put in its place, there remains a difficulty in practice which the quest for an adequate doctrine of salvation cannot dodge: the psychological force, especially amongst people who may already have low self-esteem, of the recognition that living up to being made in God's image may feel like a tough task. A sense of unworthiness may easily counter any sense of intrinsic God-given worth. The point has often been made that repeated confession, in the form of the recognition, say, that we are 'miserable offenders', can have a damaging impact on a person's self-perception.[14] When not placed within the context of a declaration of forgiveness (absolution), the reminder of misdemeanours (as symptoms of a sinful state) can be harmful. Outside the context of a spiritual discipline of regular public confession undertaken within a supportive worshipping community, repeated statements of unworthiness can prove damaging. A psychological sense of personal unworthiness, rather than a theological recognition of individual and social sin as 'lived with' realities, results.[15]

Jesus had recognized that those who were well (and perhaps the wealthy too) would not be too interested in his words and action (Mark 2.17). But Luther's insistence about the valuelessness of human actions for salvation (and not their valuelessness per se) was making a different point. In the present it may be much easier to accept

---

[13] As van der Kooi and van den Brink note, 'exegetes all agree that there is no basis for suggesting any major difference between "image" and "likeness"'(*Christian Dogmatics*, 261).

[14] The observation has often been made within Christian theology (e.g. Harry Williams), as well as by critics from outside. The language of 'miserable offenders' is from the form of the confession for Morning and Evening Prayer in *The Book of Common Prayer* of the Church of England. The issue has been well explored in Stephen Pattison in *Shame: Theory, Therapy, Theology*, (Cambridge: Cambridge University Press, 2000).

[15] This is arguably the precise point which has led Joel Osteen to adopt his particular style and content of worship (see Chapter 5 above).

that you are sinful when you are already quite confident or feeling comfortable with life on many fronts. Jesus recognized that he was more likely to be responded to by the desperate or the hopeless, the marginal and the ostracized.[16] But the question of how an appropriate sense of self-worth is to emerge when there is a theological need *not to* count human actions as contributory to salvation is an important one. It could be that people need lifting up a little even to have a chance of being receptive to what God has done and is doing in Christ. This pastoral and psychological reality is theologically important. This is why Pelagius nags at us. Let us be clear and honest about this: Augustine had already led an ill-disciplined life before he became an ascetic.

Crucial, perhaps, is not to consider whatever people may do or say as a straightforwardly human *achievement*. God surely wants us to use whatever we have and all that we are (Matt. 25.14–30). This is what is meant by the fulfilment of human potential. But what people have is to be seen as 'on loan'. And yet even though it is logical why many religious people find it conducive to work in roles in education, human resources, and management where they can enable *others* to fulfil their potential, it is also understandable why there can be a religious reserve about the notion that the meaning of life entails always doing *the most* that we might be capable of doing (as if that were thereby inevitably pleasing to God, even if we exhaust ourselves in the process).[17] Such an approach to human potential would be in danger of permitting justification (or sanctification) by works to return.[18] Much better, then, to put human activity within an appropriate theological context and acknowledge that all human agency which promotes human flourishing receives at the very least a divine prompt (and is thus a form of 'double agency', for divine and human actions work in tandem), and that it is a consequence of—a response in gratitude to—the gifts which God makes available to all.[19]

---

[16] Van der Kooi and van den Brink's comments on 'nice people' are pertinent here (*Christian Dogmatics*, 697).

[17] William T. Cavanaugh, 'Actually You Can't Be Anything You Want (and it's a Good Thing, too)', in David S. Cunningham (ed.), *At this Time and in this Place: Vocation and Higher Education* (New York: Oxford University Press, 2015), 25–46.

[18] The danger of 'sanctification by works'—a helpful signal of how 'justification by works' can sneak into view even when one thinks that one has got 'good works' appropriately understood and located—is noted by van der Kooi and van den Brink, 689.

[19] Miroslav Volf, *Free of Charge: Giving and Forgiving in a Culture Stripped of Grace* (Grand Rapids, MI: Zondervan, 2005).

These theological observations are necessary to put all human beings appropriately 'in their place', lest any individual, or any human group (religious traditions included), be inclined to stake a claim for God's particular privileging. It is simply not so. *All* human beings are made in God's image and therefore all have equal potential to be agents of God's activity. That they may be prevented from so doing is due to sin—universal, ubiquitous sin—which will function socially as well as individually in different ways for each individual human being, but will certainly affect all. Such sin is a consequence of the freedom God grants to all creatures, the rediscovery of which—freedom before and under God—is a consequence of dealing with sin (the focus of redemption).[20]

It is, then, quite wrong to suppose that Christian theology and practice, and even Reformation theologians, are against or not positive about human creativity and human endeavours.[21] The maximization of one's capabilities can be seen as a joyful response to God's generosity. That is why Handel made music and Grünewald painted. It is why (some) novelists write and film-makers make films. It can even be why some people make money. It is not inappropriate to see a person using their gift to run a highly successful business in exactly the same way as an artist (so long as people are not exploited in the process). An athlete who discovers she has tremendous physical abilities can justifiably stretch these to the maximum, and do so as a spiritual discipline before God, seeing this both as a thankful response to gifts received but also as her own development. *Not* to fulfil oneself to the maximum is not, however, a sinful response, as is sometimes supposed, and as under-pins so much educational practice.[22] There can be a world of difference between 'making a living', 'making a fortune', and 'making a name for oneself', and yet all can be legitimate expressions of gratitude

---

[20] And in that sense, and only in that sense, God can be held responsible for sin (see, for example, Schleiermacher, *The Christian Faith*, 325–6).

[21] See, for example, Gerrish on Calvin: 'Calvin was too good a classical humanist not to admire human achievements in art, science, philosophy, and civic virtue' (*Christian Faith*, 86–7).

[22] It is understandable that education, especially in relation to the education of children and young people, strives for 'the best'. But most of my higher education teaching experience has been amongst mature learners, and this has enabled me to see that going for the best and fulfilling the maximum of one's potential are not always appropriate. A student with multiple demands and pressures may accept limits to intellectual endeavour, whilst fully enjoying an educational experience, because of valuing an appropriate balance between employment, domestic responsibilities, education, and rest.

to God for talents received. Problems arise—potentially more in the last two cases than the first—where human endeavours cause a loss of sight of whose gifts are being enjoyed, and when 'works righteousness' reappears.

We may not now use the same terms as Luther to define such 'works righteousness', but, like Augustine before him, he had a point: over-stating what it is possible for humans to achieve is dangerous and ultimately undermining of an appropriate standpoint before God.[23] To say there is nothing—*nothing*—that we need to do or can do to earn God's favour sounds damning. In the context of Luther's theology, and any ensuing theology influenced by him, however, it is a liberating way of thinking and believing. The handling of such a basic theological insight is, though, a sensitive pastoral matter. This, to repeat, is what lies behind Wright's summary of the Augustine v. Pelagius debate. It was essential, on scriptural and theological grounds, for the church not to side with Pelagius. Human beings are not 'born free', for they are born into a world of social sin within which their own individual sinfulness develops. And yet they are divine creatures who are invited to participate in the love God has for the whole world. What Pelagius stands for is the recognition of how, in practice, it is necessary to keep on reminding people in all walks of life, and in vastly differing sets of circumstances, that they are (already) of worth, and that what they may think, believe, and do does matter, even if God really does require them to do nothing and not to be a particular kind of person to be able to respond to the love God offers. How, though, are people to be freed from the consequences of the sin into which they are born, so that they can live freely for and before God? That, in essence, is the task of the doctrine of salvation to articulate. To the positive aspects of the doctrine we now turn.

WHAT DOES SALVATION ACTUALLY DO FOR US?

This is a dangerous, acquisitive, almost consumerist question (like 'What do we get for our money?' or 'What's in it for me?'). It is arguably

---

[23] Luther remarks, memorably ('On Christian Liberty', in Martin Luther, *Three Treatises* (Philadelphia, PA: Fortress Press, 1970), 288):

> You see that the First Commandment, which says, "You shall worship one God," is fulfilled by faith alone. Though you were nothing but good works from the soles of your feet to the crown of your head, you would still not be righteous or worship God or fulfil the First Commandment.

quite the wrong question to be asking as we seek to articulate what salvation means, especially given the Reformation emphasis on *reception* first.[24] And yet, because of the starting point of reception (we can do nothing anyway: we have to be given something by God in the first place), it is precisely the next key question to move onto. Salvation gives us Christ, and in giving us Christ it transforms our relationships.[25] This is the response to our question that we need to unpack further.

Melanchthon's recognition that 'to know Christ means to know his benefits' has reverberated through the history of Western Christian theology.[26] Though in context Melanchthon's remark was pointing out the relative value of different kinds of theological investigation and was opposed to theoretical speculation, its significance as a pointer to the importance of practical, existential matters in theology is unavoidable. It is a wholly reasonable human question to ask 'What's in it for me?', even if the form of such a question should not then lead to self-absorbed versions of a doctrine of salvation. 'So what?' questions—Why bother getting saved?—are quite legitimate and pertinent to salvation's content. God *wants* to save us, and can only not do so without our aid *because* of the freedom granted to us. So long as we do not then turn our response into a human work which somehow merits the salvation offered, it is, in fact, a vital question to ask. 'What's in it for us?' (where 'us' means at least the whole human race and potentially the entire created order) opens up a wonderful, lavish response.

Before we get to the contemporary existential dimensions of what salvation entails, however, we need to attend to what Christian theological tradition informs us is happening to enable us to receive

---

[24] 'We have repeatedly underlined that we are only the recipients of salvation,' van der Kooi and van den Brink, *Christian Dogmatics*, 708.

[25] This was a particular emphasis of the work of Schleiermacher, both in his magnum opus *The Christian Faith* (Edinburgh: T&T Clark, 1928; German original, 1830) and, in narrative form, in his *Christmas Eve Celebration: A Dialogue* (Eugene, OR: Cascade Books, 2010; German original, 1806). An extensive and valuable study of this whole aspect of Schleiermacher's work can now be found in Matthew Ryan Robinson, *Redeeming Relationship, Relationships that Redeem* (Tübingen: Mohr Siebeck, forthcoming), esp. ch.7.

[26] Philipp Melanchthon, *Loci Communes Theologici*, (in W. Pauck (ed.), *Melanchthon and Bucer*, Philadelphia, PA: The Westminster Press, 1969), 21. In van der Kooi and van den Brink's recent work, the translation reads: 'To know Christ is to see what he did for us, and not to understand his natures,' *Christian Dogmatics*, 450.

whatever this 'salvation' is. It can be relatively simply put. Despite the centuries of debate and conflict surrounding the many and different theologies (and related traditions) which have argued about the meaning of the work of Jesus Christ, for our purposes it is possible to distil the outcome very succinctly. Salvation introduces us to the efficacious presence of Jesus Christ. To access the current meaning of that statement, however, we must note how Christian tradition has handled that insight, in the form of the conviction that Christ died for us (Rom 5.8). Whatever particular interpretation of Jesus's death as having atoning significance a person may have, the resulting conviction remains in place: the self-giving of Jesus the Christ was 'for us', and thus for anyone wishing to work through and live out the meaning of that self-giving death. It matters whether the 'self-givingness' of the commitment of Jesus to the words and deeds of the Kingdom of God was the knowing giving of the self unto death, the requirement of a bloodthirsty, wrathful God, or the unforeseen consequence of the chosen path. The choice here has consequences for other areas of systematic theology, not least the doctrine of God espoused.[27] But for our immediate purposes it is the 'dying for' aspect which has immediate repercussions.

Death was the consequence of Jesus's words and actions, but his death was, in a very clear sense, not 'the end'. In Christ, God was reconciling the world to himself (2 Cor. 5.19). Whatever is made in detail of the resurrection—as a past event, as a set of narratives, and as an ongoing reality—it is clear that God's reconciling work incorporates both the death and resurrection of Jesus Christ. That it is for *the world* invites us to examine what salvation means not just for a particular group of believers. Taking up challenges from Part II of this book and filtering our inquiry through the insights drawn together in Chapter 7, we are now pressed to consider who the 'us' are when we consider God's saving work for the world. Despite my use of two Pauline references just now, it is not just Pauline theology that comes into play here. We are asking how a Christian doctrine of salvation takes shape without Christians staking too privileged a claim to what God is offering.

---

[27] The first two could, of course, both be true. For the record I am more inclined to conclude the third option, accepting that Jesus was ready to accept that the first was a distinct possibility. The second has been extensively assumed in practical Christianity, and can be linked with much of the biblical tradition of sacrifice, but needs challenging. Sacrifice is better understood in terms of costly self-giving.

What *is* the gift of salvation that is given, and who is it given *to*? To anticipate what I shall go on to explore in more depth, it is possible to say this: salvation is the gift of the presence of Christ. It is given to anyone willing to live within the framework of costly love, recognizing that all of their relationships are affected by this commitment. It is accessed via a commitment to participation, without it necessarily being recognized (at first or ever) that such participation in costly love is indeed participation in Christ.[28] What is given, then, is not a set of skills or talents. What is given is the strength to see overcome all that, in any given situation or personal life history, could obstruct the capacity to love, be that material lack, disrupted relationships, lack of love shown to us, low self-esteem. It does not and could not mean that all that obstructs our capacity to love can be obliterated. What God makes available for us to take advantage of is the presence of Christ, who enables us to see and feel in a new way. What salvation does for us, then, is open up the possibility for us to live 'in Christ' as a result of what God in Christ has done for us.

The language of 'participation' is crucial here, and this has become a major watchword in theology in recent years.[29] It is striking that it features prominently in the two recent works of Christian dogmatics that I have been engaging with in the final phase of writing this present study.[30] The concept of participation is important for a number of reasons. Whilst retaining an individual element (the individual does the participating), there is instantly a communal and relational dimension too: participation in Christ means that one recognizes oneself within a community with others. Second, it

---

[28] Hence, the question could arise as to whether I am arguing in favour of the concept of 'anonymous Christianity' here, i.e. those who participate in love as expounded here are 'really Christians' without knowing it. It is not, however, an issue which I think needs addressing, given that it can easily be argued that what Christians believe themselves to be in touch with—the reality of God as known in Christ—goes beyond Christianity itself.

[29] I am grateful to Michael Nausner for first drawing this to my attention many years ago and for providing many 'leads' for me to follow up since then on different occasions.

[30] Gerrish notes this as a feature of Calvin's theology (*Christian Dogmatics*, 168), as an appropriate Reformation-based counterpart to notions of 'deification' (192), and as a key aspect of the New Testament idea of *koinonia* (215). Van der Kooi and van den Brink consider the term in their ecclesiology chapter (*Christian Dogmatics*, 575–6, 596), though it then features prominently in their consideration of the Christian life (where they 'link justification and sanctification together under the common category of *participation*', 683 [italics original], noting also that participation 'is a pneumatological and not an ontological category', 685).

is not a primarily cognitive act that is undertaken in order for one to be a participant. Openness to love—to the love of God, and then to the possibility of being loving—is the hallmark of membership. 'Belief' takes a step back here. Whilst not an irrational step to take, it is not simply a rational act. Feelings are involved, and faith—as opposed to belief—is a state of being rather than just thinking.[31] Third, participation is not a transaction whereby some kind of 'deal' is being done with God, or with human beings.[32] No papers need signing; no hands need shaking. This does not mean there is no commitment (either from God to us or from all those who participate in Christ to each other). It is simply that there are no clear membership requirements beyond the willingness to be open oneself to the consequences of accepting God's love for us. That said, participation, whilst neither an action nor an ideological decision, is not automatic and is a commitment. This is as much of a 'work' as participation in Christ can be. Anything more and it would indeed be in danger of undermining the quality of divine salvation as a freely given gift.

Participation is, though, an extremely useful concept for capturing something of the way in which Christian spirituality, as practical, embodied everyday theology, bridges the content of what I am exploring in this chapter and the form and media of the resources and concerns raised in Chapters 3–6. Films, TV, music, and art are all participative media evoking a variety of responses from viewers, hearers, and watchers. Whether or not viewers, hearers, and watchers are religious (let alone Christian) the practice of participation introduces respondents into an arena of feeling, embodiment, and interaction within which very basic questions about human living are posed (What *is* love? What am I to do with the sense of exhilaration I experience here? How do I handle the ways in which I am like and unlike fictional characters with whom I identify? How am I to live?).[33]

---

[31] I have found F. Gerrit Immink, *Faith: A Practical Theological Reconstruction* (Grand Rapids, MI, and Cambridge: Eerdmans, 2005) an especially helpful exploration of the phenomenon of faith.

[32] As Miroslav Volf tellingly puts it: 'God doesn't make deals. God gives' (*Free of Charge*, 26). It would, of course, be possible to make much of the background theology of 'covenant' (stressing the distinction to be drawn between 'covenant' and 'contract' for an understanding of God's relationship with creation and with humankind).

[33] Conversations with Nicola Slee have been very helpful in enabling me to see some of the aspects of the work I have done for many years in the field of theology/religion and popular culture.

The fact of sharing in such responsiveness (e.g. via the formation of fan communities) becomes important too. It is much too simple to try and pretend that any such communal response may be a form of 'proto-church'. It is, though, vital that the theological significance of what happens in any such intense act of participation in cultural life is recognized. 'Testing and distinguishing' need to occur to determine what may or may not be of God.[34] But if the presence of God in Christ in the world is not to be confined to 'church' as an identifiable phenomenon, then the notion of participation—understood as participation in Christ, in particular construals of understanding everyday life—becomes essential.[35]

How, though, does such a notion of salvation as participation relate to the concept and reality of 'church'? For is not *the church* the Body of Christ? It is possible that in trying to develop a Reformation-led theology of salvation for the present we make so much of the shift to social understandings of sin and salvation (and play down what happens to the individual), and that we pay so much attention to contemporary life (where the church in the West is weak), that we do insufficient justice to the church. We now need to address the question of where 'church' fits in in a contemporary social construal of salvation.

CHURCH IS ESSENTIAL, BUT NOT IN WAYS WE MAY ASSUME

The church is not *the* Body of Christ. It never has been, nor could it ever be. Whilst it is understandable that a theological argument might be made for concluding that all who commit themselves to God (across—and even beyond—all religions) could be deemed to become God's church universal (and this would be Christ's body), it is not a very helpful argument, as only God could know who belonged.[36] It is better to see the church as a more limited phenomenon, even if existing in visible and invisible forms, as those who have committed

---

[34] Van der Kooi and van den Brink, *Christian Dogmatics*, 522–4.

[35] I have addressed this theme in my *Christ in Practice*, and will go on to say more in the next section.

[36] Hence *Extra ecclesiam nulla salus* is simply mistaken, or can only be claimed and defended in a very attenuated or highly modified form.

themselves to Christ through the Christian religion. Christ cannot, however, be bound to Christianity. If God is love, and the demonstration of that love in Christ invites a response from anyone who seeks to live lovingly and justly, in the knowledge that such love is not earned but participated in, then the social, relational forms in which such love will be shared and enjoyed will far exceed what is known, officially, as 'church'. The church still has a role, though, and a crucial one at that.

I have been suggesting that salvation is 'from', 'for', 'by', and 'into'. In terms of the template being used, this section seeks to explore what it is we are 'saved into'. It will be apparent by now that the 'salvific communities' within which we may find ourselves, and into which we may feel drawn once we participate in the experience of salvation, may be many and various. I sought in a previous publication to map the kinds of theologically informed aspects of such communal contexts within which it is possible to say 'Christ is here'.[37] Seeking to pinpoint the presence and action of Christ in this way is a means of indicating how salvation works, and the form it takes for individuals and groups who take advantage of God's making it freely available.[38] The danger of the approach I took in that previous publication was, of course, that the features identified could themselves become an ethical programme ('Do this, and Christ will show up'). I sought to guard against this throughout the text. In the light of this chapter it will have become very clear: no such programme exists. All such actions, and celebration of all such aspects of Christ's presence, remain gifts even when they may have been 'worked for'. But 'church' remains one of the forms of Christ's presence. What, then, in the light of a soteriological approach to everyday life, does church do, and what is it for?

It is clear that one of the consequences of the line I am taking is that not everyone who participates 'in Christ' necessarily participates also in an identifiable church.[39] Nevertheless, the church remains indispensable. Churches are responsible both for articulating publicly their understanding of who and where Christ is in the world today and for

[37] Clive Marsh, *Christ in Practice: A Christology of Everyday Life*, (London: Darton, Longman, and Todd, 2006), 22–43, where I identify ten hallmarks of the presence of Christ.

[38] Again Schleiermacher is helpful here, and the study by Robinson, *Redeeming Relationship*, explores the attention Schleiermacher pays to 'free sociability' as a theological practice.

[39] This has long been an approach recognized within interfaith encounter.

fostering practices which celebrate and promote their understanding of Christ's presence. Hence, celebrating Baptism and Holy Communion (Breaking of Bread, Lord's Supper, Eucharist, Mass), organizing regular worship, and overseeing other explicit practices of Christian discipleship (study of the Bible, prayer) are explicit forms of celebrating the presence of Christ. These are occasions of, and aids to, the practice of the presence of Christ. Such practices relate to all that would be found contained within chapters in volumes of dogmatics or systematic theologies under 'ecclesiology'.[40]

Churches cannot, however, claim a monopoly on Christ, and it is important also to note where the subject matter of identifying and celebrating the presence of Christ appears *outside* the ecclesiology chapters in works of theology (for example, when exploring creation or pneumatology). This expands the Christian grasp of salvation understood as participation in Christ, and in turn highlights how Christ is not bound to the church. Hence, the creative and sanctifying work of the Spirit (in explorations of creation, soteriology, and pneumatology) amplifies the attempt to articulate the presence of Christ and informs the everyday practice of Christians. In turn, daily life is rendered more open to theological (and specifically Christological) interpretation.

What, though, is being looked for in daily life? In simplest form: the church carries the message of the Kingdom of God. Whilst it seeks itself to model in social form the kingdom it proclaims, it knows it will fail to do so. But its public role is to declare what it cannot even embody itself. Summing up the New Testament witness, Christopher Morse writes: 'To be saved is to be where Jesus Christ is.'[41] We could add to this: Christ is where the Kingdom of God is (and vice versa). The church hopes it is part of that kingdom, though bits of it clearly fall out of it at times. And there is certainly much of the kingdom beyond the church.[42] 'The Beloved Community' has been one further powerful attempt to capture linguistically what is being sought and

---

[40] Such chapters having traditionally gone under the heading of 'church, ministry, and sacraments' to show that church order and structures, and ritual and liturgical practices also come into play.

[41] Christopher Morse, 'Soteriology', in Ian A. McFarland, David A. S. Fergusson, Karen Kilby, and Iain R. Torrance (eds.), *The Cambridge Dictionary of Christian Theology* (Cambridge: Cambridge University Press, 2011), 479–81, here 480.

[42] Celebrating those other forms of Christ (domestic life, education, work) which I highlight in *Christ in Practice*. It is also necessary to identify other potentially salvific communities (fan communities, web groups, music groups, sports clubs).

welcomed.[43] It is, then, more accurate to say that there is no salvation outside the Kingdom of God than outside the church.

A challenge for churches, and their theologians, then, is to identify, without merely moralizing, what kinds of human community actually foster Christ-like living, and what the purpose is of identifying them as such. It is at this point that the strange decision to include within an exploration of the (serious) doctrine of salvation a discussion of the (seemingly lightweight) comedy *The Big Bang Theory* comes into its own. I recently led an entire session for a group of theology students entitled 'On Being True to Jesus without Mentioning Jesus: An Exercise in Practical Christology'. The session invited them to reflect critically, from a Christological standpoint, on selected excerpts from the comedy series. Alongside rather proverbial attempts to identify individual Christ figures—rarely wholly invalid, though not always very productive in practice[44]—the group began to explore, as I had hoped, ways in which what the group of friends was doing was creating a context in which 'odd' Sheldon could be at home, and the characters were doing this whilst also recognizing their own foibles and limitations. The fictional characters were creating a form of 'Beloved Community' in microcosm. They were, in their own way, practising the presence of Christ, without naming this as such, through the love, loyalty, willingness to grow and be challenged.

There is work to be done on the significance of the fact that, even if in rather attenuated form, this group of friends is multifaith (Jewish, atheist, Hindu, and—at one stage removed—evangelical Christian).[45] The point is significant, however, in meshing with the sense that salvation understood as participation in Christ takes us beyond a single religious tradition even if, in Christian perspective, there is a specifically

---

[43] This was especially prominent in the speeches and activity of Martin Luther King Jr (see, for example, his correlation of redemption and reconciliation with the creation of the beloved community via nonviolence in 'Nonviolence and Racial Justice', in James M. Washington (ed.), *A Testament of Hope: The Essential Writings of Martin Luther King Jr.* (San Francisco: Harper & Row, 1986), 8).

[44] For a rather extreme summary of the features for which viewers seek, see Anton Karl Kozlovic, 'The Structural Characteristics of the Cinematic Christ-Figure', *The Journal of Religion and Popular Culture*, 8.1 (2004), 29 pp., https://dspace2.flinders.edu.au/xmlui/bitstream/handle/2328/14295/2004054629.pdf, accessed 1 December 2017.

[45] I began to spell out what this might mean in an as yet unpublished contribution to the University of Notre Dame TV Comedy Symposium, London, 17 November 2017: 'Religion's Public Visibility: *The Big Bang Theory* as a Test-Case'.

Christian way of viewing the divine action at work (it being recognized and interpreted as being 'in Christ'). As I stressed in Chapter 5, I am not suggesting that the group of friends should in any direct sense be seen as 'church'. Churches will still exist alongside such groups of friends, though it is the job of churches to identify and celebrate, in the light of Christ and through a soteriological and Christological lens, the quality of such friendships as they occur. In so doing, churches locate the real presence of Christ in the midst of the societies and cultures in which they are situated.[46]

SALVATION NOW AND IN THE FUTURE

For much of Christian history, salvation has looked more like something to do with the future rather than to be enjoyed or experienced in the present. This is deceptive, for even the Apostle Paul could say 'since we are justified by faith, we have peace with God through our Lord Jesus Christ' (Rom. 5.1). Much of the concern across the New Testament about how Christians are to live, which may be called the way of sanctification, relates to the present aspect of salvation: 'we are what he has made us, created in Christ Jesus for good works, which God prepared beforehand to be our way of life' (Eph. 2.10). Once the 'good works' are put in their appropriate place, then it is clear how salvation is to be experienced and enjoyed *now*.

But whether this present aspect is, in practice, how Christians have often lived the faith, and understood salvation to take effect, is a moot point. Paul's emphasis upon salvation as relating to a moment in the future, through his extensive use of law court imagery with respect to a final judgement, when believers would be 'declared righteous' inevitably throws attention forward and away from this present life. For example, if one's circumstances did not promise a long life expectancy or a comfortable present existence, then it would be understandable to look for the promise of more 'beyond' (in the next life). This

---

[46] This happens intradiegetically within the fictional story. The real presence of Christ can also be identified and celebrated in the way the series is received, explored, and 'used'—consciously or unconsciously—in and beyond the humour, as people's relationships are affected positively.

would have been the reality for most people across Europe for most of Christian history up to and through the Reformation[47]

The modern-world context in which much Christian theology is now done has changed matters considerably. Increased life expectancy, greater levels of material comfort (in practice, in global terms, still for the minority, but that minority includes many Western Christians, of course), and, it should be said, less confidence that there is 'life beyond' in any form have inevitably had an impact on how salvation is understood. The concerns addressed in Chapter 6 of this study are all the more necessary because of these changes.[48] It is thus understandable that it has to be a priority, for the purposes of sheer comprehensibility, to address the question of what salvation means for the present, regardless of what the future may hold and of how that future is understood. Even though it can be claimed that what happens now includes 'a view from the future' and anticipates a conviction about what God has in store for creation, the current impact of such a view and the present meaning of salvation still need spelling out.

There is also a moral argument in favour of accentuating the present: we cannot let the next life play too great a role in shaping how we live now. Even if we use an end of life/judgement/next life set of images in order to help shape the meanings and conduct of this life, they need to remain as imaginative images so that they do not displace and devalue the stark concreteness of the present world. The danger of being too confident about what happens in the world beyond has become all too apparent in cases of terrorism.[49]

What form, then, does an emphasis on the present aspect of salvation amount to in practice? Has salvation indeed been reduced to happiness, as Roy Porter supposed? I shall offer in the concluding

---

[47] Darrin McMahon, *The Pursuit of Happiness: A History from the Greeks to the Present*, London: Penguin Books, 2007, 205:

It is all too easy to forget... that the pursuit of earthly happiness as something more than good fortune or a millenarian dream is a luxury in itself... it is estimated that in the first half of the seventeenth century, a third of the population of Central Europe was killed off by war, starvation, and disease.

[48] And, it has to be acknowledged, reflect the Western bias of this study too.

[49] I am referring here to the heavenly rewards which are reported as being believed in by suicide bombers. I do not think this is simply an issue for Islam. It is an aspect of the psychology of religion per se. Recognizing the dangers of such belief does not, of course, of itself refute all such beliefs, or religion as a whole. It merely presses for clarification of what such beliefs amount to, how they function, and how powerful they can be.

chapter a final answer to the question whether 'happiness' is a helpful term to use. For the moment we must distil from the sifting process of Chapter 7 some insights into how the contextual, cultural discussions of Chapters 3–6 inform our present understanding.

We can see that salvation, understood as present participation in Christ, is a multidimensional experience, affecting body, mind, and heart. It comes into play as we seek to be loving people, whilst we also interact with all of the cultural stimuli in and through which we expand our grasp of what it means to be free and loving. More precisely, we are being expanded by God in our understanding of what it means to be free and loving, the more we open ourselves up to learning what it means to live 'in Christ'.

Chapter 6 challenged us, however, to consider whether there are minimal material conditions which are necessary for salvation to be made available. Though the answer to this question has to be no, it also became clear that material lack can prove a blockage to being able to respond to the goodness of God. The social sin of material inequality gets in the way of God's love. No amount of economic or material well-being, however, brings salvation about. Salvation in the present is much more about quality of relationship, inner well-being, openness to others, being willing to be challenged, accepting the struggle and costs of growth, and recognizing that one's own well-being is bound up with that of others.[50] I shall draw out the practical consequences of this summary in the final chapter.

SALVATION BROAD AND NARROW

It will by now be clear that there can be very broad—and also more contained—Christian understandings of salvation. There is a genuine

---

[50] This leads in turn to the challenging question of whether anyone can feel comfortable about being a saved person unless all are saved. This is a psychological aspect, if not the psychological basis, of a belief in universal salvation (i.e. not that all *can* be saved, but that all *will* be). On recent studies which pick up this discussion in relation to the theologies of Schleiermacher and Barth, see Anette I. Hagan, *Eternal Blessedness for All?: A Historical-Systematic Examination of Friedrich Schleiermacher's Reinterpretation of Predestination* (Cambridge: James Clarke, 2014) and Tom Greggs, *Barth, Origen, and Universal Salvation: Restoring Particularity* (Oxford: Oxford University Press, 2009).

sense in which a Christian doctrine of salvation encompasses the whole of Christian theology.[51] So long as salvation is not rendered anthropocentrically, as if we do 'God talk' *for us* alone, so that God serves our purposes without remainder, there is truth in the notion that God acts for 'us', where 'us' means the whole created order. God's self-giving lies at the heart of creation. Things are, because God is, and things (and people) develop because of God's continuing interaction with them. God's salvific work is, then, an act of self-expenditure by God for the sake of what God has, in love, let be. The whole of theology's task is, therefore, about getting to grips with this. Doctrines of the Trinity, creation, human being, Christ, Holy Spirit, church, sacraments, and eschatology all play their appropriate part in that process of understanding.

More narrowly, salvation is about how created beings deal with the limitations of their creatureliness, especially with how to deal with imperfection, with flaws and frailty, and with wilful wickedness. Freedom brings both risk and responsibility. God's 'letting be' of creation means that so much is not as it should be. How, then, God works with those creatures who, in freedom, choose to work with God and accept the way in which God enables frailties to be faced, burdens to be lifted, and evil to be overcome forms the core of the doctrine of salvation more narrowly construed.

I have been trying to find a way which speaks not only for and to Christians who 'know the language', but also relates to, and engages with, the variety of cultural forms in which the theological concerns here being explored manifest themselves in Western culture. Having wrestled for my whole Christian and academic life with the tension between world and church, I have wanted to find a working theology which is not couched only in in-house language, using internal resources, even though, inevitably, traditional sources and resources do have to be made use of in the testing process.

Much recent Western theology has seen fit to reassert 'the Christian story' over against all others, sometimes over-assertively, even bombastically. It has seemed as though we have been encouraged simply to 'tell the tale' better and more forcibly. Paying too much attention to context or listening too closely to 'the world' would, it is implied, contaminate the story. I fundamentally disagree.

---

[51] Dorothea Sattler, *Erlösung: Lehrbuch der Soteriologie* (Freiburg im Breisgau, Basle, and Vienna: Herder, 2011), 13.

The God about whom the story is told is so embedded (incarnated) in, committed to, and suffers with the created world that essence and context are interwoven to a degree that is problematic most of the time. But it is still the same story that is being told. To have that conviction, whilst accepting theology's complex engagement with context, is to demonstrate faith in an incarnate God. In the final chapter I shall seek to draw all the threads of the study together in a practical way.

Conclusion: What, then, *Is* Salvation?

I began this study by locating my theological inquiry within current interest in happiness. I saw this as necessary, for although theology must work with explicit past and present theological resources (Bible and doctrinal tradition), it cannot use only these in seeking to discern and articulate what God is doing. Happiness set the agenda and then the contents of Part II explored, through a series of case studies, the current Western context for theology, within which the cultural-theological method outlined in Chapter 2 could be used. Chapters 7 and 8 distilled key themes and issues before offering, in a fresh way, the main emphases of a current version of the Christian doctrine of salvation. It is now necessary to draw all the threads together in this practical conclusion. I shall do this in three steps. First, I offer a brief statement of what, in theoretical terms, I have offered in this book. Second, I recap on the form and content of what I have called the 'salvation template' and spell out how it is best used. Finally, in a series of summary headings I seek to encapsulate ways in which salvation may be best understood.

SO WHAT HAS THIS ALL BEEN ABOUT?

This book has in part resulted from the frustration of reading so many works of theology which barely seem to have acknowledged explicitly the world within which the theology is being done.[1] In other words,

---

[1] I speak here mostly of Christian systematic theology. My comment is not, of course, true of practical, liberation and contextual theologies. The challenge remains to press for such contextual and liberation (and 'adjectival') theologies to unsettle

whilst I am indebted to a great many fine works of theology, there have been times when I have wondered how the theologians I am reading actually live their lives, how they process their everyday experiences, or what they do with what they consume on a regular basis, culturally speaking, whilst thinking and acting theologically. This comment is not meant to imply that theology is a thinly veiled form of autobiography or that context so controls theology's content that there is no room any more for 'working with tradition'. Far from it. Self-aware theologians have the chance of being the best theologians because they ask themselves critically, with the help of others, where their life experience is informing and distorting their theological work. What I mean is that theology which gives little clue as to how it has been worked out in 'real life' is unlikely to connect or convince. Systematic theology will always be especially prone to this difficulty, as there is a clear sense in which it 'abstracts' its findings from the vicissitudes of living.

Cultural theology of the kind I have been trying to undertake in this book blurs the lines. It has to. It wants to be 'systematic' in so far as it treats doctrines in a 'traditional way', i.e. recognizing that there are specific topics which have to be dealt with, that there is a past to be drawn on, and that there will be interconnections between these topics. But it looks 'unsystematic' in that it borrows insights and methodological approaches from practical theology, contextual and liberation theologies, and missiology, as well as listening to other disciplines' treatments of the sources and resources it deems it important to consider. It is complex and messy, uneven and incomplete, but, I suggest, all the more 'real', energizing, stimulating, and, yes, useful as a result.

What I have done is offered a 'theological phenomenology of the experience of salvation' which has resisted simply extracting from identifiably Christian experience what salvation means. It has sought also to look at life experience and cultural explorations of human living to see what 'salvation-like' and 'salvation-related' aspects of life

systematicians. I also need to acknowledge that amongst white, male systematic theologians there are some exceptions, i.e. those who attend to 'non-theological' resources or move beyond the realm of solely internal Christian discourses (e.g. Mike Higton, Keith Ward, Veli-Matti Kärkkäinen, David Brown, Cornelis van der Kooi, and Gijsbert van den Brink). The crucial question, of course, is how constitutive, as opposed to merely illustrative, any of these theologians' engagements with the arts and broader culture prove for their theological conclusions.

look like and how they, in turn, inform Christian understanding of salvation. Christians must not simply rework their own traditions but probe ('test and distinguish') everyday life to clarify their understandings in the light of fresh insights into how God is at work.

That process produces a living form of systematic theology. I have been seeking Tillich's *Gehalt* of culture not as something theologically hidden within the original artistic or cultural creations, producing a neatly packaged set of theological insights, but as the result of critical, dialogical interaction with the resources examined, in search of God's envisaged future. The Gospel of the Kingdom of God comes to us from the future,[2] and needs to be worked out and expressed in anticipatory linguistic form and in lived practice as we constantly wrestle with Christian tradition and daily life experience in relation to all the cultural activity that we undertake. That is how a living theology comes about.

'FROM', 'FOR', 'BY', AND 'INTO'

I have sought to use a template of salvation throughout this study. This template has long been in place implicitly within the tradition, and other scholars have used a version of it, or parts of it, in the past. It is not new. Asking what a person is saved from, for, by, and into are all standard components of a doctrine of salvation. 'Into' may be the most unusual element, though 'church' has always been there by implication or explicitly in many theological accounts which may not have used all four elements of the template. There has to be some relational aspect to soteriology. I have simply opted not to see that relational element to be absorbed into, or consumed by, ecclesiology. Salvific communities are, in practice, more diverse than that. Being 'in Christ', as we saw, is not simply to be equated with being 'in church'.

The pre-existence of the template should not, though, be taken to mean that the filling of the template with content was also wholly predetermined. Form and content can never be wholly detached. Hence, whilst the from/for/by/into structure was shaped by a basic

---

[2] As noted in Chapter 2, with reference to the work of Gorringe and Pannenberg.

soteriological model deriving from both Judaism and Christianity, how the doctrine is then received, reworked, and re-expressed for the present constitutes a new piece of work. The template *implies* a structure, and the structure presupposes a 'working content'. But the content is reworked as the template gets filled, even if with respect to the Christian tradition as a whole this change happens slowly. Here, in highly compressed form, is what I have proposed.

We are, or can be, saved *from*:

- Inner turmoils of many kinds (addictions, lack of confidence, self-absorption, our propensity to nastiness);
- the impact of external factors upon us (summarized earlier as life's 'shittiness');
- grinding poverty, or other forms of material lack;
- being sinned against—where we are always pressed to forgive, but may not be able to;
- the consequences of abuse—a specific form of the external factors which affect our lives, where our inner turmoil (low self-esteem, or lack of a sense of worth) may result from damaging behaviour towards us;
- political and economic exploitation.

The composite picture I have sought to present reworks 'sin' through the above themes, thus challenging what can sometimes be a dangerous abstractness in theological writing or an over-individualizing when focusing on an individual's inner life, with insufficient reference to the sociopolitical context in which a person lives.

We are saved *for* a life of flourishing, the detail of which I shall unpack under ten headings in the next section. This has clearly been underplayed in the Christian tradition with respect to life in this world. Eternal life has often primarily meant never-ending life beyond the grave rather than an anticipatory quality of life beginning now. When linked to Christianity's propensity to overemphasize individual salvation, however, this can mean that well-being is sought by and for individual human beings, without reference to humanity as a whole or to the well-being of creation. To consider what we are saved *for* therefore requires us to work back from the well-being of creation, through the well-being of humanity as a whole, to consideration of our/my place as a being-saved individual. We are saved for a state of ultimate bliss, but are not to claim this for ourselves without considering the entire created order in the process.

We are saved *by* Christ, grace, faith, and others. More precisely we are saved by God, full stop. But we perceive who God is and how God is at work in and through the person of Jesus Christ (past, present, and future). We are saved 'by' grace in the sense that this term characterizes the fact that salvation is a gift. We are saved 'in' faith rather than 'by' it in the sense that we must be careful not to let our own believing become a causal means by which grace is received. 'Faith' denotes a state of being and self-understanding within which we have a chance of grasping what God is doing to and for us. We are saved 'by' others in the sense that our being 'in Christ' (our being-saved state) is not a solitary state. We will always be connected with and to others in some way if we are to experience salvation. God is at work in others in order to enable us to perceive and receive grace. God seeks to be at work in us so that others may recognize and receive salvation as a result of God's working through us.

We are saved *into* new states of being, and into all manner of communities which become for us salvific communities. These are the communal 'forms of Christ' today. Christ is where we are fully alive and fully ourselves, but when we are also conscious of having been released from all that enslaves us or obstructs the possibility of our relating to God and to others. The salvific communities in which we find ourselves do not all become 'churches'. Nor are churches necessarily always salvific (though God can do astonishing things with rather meagre human efforts to be communal). As a concept, however, church is a challenge to tribalism and kin worship. Communities which are 'in Christ' will always make us both secure and uncomfortable at one and the same time, confirming that we are being saved and reminding us too that the world is not yet redeemed.

The template of salvation becomes, then, a very practical tool, even though its content results from demanding and ongoing theological discussion and analysis. Constructed out of critical reflection upon what is perceived to be the activity of God in the world, formed by the four dimensions I explored, and able, in turn, to shape human experience, it is a lens, a filter, through which life experience may not merely be 'understood' but also enhanced. This template could, admittedly, be 'just words' in the sense that it is an imaginative imposition placed upon life experience in order to help people make sense of life. This amounts to a 'religion as coping mechanism' approach. I am, though, often amused when people say of any aspect of Christian belief or tradition being talked about 'But it's just a story, right?', as if any form of words or narrative that actively shapes life experience can be 'just words'. I know what is meant. There may be nothing behind or beyond the words in the sense of an 'ontological reality' to which the words relate other than the thoughts and actions of those who speak them.[3] But here is not the place to open up this debate. It simply has to be left open whether salvation narratives are 'just words' (informing thoughts, beliefs, and actions) which shape life or whether, as they shape life, they are also tapping into a greater ontological reality. Either way, salvation as a doctrine and practice faces the present and contributes to the shaping of what-is-coming-to-be. Even whilst a specific Christian contribution, this is not to be confused with a strategy of trying to impose Christianity onto everyone.

How does it work, though, this template? It is important to recognize that whilst it has a certain trajectory (from—for—by—into), it is wrong to suggest that 'from' is somehow left behind. *Simul iustus et peccator* means that we do indeed go on sinning. 'From' is always there. Similarly, 'for' is always being newly discovered, as new dimensions of flourishing continue to be encountered. 'By' is constant in the sense that God has saved, is saving, and will save 'in Christ', 'by the Spirit'. The relational forms in which people experience what it means to be 'in Christ' will keep on being refreshed.

In short, all four 'moments' of the template remain active at any time. And people may pitch in to the template at different starting points. Those who find themselves in a deep new set of relationships or in a new communal setting where they begin to grasp what others who have spoken of being 'in Christ' have been referring to may then be able to use the template to reach greater self-understanding (Whom am I among? How have I got here? What did I need rescuing from?). Likewise, those who already have a strong sense of what they need to overcome may see very clearly what they are saved from and even a glimpse of what they know they need saving for, but may take time to discover and trust the relational setting into which they are

---

[3] This is the background to discussion about the distinction between theological realism (There is a God) and theological non-realism (God language is vital for human well-being, but no reality 'out there' or 'in here' is actually being referred to). 'God' thus becomes a necessary figment of the human imagination. On the British scene this discussion was provoked throughout the 1980s and 1990s in particular by Don Cupitt, beginning with *Taking Leave of God* (London: SCM Press, 1980).

brought, lest it look, having experienced a sense of personal, individual salvation, as though they have to 'go it alone'.

Once all four 'moments' are glimpsed, however, the soteriological template can be drawn on consciously in the midst of daily life, in interpersonal relationships, in the midst of economic and political decisions, and in interacting with media and culture. It can function as a 'schema' or a 'hermeneutical key' to assist with sense-making in daily living and fruitful shaping of present and future thoughts and actions.

SALVATION IN TEN HEADINGS: CONSEQUENCES FOR EVERYDAY LIFE

How, though, is it best to fill out this template with theological content? Are there helpful contemporary terms, whether with an explicitly theological provenance or history or not, which can help us capture appropriately something of what salvation is and is for? In this third section I present ten concluding working concepts and catchwords which articulate what salvation means. No single term presented here will suffice. Each does grasp *something* of salvation's meaning. But in truth *all* are needed to capture successfully what the 'flourishing' feels like and is about.

At its most expansive, salvation is **'ultimate well-being'**, beginning now. The sense of 'ultimacy' here alludes to the fact that, whatever is made of salvation in the present, a future state of well-being—perhaps greater than anything that could even be imagined in this life—is envisaged. The vision of well-being affects reality now. This is the case whether or not it will be 'real' in the sense of being an embodied or conscious existence beyond this life, or is an imagined future out of which beliefs, feelings, and actions in the present emerge. 'Well-being', as we have seen throughout this study, must not be confined to the inner life, though it includes it. Well-being may refer to material, economic, social, mental, psychological dimensions of experience. Salvation relates to them all. Whatever blocks the capacity to flourish in all those dimensions is what people need saving from. 'Beginning now' highlights that whatever is envisaged for the future can be anticipated in this life. In no way can it be guaranteed. Life is a struggle not only because of sin or lack, but because all forms of flourishing can be hampered due to the effects of (universal, ubiquitous) social sin. It would, though, be wrong to throw all aspects of salvation into the future. God wants flourishing *now*, for the whole of creation.

Salvation is **health**. It is not the health produced by a rigorous, expensive daily gym workout. Nor can it mean total freedom from illness or disease. I offer this as one of the readings of salvation cautiously, as it needs careful defining. It is admittedly not surprising that the Bible contains an image of a future paradise, a new earth, a new Jerusalem, where 'Death will be no more; mourning and crying and pain will be no more' and where God 'will wipe [away] every tear' (Rev. 21.4). For God wills wholeness. And there is clearly a strand within the Gospel tradition which, through the healing stories of Jesus, may suggest that physical restoration is always to be brought about in the face of disease or disability. Saving and healing are brought together at a number of points, and their ramifications are to be contained under this heading of 'health', incorporating also senses of 'rescue', 'deliverance', and 'recovery'.[4]

It is difficult, of course, to subscribe to the view that salvation means inevitable release from physical pain, disease, or the consequences of constrained mobility.[5] As we saw in our treatment of the reception of art in the monastery hospital at Isenheim, health clearly cannot always mean physical healing. The emphasis, in any case, in some Gospel stories is on the social restoration, the reconnection of people who have been suffering (lepers who may still be physically disfigured as a

---

[4] Again, detailed exposition and exploration of each of these three further terms is not possible here. And as with health, I am not suggesting that rescue (e.g. from physical harm or threat), deliverance (from danger, or from a sense of 'possession'), and recovery (e.g. from illness or addiction) all immediately or automatically follow from an openness to salvation and its benefits. I am signalling simply that it is under this heading where such explorations would sit, and that these very concrete and practical aspects of what salvation can mean are not to be ignored within a practical, doctrinal inquiry.

[5] This insight—and the sustained, theologically responsible responses which flow from it—has been a feature of the work of John Swinton; see, for example, *Raging with Compassion: Pastoral Responses to the Problem of Evil* (Grand Rapids, MI: Eerdmans, 2007). Interestingly, Swinton does not speak at all of 'health' in that work, as his focus is on responses to evil, though he does discuss four redemption practices of resistance: lament, forgiveness, thoughtfulness, and hospitality. I think it would be possible to argue that, as positive dimensions of salvation, these are, as resistance strategies, signs of health and healthy communities.

result of disease, and yet are welcomed back into healthy social relationships). Health, therefore, means healthy inclusion wherever there has been the experience of exclusion, and can at this point mean 'restoration'. The fragility of the created order is squarely and honestly faced. It is not a matter of calling the unwell well or pretending that physical things can be 'fixed' that cannot. There is even a sense in which it is wrong to place physical conditions within the realm of salvation *at all*. Sickness is not sin (John 9.3). When health is seen in social terms as the physical inclusion of all, whilst acknowledging the limitations of all physically imperfect people (i.e. all), then it can be seen in an appropriate soteriological light.[6]

Salvation is **acceptance**. In Tillich's terms: 'Simply accept the fact that you are accepted!'[7] Acceptance by God precedes all else. We are accepted, as creatures made in God's image, before we even know that we are in need. We gain a sense, it could be said, that we are saved *for* something, before we knew what we needed saving *from* (whatever form of 'sin' that may have been). If we accept our acceptance by God, however, then a full life of flourishing can begin.

We must note, though, that this acceptance does not mean self-acceptance in the sense that we cannot or do not need to change. Acceptance will include within it self-acknowledgement: the fact that we recognize who we are and who it is that God is accepting. God is not requiring us to change in order to accept us. Conditions are not applied. Acceptance can even precede repentance. We may need to feel accepted to regain enough self-esteem even to be able to repent. This 'self-acknowledgement' is not, then, 'self-acceptance' in the sense that we do not think God can do anything with us. But nor is it straightforward—'This is who we are, and that's it.' Salvation as acceptance actually says more about God than it does about us. God accepts us even if we cannot accept ourselves but then invites us to grow in grace, in Christ. Though not an explicitly theological resource, *The Big Bang Theory*, in its best moments, functions beautifully as a light-hearted, comic 'take' on a very serious subject: how to

---

[6] The words of caution uttered by John Swinton—that 'inclusion' is too vague and 'belonging' is what is needed—should be heard here ('From Inclusion to Belonging: A Practical Theology of Community, Disability and Humnanness', *Journal of Religion, Disability and Health* 16 (2012), 172–90). The Christological basis of Swinton's argument is crucial.

[7] Paul Tillich, *The Shaking of the Foundations* (New York: Charles Scribner's Sons, 1948), from the sermon 'You Are Accepted', 153–63, here 162.

222 A Cultural Theology of Salvation

accept the possibility of needing to change and grow, whilst having to live with who one is.

Salvation is **being forgiven**. Salvation as acceptance may also already mean 'being forgiven'. God is willing to accept us, though, even if we have not repented in the sense that we are already known to be made in God's image.[8] And yet the realization that we will, without question, have wronged others, been devious, been untrue to ourselves, and potentially much more besides will mean that, at some point, one of the aspects of what we need 'saving from' will be the harm we have caused and the evil in which we have participated. Forgiveness is needed by all (for sin is universal, ubiquitous), though it will not necessarily easily be recognized as essential for full flourishing. Why, after all, would one need to be forgiven or to acknowledge any kind of lack, or remorse, or frailty, or fallibility, if everything is going well? People who feel bad about themselves already know there is something amiss even if they do not know what to do about it. It is those who feel good about themselves (and perhaps smug) who have problems here (Mark 2.17).[9] But whenever a person recognizes their need of forgiveness, then God is always ready to say the word of forgiveness. In a Christian liturgical context this will be through an agent (a preacher, pastor, or priest). But the word is ready to be said, and a supportive, communal context awaits (church as a form of the body of Christ) within which a being-saved person can (constantly) seek amendment of life, as a path towards flourishing.

As we have seen throughout this study, other communal forms of Christ—where people are 'in Christ' fully acknowledging who they are, with all their flaws, but being accepted and forgiven—function 'as church' without being church. In the daily round of human interaction, giving and forgiving occur. One-to-one interactions are glimpses of salvation. Groups which embody such a practice, in whatever form that may be, are salvific manifestations of what it means to be 'in Christ'.

Salvation means participation in **forgiving**. Miroslav Volf offers an accessible (but fully theologically informed) treatment of both giving

---

[8] Though there is much in the Bible as a whole which suggests otherwise, i.e. that repentance is the condition for divine acceptance, Jesus does not seem to see this as a prerequisite for entry into the Kingdom of God (Matt. 21.31).

[9] This is why it is understandable that missiologists and evangelists are inclined to talk about needing people to be 'convicted of their sin'. It is not really a very good evangelistic strategy, as it makes most people run a mile, but the logic is clear.

and forgiving in *Free of Charge: Giving and Forgiving in a Culture Stripped of Grace.*[10] Within his exploration of the relationship between giving/receiving and being forgiven/forgiving he emphasizes that 'Christ forgives through us, and that is why we can forgive.'[11] Volf speaks more of Christ living in people than of their being 'in Christ', but the result is the same. It is humanity's dependence on God acting in Christ, and human beings' relation to that action, which makes salvation effective. The forgiveness aspect of what it means to be a saved person includes being open to the potential of God's working in us to forgive.[12] Despite the challenge presented by this dynamic aspect of salvation (for it is an active response to what one receives), it is nevertheless a clear signal and symbol of the relational, restorative dimension which the practice of salvation entails.

Salvation is **safety**. Whatever are the circumstances in which salvation is experienced, salvation denotes a movement (mental, emotional, spiritual, physical, spatial-geographical) to a place of safety. Where God is, there is peace, rest, protection. Such sentences are easier for someone to write who has the luxury of an income, time, space, and quiet to write them than for someone who may have to face the radical disjuncture between salvation understood as 'inner space' and the challenge of being in the midst of major personal turmoil or tragic or tortuous physical circumstances. But being 'in Christ' has to mean being moved to a protected environment in some sense. No physical form of what it means to be 'in Christ' can be beyond risk. Churches—understood both as physical spaces and as gatherings of people—have been 'safe spaces' at key points in history, even in very recent history (South Africa and Eastern Europe), at the same time as being part of courageous political movements. But as many sad recent examples show—where churches appeared to be 'safe havens', yet have experienced violence (Democratic Republic of Congo, Egypt, USA)—churches are far from immune to hostile attack. Furthermore, because churches attract the vulnerable, they can also themselves be vulnerable communities within which—as the cases of

---

[10] Miroslav Volf, *Free of Charge: Giving and Forgiving in a Culture Stripped of Grace* (Grand Rapids, MI: Zondervan, 2005).

[11] Volf, *Free of Charge*, 200.

[12] Whilst recognizing how difficult this may be, depending on what it is that we are being 'saved from', if this includes utter, appropriate rage if one has been mistreated or abused.

historic child abuse have demonstrated—their own frail leaders can sometimes become abusers. Churches have had to be prominent in tackling safeguarding as a practice precisely because of their role in welcoming all and supporting the weak and challenging evil.

Thankfully there are also a great many other examples of where churches (and church buildings, as homes and symbols of church communities) are able to function as havens, centres of peacefulness, and places of safety. In similar ways, families, workplaces, educational contexts, leisure and sports clubs, voluntary organizations, and political groups, which can all also be places of risk or places of safety, can function as structured means through which salvation can be experienced relationally as a place of safety.[13]

Salvation is **celebration**. In filling out the joyful aspects of the experience of salvation, salvation as the sheer enjoyment of the blessings and benefits received by being accepted, forgiven, and brought to a place of safety and peace should be emphasized.[14] The important point here is not the inner, subjective element of that experience but the almost public recognition of what has occurred. In so many ways, the practices and rituals of the Christian faith exist to celebrate the fact of salvation's possibility, due to the work that God in Christ has done, is doing, and will do. If participants in salvation do not feel joyful or do not foster and then support a sense of joyful living, then something is amiss. That is not to say that there are not important moments within such rituals which acknowledge life's struggles and our own inner turmoil (confession and lament, for example), where underlying joy is qualified and both joy and sadness are acknowledged, expressed, and faced. But if worship is not geared towards celebration, then this joyful dimension of salvation is being overlooked. The corporate dimension of worship (and commensurate with that, the communal element in any understanding of a

[13] As I write, there is major debate on whether universities can be considered 'safe spaces', the term having come to mean that people are immune from criticism, lest they be offended. This overturns the notion of higher education as a realm in which all exploration must be possible, involve risk-taking, and include the risk of giving and taking offence, in order for critical analysis and investigation to happen. On this question see Frank Furedi, *What's Happened to the University?: A Sociological Exploration of its Infantilisation* (Abingdon and New York: Routledge, 2017).

[14] Randal Zachmann highlights how even Calvin noted that learned pagans could celebrate through artistic activity the many gifts showered by God on humanity ('John Calvin', in Keith L. Johnson and David Lauber (eds.), *T&T Clark Companion to the Doctrine of Sin* (London and New York: Bloomsbury T&T Clark, 2016), 235–50, here 246.

'salvific community' which is 'in Christ') becomes especially significant here in so far as it can legitimately be said that the congregation/ community collectively carries the joy, so that whenever a person is low, joy is not lost.

Salvation is **happiness**. At this point our contemporary theological journey comes full circle. The context in which I began to ask the question what salvation might mean today (within the world of 'happiness studies') commands attention. I do think it is important to consider happiness as an appropriate term to use for salvation. Care though is needed in how this is understood. To return to the three possible understandings offered by Daniel Haybron, it is possible to locate the experience of salvation within the range of the 'emotional state' theory of happiness.[15] Salvation is, then, subjectively experienced as a basic, underpinning sense of well-being as a result of, and in direct interaction with, the other dimensions of salvation being explored in this section. It would, though, be mistaken to lift happiness out as a single, catch-all term to describe what salvation entails. To do this would be to truncate salvation's many aspects, to over-subjectivize it, and to cause confusion given the other usual emphases evident in attention to happiness.

That said, it would be equally wrong to underplay the human, subjective element of enjoyment which salvation has the potential to bring. Whether or not theologians are wise to take the line that what salvation brings is 'true happiness', as opposed to 'what the world gives', is a moot point. There is little doubt that bringing theological discussion of salvation alongside studies and explorations of happiness muddies the theological waters. But it also makes a crucial point of connection between theological discourse and lived experience.

Salvation is **contentment**. This heading provides an important gloss to the 'emotional state' theory of happiness just affirmed. Contentment could be heard as a synonym for happiness or as a

---

[15] Daniel M. Haybron, *The Pursuit of Unhappiness: The Elusive Psychology of Well-Being* (Oxford: Oxford University Press, 2008), 109 and 139:

the *default emotional state theory*...maintains that happiness consists in a person's overall emotional condition, which in turn consists in the aggregate of her moods and conditions. To be happy, on this view, is for one's emotional condition to be, on the whole, positive...Whereas the hedonist regards happiness merely as a state of one's consciousness, the emotional state view takes it to be a state of one's being. When you're happy, everything is different.

background state of welcome emotional equilibrium. These would both be appropriate.[16]

An important passage from the Apostle Paul's letter to the Philippians does, however, come into play here.[17] Phil 4.11 includes the statement: 'I have learned to be content with whatever I have.' It occurs in the context of Paul's talking about very practical matters (where he gets his food, whether he has enough to live on); he thanks the church at Philippi for their practical help. It does not, at first sight, seem a very weighty theological statement. It also gets tangled up, as the exegetes remind us, with Stoic understandings of 'contentment' which emphasize frugal self-sufficiency.[18] Paul is wanting the Philippians to hear that he is 'doing OK' and is not too demanding in his expectations. (He does not need a large expenses budget whilst on his travels.) The drawback of this passage in its active use in Christian practice, however, is that it has led Christians to underplay their actual enjoyment of the world's goodness, as if Paul is recommending rigorous frugality or acceptance of one's situation, regardless of how constrained that may be or of how meagre the resources one might have for living. Such 'contentment' would be a distortion of salvation in the fullest sense being explored here. Salvation as flourishing does not mean wasteful extravagance, but should mean appropriate enjoyment of the world's riches. Such a conclusion would not be a strict

---

[16] Though it must also be said that people are saved whilst still being in emotional turmoil. If this were not so, then there would not be hope for many! Again, it is important to stress that there are no conditions for acceptance by God. Emotional equilibrium would not necessarily follow instantly for someone who recognized their need of salvation and was open to salvation's template being put to work.

[17] There is a sense in which Phil. 4.11 is the biblical prompt for this entire study. I have spent most of my Christian life trying to work out the full theological meaning and practical significance of this verse.

[18] For discussion of the meanings of this verse, see, for example, Howard Marshall, *The Epistle to the Philippians* (London: Epworth Press, 1992), 119–20, Gordon Fee, *Paul's Letter to the Philippians: The New International Commentary on the New Testament* (Grand Rapids, MI, and Cambridge: Eerdmans, 1995), 430–2, and Markus Bockmuehl, *The Epistle to the Ephesians* (London: A&C Black, 1997), 260–1, who challenges the Stoicism-related reading of self-sufficiency, arguing that Paul is promoting 'a Christian "God-sufficiency"', concluding that 'no reader of Philippians could fail to be struck by the powerfully Christ-centred redefinition of this "contentment"' (261). Troels Engberg-Pedersen, *Paul and the Stoics* (Edinburgh: T&T Clark, 2000) supplies a fuller background to the text with respect to its Stoic hinterland (100–3) and Justin J. Meggitt, *Paul, Poverty and Survival* (Edinburgh: T&T Clark, 1998) examines the economic context in which Paul's words take shape (155–63).

exegesis of this passage, but denotes a context within which to receive it in order to prevent its misuse.

Salvation is **blessedness** (or a blessed state, or bliss). This may be read simply as a more religious term for the 'contentment' referred to earlier, as the term seeks to characterize a welcome state of being. Blessedness accentuates, however, in relation to the subjective state of feeling content, the sense of being blessed (by God). Thus, although there is a strong emphasis on what the saved person experiences, the notion of what one *receives* is prominent. Friedrich Schleiermacher's contribution is at this point especially striking, given how Schleiermacher unpacks the experience of what it means to be 'in Christ' (being assumed 'into vital fellowship with Christ').[19] Human beings do not have the source of blessedness in themselves, but a 'corporate feeling of blessedness' flows from the sense of being in Christ.[20]

This state of bliss could be seen as a mere glimpse, of interim anticipation, of a state to be fully enjoyed beyond this present life. But even so, it is clearly to be anticipated now. It is more than just imaginary, because it is recognized to be the form of God in Christ at work in human individuals and communities. We may perhaps call it the lived experience of the lure of the hopeful future (the fullest meaning of the *Gehalt* of any cultural product or practice). Blessedness should, though, be distinguished from perfection, lest too much be expected of what is possible in human experience.[21] Blessedness, like contentment, is not to be reduced to being a collection of 'happy moments'. It is a much deeper state of being, one which can also be related to *shalom* (peace), from which a link is forged to the notion also of salvation as a state of safety and security.

As noted in Chapter 8, salvation entails participation. But rather than this becoming an eleventh term in the quest for a dynamic definition of salvation, it is to be seen rather as a way in which the meanings of the ten definitions are appropriated, underpinning them by denoting active reception, rather than adding new content. It is significant that the term picks up again the notion that salvation is

---

[19] Friedrich Schleiermacher, *The Christian Faith* (Edinburgh: T&T Clark, 1928), 432.

[20] Schleiermacher, *The Christian Faith*, 435, 433.

[21] Though Schleiermacher might disagree with this statement, declaring that 'the communication of blessedness no less than the communication of perfection is given immediately in the assumption into vital fellowship with Christ' (*The Christian Faith*, 432). It could, of course, be argued that the *communication* of perfection is different from its possession.

something which is not won, but received. It is received relationally, in the company of others. All of the other terms used to offer a composite picture of salvation presuppose a participatory understanding of the doctrine and its working.

These ten headings, underpinned by the notion that salvation is something which one receives and in which one participates, distil in a practical way the theological inquiry conducted throughout this work. I contend that they are a workable entry point into a contemporary public theological discussion of what salvation means and brings about. By following a cultural-theological approach, using Christian insights to inform the inquiry, I have sought to show how public theological discussion can contribute to contemporary reflection on daily life. Daily life is, after all, much too important to be lived without reference to God.

APPENDIX

The Salvation Template

The chart below presents in a structured, diagrammatic way the explorations and findings of the discussions conducted in Chapters 3–6 of this book. For some ('visually thinking') readers, this chart may work better as a way of understanding what the chapters were getting at. It is designed to help all readers in four ways:

- It 'maps' the different dimensions of salvation—aesthetic (Chapter 3), affective (Chapter 4), therapeutic (Chapter 5) and material/economic (Chapter 6)—in relation to each cultural product or practice examined.

- It provides a visual framework which could be filled in differently by readers with other material which has helped or stimulated their theological thinking in similar ways.

- It creates an overall picture which, whilst not random, serves as a reminder of the multiple ways in which salvation impinges upon everyday life. If this picture 'overwhelms' a little, then this is in itself informative.

- The overall map shows how a theologically informed life is lived: as a rich, reflected-upon set of diverse experiences and cultural engagements.

Resource ▼	Dimension of Salvation			
	From	To/For	By	Into
Example 1 / Chapter 3 Isenheim Altarpiece [Fine Art]	Illness Despair Hopelessness	Health Comfort Safety Communal support Hope	God in Jesus the Messiah/Christ Christ's presence in/through other people Imaginative activity	A supportive therapeutic community Eternal life (beyond the grave)
(Current viewers)	Gloom Indifference Mundaneness Despair Personal struggle with pain	Exhilaration/Uplift Transcendence	Individual visual-aesthetic experience Communal viewing (in gallery setting)	A state of hopefulness A virtual community of art-lovers
Example 2 / Chapter 3 Handel's *Messiah* [Music]	Lostness Sinfulness Lack of hope	Rescue from hopelessness Deliverance from the consequences of human wickedness	God in Jesus the Messiah/Christ Christ's presence in/through music	A church uplifted in this earthly life by such aesthetic moments Eternal life (beyond the grave)
(Current listeners)	Mundaneness	Transcendence Emotional exhilaration	Musical-aesthetic experience Escapism	A community of listeners / (classical) music fans
Example 3 / Chapter 4 *Crazy Heart* (dir. Scott Cooper) [Film]	Alcohol addiction Ruined relationships	A more stable, healthy life Recovery Reorientation/amendment of life	Intimacy A group of friends Meaningful relationships	A supportive environment A purposeful life
(Current viewers)	Loneliness Loss of purpose Whatever links with Blake's experience	A more resilient, purposeful life	Experience of the affective reception of film Emotional engagement	A safer, healthier emotional space
Example 4 / Chapter 4 *Breaking Bad* (dir. Vince Gilligan) [TV]	Self-reliance/Destructive individualism Addiction to acquisition Fractured relationships	Restored relationships	[Walter White's death – though in no sense as sacrificial]	Survival (Jesse Pinkman, Skyler White, Walter White Jr.) [Oblivion (there being no apparent salvation for Walter White)]
(Current viewers)	Mundaneness/Boredom Purposelessness	A tense, pleasurable viewing experience An opportunity to reflect on life's purpose and meaning/s	Reflection on a thrilling viewing experience	A community of meaning-making viewers /fan community
Example 5/ Chapter 5 Positive Psychology	Low self-esteem	Flourishing/happiness Emotional health	Self-acceptance Self-understanding A structured life	An accepting community
Example 6 / Chapter 5 *The Big Bang Theory* [TV]	Isolation as incomplete individuals Social exclusion A lack of confidence	Flourishing amongst friends New-found confidence	Acceptance by others The social stability provided by their social worlds (including the role played by different faiths)	A diverse, supportive community A structured life (e.g. marriage, co-habitation)
(Current viewers)	Social awkwardness/exclusion Hostility to 'geeks' Gloom	Social acceptance Being valued as one is Pleasure	Recognition of humanity of those who are different Humour/Laughter Pleasure	A fan community A community of acceptance
Example 7 / Chapter 6 Social and Cultural Capital	Absence of purpose Social detachment/isolation	Meaningful relationships A more fulfilled life	Acquisition of (cognitive, aesthetic and affective) capital Growth in cultural confidence and competence	A community of learners An informed society
Example 8 / Chapter 6 Money	Poverty Material acquisitiveness Disregard for the body	Physical well-being Material comfort Having 'enough to live on'	Sharing and acquisition of material wealth Having sufficient goods and resources to enable healthy living	A fair and just society Community groups working for the well-being of all

Resources Used

Action for Happiness, www.actionforhappiness.org/about-us, accessed 18 December 2015.

Anderson, Jami, 'A Life Not Worth Living', in David P. Pierson, (ed.), *Breaking Bad: Critical Essays on the Contexts, Politics, Style, and Reception of the Television Series* (Lanham, MD: Lexington Books, 2014), 103–18.

Arendt, Hannah, *Eichmann in Jerusalem: A Report on the Banality of Evil* (Harmondsworth: Penguin Books, 1977).

Arnold, Matthew, 'Culture and Anarchy: An Essay in Political and Social Criticism' (first published, 1867), in *Culture and Anarchy and Other Writings* (Cambridge: Cambridge University Press, 1993), 53–187.

Astley, Jeff, *Ordinary Theology: Looking, Listening and Learning in Theology* (Aldershot: Ashgate, 2002).

Astley, Jeff, *SCM Studyguide to Christian Doctrine* (London: SCM Press, 2010).

Astley, Jeff and Leslie J. Francis (eds.), *Exploring Ordinary Theology: Everyday Christian Believing and the Church* (Farnham and Burlington, VT: Ashgate, 2013).

Atherton, John, *Challenging Religious Studies: The Wealth, Wellbeing and the Inequalities of Nations* (London: SCM Press, 2014).

Augustine, *Confessions* (Harmondsworth: Penguin Books, 1961).

Baker, Chris, 'Exploring Spiritual Capital: Resource for an Unknown Future?', in Michael O'Sullivan and Bernadette Flanagan (eds.), *Spiritual Capital: Spirituality in Practice in Christian Perspective* (Farnham and Burlington, VT: Ashgate, 2012), 7–22.

Barclay, John, *Paul and the Gift* (Grand Rapids, MI: Eerdmans, 2015).

Batstone, David, 'Transcendence and Material Culture', in Dwight N. Hopkins and Sheila Greeve Davaney (eds.), *Changing Conversations: Religious Reflection and Cultural Analysis* (New York and London: Routledge, 1996), 59–77.

Battin, J., 'Saint Anthony's Fire or Gangrenous Ergotism and its Medieval Iconography' (in French), *Histoire des Sciences Medicales* 44 (2010), 373–82.

Beckerlegge, Oliver A., *A Methodist Life* (Loughborough: Teamprint, 2000).

Begbie, Jeremy, 'Beauty, Sentimentality and the Arts', in Daniel J. Treier, Mark Husbands, and Roger Lundin (eds.), *The Beauty of God: Theology and the Arts* (Downers Grove, IL: IVP Academic, 2007), 45–69.

Béguerie-De Paepe, Pantxika and Magali Haas, *The Isenheim Altarpiece: The Masterpiece of the Musée Unterlinden* (Colmar: Musée Unterlinden and Paris: Artlys, 2015).

Billings, J. Todd, *Calvin, Participation, and the Gift: The Activity of Believers in Union with Christ* (Oxford and New York: Oxford University Press, 2007).

Blevins, Jacob and Dafydd Wood (eds.), *The Methods of Breaking Bad: Essays on Narrative, Character and Ethics* (Jefferson, NC: McFarland and Co., 2015).

Bockmuehl, Markus, *The Epistle to the Ephesians* (London: A&C Black, 1997).

Booker, Christopher, *The Seven Basic Plots: Why We Tell Stories* (London and New York: Continuum, 2004).

Borg, Marcus, 'Root Images and the Way We See: The Primordial Tradition and the Biblical Tradition', in Arvind Sharma (ed.), *Fragments of Infinity: Essays in Religion and Philosophy* (Bridport: Prism, 1991), 31–45.

Bourdieu, Pierre, *Distinction: A Social Critique of the Judgement of Taste* (New York and London: Routledge, 1986).

Bowler, Kate, *Blessed: A History of the American Prosperity Gospel* (New York: Oxford University Press, 2013).

Bradley, Ian, *You've Got to Have a Dream: The Message of the Musical* (London: SCM Press, 2004).

Brant, Jonathan, *Paul Tillich and the Possibility of Revelation through Film* (Oxford: Oxford University Press, 2012).

Brown, Frank Burch, *Good Taste, Bad Taste, and Christian Taste: Aesthetics in Religious Life* (Oxford: Oxford University Press, 2000).

Brümmer, Vincent and Marcel Sarot (eds.), *Happiness, Well-Being and the Meaning of Life* (Kampen: Kok Pharos, 1996).

Bullard, Roger A., *Messiah: The Gospel According to Handel's Oratorio* (Grand Rapids, MI: Eerdmans, 1993).

Bulman, Raymond F. and Frederick J. Parrella (eds.), *Religion in the New Millennium: Theology in the Spirit of Paul Tillich* (Macon, GA: Mercer University Press, 2001).

Burkhard, Arthur, *Matthias Grünewald: Personality and Accomplishment* (New York: Hacker Art Books, 1976; first published, 1936).

Burrows, Donald, *Handel: Messiah* (Cambridge: Cambridge University Press, 1991).

Butt, John, 'George Friedric Handel and *The Messiah*', in Michael Lieb, Emma Mason, and Jonathan Roberts (eds.), *The Oxford Handbook of the Reception History of the Bible* (Oxford: Oxford University Press, 2011), 294–306.

Calland, Chris, 'From rogue to redemption: what can brands learn from persona non grata?' (30 September 2013) www.theguardian.com/media-network/media-network-blog/2013/sep/30/rogue-redemption-brands-reputation-lessons, accessed 14 January 2016.

Callaway, Kutter and Dean Batali, *Watching TV Religiously: Television and Theology in Dialogue* (Grand Rapids, MI: Baker Academic, 2016).

Campbell, Heidi A. and Stephen Garner, *Networked Theology: Negotiating Faith in Digital Culture* (Grand Rapids, MI: Baker Academic, 2016).

Capps, Donald, *The Depleted Self: Sin in a Narcissistic Age* (Minneapolis, MN: Fortress Press, 1993).

Capps, Donald, *A Time to Laugh: The Religion of Humor* (London and New York: Continuum, 2005).

Carew, Nick, 'The Magdalenes' (2013), www.truetube.co.uk/film/magdalenes, accessed 23 March 2016.

Carey, James W., *Communication as Culture: Essays on Media and Society* (rev. edn, Abingdon and New York: Routledge, 2009).

Cavanaugh, William T., 'Actually You Can't Be Anything You Want (and it's a Good Thing, too)', in David S. Cunningham (ed.), *At this Time and in this Place: Vocation and Higher Education* (New York: Oxford University Press, 2015), 25–46.

Cavicchi, Daniel, *Tramps like us: Music & Meaning among Springsteen Fans* (New York: Oxford University Press, 1999).

Charry, Ellen, *God and the Art of Happiness* (Grand Rapids, MI: Eerdmans, 2011).

Chester, Jason, 'My how you've changed! A look back at Sam Frost's transformation during a life changing year . . . ' (30 December 2015), www.dailymail.co.uk/tvshowbiz/article-3378294/A-look-Sam-Frost-s-transformation-life-changing-year-chart-journey-heartbreak-happiness.html, accessed 14 January 2016.

Christie, Ann, *Ordinary Christology* (Farnham and Burlington, VT: Ashgate, 2012).

Christie, Ann and Jeff Astley, 'Ordinary Soteriology: A Qualitative Study', in Leslie J. Francis, Mandy Robbins, and Jeff Astley (eds.), *Empirical Theology in Texts and Tables: Qualitative, Quantitative and Comparative Perspectives* (Leiden: Brill, 2009), 177–96.

Clayton, John P., *The Concept of Correlation: Paul Tillich and the Possibility of a Mediating Theology* (Berlin: De Gruyter, 1980).

Cobb, Kelton, 'Reconsidering the Status of Popular Culture in Tillich's Theology of Culture', *Journal of the American Academy of Religion* 53 (1995), 53–85.

Cobb, Kelton, *The Blackwell Guide to Theology and Popular Culture* (Malden, MA, and Oxford: Blackwell, 2005).

Cobb, Thomas, *Crazy Heart* (London: Corsair, 2010).

Cochrane, James R., 'Salvation and the Reconstruction of Society', in Vincent Brümmer and Marcel Sarot (eds.), *Happiness, Well-Being and the Meaning of Life* (Kampen: Kok Pharos, 1996), 76–98.

Connolly, Hugh, *Sin* (London and New York: Continuum, 2002).

Cook, Christopher C. H., *Alcohol, Addiction and Christian Ethics* (Cambridge and New York: Cambridge University Press, 2006).

Coward, Harold, *Sin and Salvation in the World Religions: A Short Introduction* (Oxford: Oneworld, 2003).

Crazy Heart, 20th Century Fox Home Entertainment (2010).

Csikszentmihalyi, Mihaly, *Flow: The Psychology of Happiness: The Classic Work on How to Achieve Happiness* (London: Rider, 2002).

Cuidon, Jackson, 'Why We Need *Breaking Bad*', www.christianitytoday.com/ct/2013/july-web-only/breaking-bad.html, accessed 12 April 2016.

Cupitt, Don, *Taking Leave of God* (London: SCM Press, 1980).

Davaney, Sheila Greeve, 'Mapping Theologies: An Historicist Guide to Contemporary Theology', in Dwight N. Hopkins and Sheila Greeve Davaney (eds.), *Changing Conversations: Religious Reflection and Cultural Analysis* (New York and London: Routledge, 1996), 25–41.

Davidson, Ivor J. and Murray A. Rae (eds.), *God of Salvation: Soteriology in Theological Perspective* (Farnham and Burlington, VT: Ashgate, 2011).

Davies, William, *The Happiness Industry* (London and New York: Verso, 2015).

Davis, Stephen T., Daniel Kendall, SJ, and Gerald O'Collins, SJ (eds.), *The Resurrection* (Oxford: Oxford University Press, 1999).

Davis, Stephen T., Daniel Kendall, SJ, and Gerald O'Collins, SJ (eds.), *The Redemption* (Oxford: Oxford University Press, 2004).

D'Costa, Gavin (ed.), *Resurrection Reconsidered* (Oxford: Oneworld, 1996).

D'Costa, Gavin, *Theology in the Public Square: Church, Academy and Nation* (Oxford: Wiley-Blackwell, 2005).

Deacy, Christopher, 'Redemption Revisited: Doing Theology at Shawshank', *Journal of Contemporary Religion* 21 (2006), 149–62.

Deacy, Christopher, *Christmas as Religion: Rethinking Santa, the Secular, and the Sacred* (Oxford: Oxford University Press, 2016).

DeCou, Jessica, 'Relocating Barth's Theology of Culture: Beyond the "True Words" Approach of *Church Dogmatics* IV/3', *IJST* 15 (2013),154–71.

De Gruchy, John, *Christianity, Art and Transformation: Theological Aesthetics and the Struggle for Justice* (Cambridge: Cambridge University Press, 2001).

DeLashmutt, Michael W., 'Theology and Popular Culture', in Mike Higton and Jim Fodor (eds.), *The Routledge Companion to the Practice of Christian Theology* (London and New York: Routledge, 2015), 422–34.

Dillenberger, John, *A Theology of Artistic Sensibilities: The Visual Arts and the Church* (London: SCM Press, 1987).

Dolan, Paul, *Happiness by Design: Finding Pleasure and Purpose in Everyday Life* (London: Penguin Books, 2015).

Downing, Crystal, *Salvation from Cinema: The Medium is the Message* (New York and Abingdon: Routledge, 2015).

Ebert, Roger, Review of *Crazy Heart*, www.rogerebert.com/reviews/crazy-heart-2009 /, accessed 14 April 2016.

Edwards, Jonathan, *Religious Affections (The Works of Jonathan Edwards: Volume 2)* (New Haven, CT: Yale University Press, 2009).

Ehrenreich, Barbara, *Smile or Die: How Positive Thinking Fooled America and the World* (London: Granta, 2009).

Engberg-Pedersen, Troels, *Paul and the Stoics* (Edinburgh: T&T Clark, 2000).

Faucette, Brian, 'Taking Control: Male Angst and the Re-Emergence of Hegemonic Masculinity in *Breaking Bad*', in David P. Pierson (ed.), *Breaking Bad: Critical Essays on the Contexts, Politics, Style, and Reception of the Television Series* (Lanham, MD: Lexington Books, 2014), 73–86.

Fee, Gordon, *Paul's Letter to the Philippians: The New International Commentary on the New Testament* (Grand Rapids, MI, and Cambridge: Eerdmans, 1995).

Fergusson, David A. S., 'Theology and Laughter', in Paul Middleton (ed.), *The God of Love and Human Dignity: Festschrift for George Newlands* (London and New York: T&T Clark, 2007), 107–16.

Fiddes, Paul, 'Salvation', in John Webster, Kathryn Tanner, and Iain Torrance (eds.), *The Oxford Handbook of Systematic Theology* (Oxford: Oxford University Press, 2007), 176–96.

Field, John, *Social Capital* (2nd edn, Abingdon and New York: Routledge, 2008).

Ford, David F. and Mike Higton, with Simeon Zahl (eds.), *The Modern Theologians Reader* (Oxford and Malden, MA: Wiley-Blackwell, 2012).

Fulkerson, Mary McClintock, 'Toward a Materialist Christian Social Criticism: Accommodation and Culture Reconsidered', in Dwight N. Hopkins and Sheila Greeve Davaney (eds.), *Changing Conversations: Religious Reflection and Cultural Analysis* (New York and London: Routledge, 1996), 43–57.

Furbey, Robert et al., *Faith as Social Capital: Connecting or Dividing?* (Bristol: Policy Press, 2006).

Furedi, Frank, *Therapy Culture: Cultivating Vulnerability in an Uncertain Age* (London and New York: Routledge, 2004).

Furedi, Frank, *What's Happened to the University?: A Sociological Exploration of its Infantilisation* (Abingdon and New York: Routledge, 2017).

Furnal, Joshua R., 'On the Hermeneutics of Religious Film Criticism', *Literature and Theology* 26 (2012), 77–92.

Ganzevoort, R. Ruard and Heye K. Heyen (eds.), *Weal and Woe: Practical-Theological Explorations of Salvation and Evil in Biography* (Münster: LIT Verlag, 2004).

Gerrish, Brian A., *Christian Faith: Dogmatics in Outline* (Louisville, KY: Westminster John Knox Press, 2015).

Gill, Andy, 'Garvey goes down a storm with songs straight from the heart', *The Independent*, (Radar section), 31 October 2015.

Gillibrand, John, *Disabled Church—Disabled Society: The Implications of Autism for Philosophy, Theology and Politics* (London: Jessica Kingsley, 2010).

Goodchild, Philip, *Theology of Money* (London: SCM Press, 2007).

Gorringe, Timothy J., *Furthering Humanity: A Theology of Culture* (Aldershot and Burlington, VT: Ashgate, 2004).

Graham, Carol, *Happiness around the World: The Paradox of Happy Peasants and Miserable Millionaires* (New York and Oxford: Oxford University Press, 2012).

Graham, Elaine (ed.), *Grace Jantzen: Redeeming the Present* (Farnham and Burlington, VT: Ashgate, 2009).

Graham, Elaine, 'The "Virtuous Circle": Religion and the Practices of Happiness', in John Atherton, Elaine Graham, and Ian Steedman (eds.), *The Practices of Happiness: Political Economy, Religion and Wellbeing* (Abingdon and New York: Routledge, 2011), 224–34.

Graham, Elaine, Heather Walton, and Frances Ward, *Theological Reflection: Methods* (London: SCM Press, 2005).

Graham, Elaine, Heather Walton, and Frances Ward, *Theological Reflection: Sources* (London: SCM Press, 2007).

Grau, Marion, *Of Divine Economy: Refinancing Redemption* (New York and London: T&T Clark, 2004).

Greggs, Tom, *Barth, Origen, and Universal Salvation: Restoring Particularity* (Oxford: Oxford University Press, 2009).

Gregory, Brad S., *The Unintended Reformation: How a Religious Revolution Secularized Society* (Cambridge, MA: Harvard University Press, 2012).

Grey, Mary, 'Natality and Flourishing in Contexts of Disability and Impairment', in Elaine Graham (ed.), *Grace Jantzen: Redeeming the Present* (Farnham and Burlington, VT: Ashgate, 2009), 197–211.

Gunton, Colin E. (ed.), *The Cambridge Companion to Christian Doctrine* (Cambridge: Cambridge University Press 1997).

Guthrie, Steven R., *Creator Spirit: The Holy Spirit and the Art of Becoming Human* (Grand Rapids, MI: Baker, 2011).

Hagan, Anette I., *Eternal Blessedness for All?: A Historical-Systematic Examination of Friedrich Schleiermacher's Reinterpretation of Predestination* (Cambridge: James Clarke, 2014).

Häger, Andreas, 'The Transcendences of Listening to Music: How Listening to Bob Dylan Moves His Fans', *Temenos* 48.1 (2012), 65–85.

Hart, Trevor, 'Redemption and Fall', in Colin E. Gunton (ed.), *The Cambridge Companion to Christian Doctrine* (Cambridge: Cambridge University Press, 1997), 189–206.

Hastings, Ross, *Missional God, Missional Church: Hope for Re-Evangelizing the West* (Downers Grove, IL: IVP Academic, 2012).

Hauerwas, Stanley, '"Salvation even in Sin": Learning to Speak Truthfully about Ourselves', in *Sanctify Them in the Truth: Holiness Exemplified* (Edinburgh: T&T Clark, 1998), 61–74.

Haybron, Daniel M., *The Pursuit of Unhappiness: The Elusive Psychology of Well-Being* (Oxford: Oxford University Press, 2008).

Haybron, Daniel M., *Happiness: A Very Short Introduction* (Oxford: Oxford University Press, 2013).

Hayum, Andrée, *The Isenheim Altarpiece: God's Medicine and the Painter's Vision* (Princeton, NJ: Princeton University Press, 1989).

Hector, Kevin W., *The Theological Project of Modernism: Faith and the Conditions of Mineness* (Oxford: Oxford University Press, 2015).

Hibbs, John, *The Country Chapel* (Newton Abbott: David and Charles, 1988).

Higton, Mike, *Christian Doctrine* (London: SCM Press, 2008).

Higton, Mike and Jim Fodor (eds.), *The Routledge Companion to the Practice of Christian Theology* (Abingdon and New York: Routledge, 2015).

Higton, Mike, Jeremy Law, and Christopher Rowland (eds.), *Theology and Human Flourishing: Essays in Honor of Timothy J. Gorringe* (Eugene, OR: Cascade Books, 2011).

Hogan, Nanci, 'The Implications of a Politics of Natality for Transformational Feminist Advocacy: Transforming the Human Rights Moral Imaginary', in Elaine Graham, (ed.), *Grace Jantzen: Redeeming the Present* (Farnham and Burlington, VT: Ashgate, 2009), 227–45.

Hoggart, Richard, *The Use of Literacy: Aspects of Working-Class Life* (first published, 1957, London: Penguin Books, 2009).

Holmes, Stephen R. (ed.), *Public Theology in Cultural Engagement* (Milton Keynes, Colorado Springs, CO, and Hyderabad: Paternoster, 2008).

Hoose, Bob and Paul Asay, '*The Big Bang Theory*', www.pluggedin.com/tv-reviews/bigbangtheory/, accessed 17 April 2016.

Hopkins, Dwight N. and Edward P. Antonio (eds.), *The Cambridge Companion to Black Theology* (Cambridge: Cambridge University Press, 2012).

Hopkins, Dwight N. and Sheila Greeve Davaney (eds.), *Changing Conversations: Religious Reflection and Cultural Analysis* (New York and London: Routledge, 1996).

Horne, Brian, 'The Legacy of Romanticism: On Not Confusing Art and Religion', in Stephen Holmes (ed.), *Public Theology in Cultural Engagement* (Milton Keynes, Colorado Springs, CO, and Hyderabad: Paternoster, 2008), 153–69.

Howes, Graham, *The Art of the Sacred: An Introduction to the Aesthetics of Art and Belief* (London and New York: I. B. Tauris, 2007).

Humanists UK, '53% of Britons are Non-Religious, Says Latest British Social Attitudes Survey', https://humanism.org.uk/2017/07/05/53-of-britons-are-non-religious-says-latest-british-social-attitudes-survey/, accessed 5 Sept 2017.

Hunsinger, Deborah van Deusen, 'Forgiving Abusing Parents: Psychological and Theological Considerations', in Alistair McFadyen and Marcel Sarot (eds.), *Forgiveness and Truth: Explorations in Contemporary Theology* (Edinburgh and New York: T&T Clark, 2001), 71–98.

Huysmans, J-K., 'Two Essays on Grünewald', in *Grünewald: The Paintings* (London: The Phaidon Press, 1958), 7–25.

Immink, F. Gerrit, *Faith: A Practical Theological Reconstruction* (Grand Rapids, MI, and Cambridge UK: Eerdmans, 2005).

Inge, William Ralph, *More Lay Thoughts of a Dean* (London: Putnam, 1931).

Iqbal, Razia, 'Pain and Trauma Live just under the Skin', *The Independent* (Radar section), 11 April 2015.

Jackson, Tim, *Prosperity without Growth: Economics for a Finite Planet* (London and Washington DC: Earthscan, 2009).

Jantzen, Grace, 'The Gendered Politics of Flourishing and Salvation', in Vincent Brümmer and Marcel Sarot (eds.), *Happiness, Well-Being and the Meaning of Life* (Kampen: Kok Pharos, 1996), 58–75.

Johnson, Keith L. and David Lauber (eds.), *T&T Clark Companion to the Doctrine of Sin* (London and New York: Bloomsbury T&T Clark, 2016).

Jones, Gareth (ed.), *The Blackwell Companion to Modern Theology* (Oxford: Blackwell, 2004).

Jones, Serene, 'What's Wrong with Us?', in William C. Placher (ed.), *Essentials of Christian Theology* (Louisville, KY, and London: Westminster John Knox Press, 2003), 141–58.

Kaczor, Christopher, *The Gospel of Happiness: Rediscover your Faith through Spiritual Practice and Positive Psychology* (New York: Image, 2015).

Kalder, Daniel, 'Joel Osteen: The New Face of Christianity', *The Observer*, 7 March 2010, www.theguardian.com/world/2010/mar/07/joel-osteen-america- pastor, accessed 1 February 2017.

Kallenberg, Brad J., 'Some Practices of Theological Reasoning, or, How to Work Well with Words', in Mike Higton and Jim Fodor (eds.), *The Routledge Companion to the Practice of Christian Theology* (Abingdon and New York: Routledge, 2015), 23–42.

Kapic, Kelly M. and Bruce L. McCormack (eds.), *Mapping Modern Theology: A Thematic and Historical Introduction* (Grand Rapids, MI: Baker Academic, 2012).

Kelsey, David H., *Imagining Redemption* (Louisville, KY: Westminster John Knox Press, 2005).

Kerwick, Jason, 'The Philosophy, and Theology, of "Breaking Bad"', www. beliefnet.com/columnists/attheintersectionoffaithandculture/2015/09/the-philosophy-and-theology-of-breaking-bad.html, accessed 12 April 2016.

Kilby, Karen, *A (Very) Critical Introduction to Balthasar* (Grand Rapids, MI: Eerdmans, 2012).

Klammer, Arjo, 'Property and Possession: The Moral Economy of Ownership', in William Schweiker and Charles Mathewes (eds.), *Having: Property and Possession in Religious and Social Life* (Grand Rapids, MI: Eerdmans, 2004), 337–52.

Klemm, David E., 'Introduction: Theology of Culture as Theological Humanism', *Literature &Theology* 18 (2004), 239–50.

Klemm, David E. and William Schweiker, *Religion and the Human Future: An Essay on Theological Humanism* (Malden, MA, and Oxford: Blackwell, 2008).

Koepsell, David R. and Robert Arp (eds.), *Breaking Bad and Philosophy: Badder Living through Chemistry* (Chicago and LaSalle, IL: Open Court, 2012).

Kowalski, Dean. A. (ed.), *The Big Bang Theory and Philosophy: Rock, Paper, Scissors, Aristotle, Locke* (Hoboken, NJ: John Wiley, 2012).

Kozlovic, Anton Karl, 'The Structural Characteristics of the Cinematic Christ-Figure', *The Journal of Religion and Popular Culture*, 8.1 (2004), 29 pp., https://dspace2.flinders.edu.au/xmlui/bitstream/handle/2328/14295/2004054629.pdf, accessed 1 December 2017.

Kuschel, Karl-Josef, *Laughter: A Theological Reflection* (London: SCM Press, 1994).

Lancaster, Sarah Heaner, *The Pursuit of Happiness: Blessing and Fulfillment in Christian Faith* (Eugene, OR: Wipf and Stock, 2010).

Lane, Anthony N. S., 'Lust: The Human Person as Affected by Disordered Desires' *Evangelical Quarterly* 78 (2006), 21–35.

Lansley, Peter, 'Aston Villa derby woe leaves Tim Sherwood relishing shot at redemption', www.theguardian.com/football/2015/sep/20/aston-villa-west-bromwich-albion-premier-league-match-report, accessed 14 January 2016.

Layard, Richard, *Happiness: Lessons from a New Science* (London: Penguin, 2005).

Lent, Jeffrey. 'Top 10 books about justice and redemption', www.theguardian.com/books/2015/dec/16/top-10-books-about-justice-redemption-jeffrey-lent, accessed 14 January 2016.

Lindbeck, George, *The Nature of Doctrine* (London: SPCK, 1984).

Lints, Richard, 'Soteriology', in Kelly M. Kapic and Bruce L. McCormack (eds.), *Mapping Modern Theology: A Thematic and Historical Introduction* (Grand Rapids, MI: Baker Academic, 2012), 259–91.

Logan, Elliott, *Breaking Bad and Dignity: Unity and Fragmentation in the Serial Television Drama* (Basingstoke and New York: Palgrave Macmillan, 2016).

Long, Stephen, 'Moral Theology', in John Webster, Kathryn Tanner, and Iain Torrance (eds.), *The Oxford Handbook of Systematic Theology* (Oxford: Oxford University Press, 2007), 456–75.

Loughlin, Gerard, 'Cinéma Divinité: A Theological Introduction', in Eric S. Christianson, Peter Francis, and William R. Telford (eds.), *Cinéma Divinité: Religion, Theology and the Bible in Film* (London: SCM Press, 2005), 1–12.

Luther, Martin, 'On Christian Liberty' (1520) in Martin Luther, *Three Treatises* (Philadelphia, PA: Fortress Press, 1970).

Luther, Martin, 'A Treatise on Good Works' (1520), www.ccel.org/l/luther/good_works/cache/good_works.pdf, accessed 29 November 2017.

Luther, Martin, *The Small Catechism* [1529], http://bookofconcord.org/smallcatechism.php, accessed 23 August 2016.

McCabe, Janet and Kim Akass (eds.), *Quality TV: Contemporary American Television and Beyond* (London and New York: I. B. Tauris, 2007).

McFadyen, Alistair and Marcel Sarot (eds.), *Forgiveness and Truth* (Edinburgh and New York: T&T Clark, 2001).

McFarland, Ian, 'The Fall and Sin', in John Webster, Kathryn Tanner, and Iain Torrance (eds.), *The Oxford Handbook of Systematic Theology* (Oxford: Oxford University Press, 2007), 140–59.

McGilchrist, Iain, *The Master and his Emissary: The Divided Brain and the Making of the Western World* (New Haven, CT, and London: Yale University Press, 2009; pbk edn, 2012).

McIntyre, John, *The Shape of Soteriology* (Edinburgh: T&T Clark, 1992).

MacKinnon, Donald, 'Tillich, Frege, Kittel: Some Reflections on a Dark Theme', in *Explorations in Theology 5* (London: SCM Press, 1979), 129–37.

McMahon, Darrin, *The Pursuit of Happiness: A History from the Greeks to the Present* (London: Penguin Books, 2007).

Macnab, Geoffrey, 'Old devils charm on a slow voyage of discovery' *The Independent*, 18 September 2015.

Mann, Alan, *Atonement for a Sinless Society* (2nd edn, Eugene, OR: Cascade Books, 2015).

Markham, Ian S., *A Theology of Engagement* (Oxford and Malden, MA: Blackwell, 2003).

Marquard, Reiner, *Karl Barth und der Isenheimer Altar* (Stuttgart: Calwer Verlag, 1995).

Marsh, Clive, 'Film and Theologies of Culture', in Clive Marsh and Gaye Ortiz (eds.), *Explorations in Theology and Film* (Oxford: Blackwell, 1997), 21–34.

Marsh, Clive, *Cinema and Sentiment: Film's Challenge to Theology* (Carlisle: Paternoster Press, 2004).

Marsh, Clive, *Christ in Focus: Radical Christocentrism in Christian Theology* (London: SCM Press, 2005).

Marsh, Clive, *Christ in Practice: A Christology of Everyday Life* (London: Darton, Longman, and Todd, 2006).

Marsh, Clive, 'Protestant Themes within Secular Models of Salvation—"Redeemed" or just "a bit Happier"?: The Example of *Crazy Heart*', paper delivered at the 'Protestantism on Screen' Conference, Wittenberg, 25 June 2015 (unpublished).

Marsh, Clive, 'Films, Values, Absolutes: Why Theological Readings of Films are Morally and Politically Essential', *Journal of Religion and Film* 20.1 (2016), article 11, 1–22.

Marsh, Clive, 'The Feeling of Engagement: Lifelong Learning about Religion in Part-Time, Secular Higher Education as a Private and Public Good', *Widening Participation and Lifelong Learning* 19 (2017), 8–32.

Marsh, Clive, 'Theology's Part-Time Future: A Fresh Initiative in Theological Education and Religious Literacy?', *Theology* 121 (2018), 171–9.

Marsh, Clive and Vaughan S. Roberts, *Personal Jesus: How Popular Music Shapes our Souls* (Grand Rapids, MI: Baker Academic, 2013).

Marshall, I. Howard, *The Epistle to the Philippians* (London: Epworth Press, 1992).

Meggitt, Justin J., *Paul, Poverty and Survival* (Edinburgh: T&T Clark, 1998).

Meister, Chad and James Beilby (eds.), *The Routledge Companion to Modern Christian Thought* (London and New York: Routledge, 2013).

Mercadante, Linda A., *Victims and Sinners: Spiritual Roots of Addiction and Recovery* (Louisville, KY: Westminster John Knox Press, 1996).

Merriam-Webster Dictionary, 'Ergotism', www.merriam-webster.com/dictionary/ergotism, accessed 28 December 2017.

Míguez Bonino, José, 'Rereading Tillich in Latin America: From Religious Socialism to the Exile', in Raymond F. Bulman and Frederick J. Parrella (eds.), *Religion in the New Millennium: Theology in the Spirit of Paul Tillich* (Macon, GA: Mercer University Press, 2001), 19–33.

Milbank, John, *Theology and Social Theory: Beyond Secular Reason* (Oxford and Cambridge, MA: Blackwell, 1990).

Milbank, John, 'Can a Gift Be Given?: Prolegomena to a Future Trinitarian Metaphysic', *Modern Theology* 11 (1995), 119–61.

Morisy, Ann, *Journeying Out: A New Approach to Christian Mission* (London and New York: Continuum, 2006).

Morris, Wayne, *Salvation as Praxis: A Practical Theology of Salvation for a Multi-Faith World* (London: Bloomsbury T&T Clark, 2014).

Morse, Christopher, 'Soteriology', in Ian A. McFarland, David A. S. Fergusson, Karen Kilby, and Iain R. Torrance (eds.), *The Cambridge Dictionary of Christian Theology* (Cambridge: Cambridge University Press, 2011), 479–81.

Nelson, Derek R., *What's Wrong with Sin?: Sin in Individual and Social Perspective from Schleiermacher to Theologies of Liberation* (London and New York: T&T Clark, 2009).

Nelson, R. David, Darren Sarisky, and Justin Stratis (eds.), *Theological Theology* (London and New York: Bloomsbury T&T Clark, 2015).

Newlands, George, *The Transformative Imagination: Rethinking Intercultural Theology* (Aldershot and Burlington, VT: Ashgate, 2004).

Nuovo, Victor, *Visionary Science: A Translation of Tillich's 'On the Idea of a Theology of Culture' with an Interpretive Essay* (Detroit, MI: Wayne State University Press, 1987).

O'Collins, SJ, Gerald, *Jesus Our Redeemer: A Christian Approach to Salvation* (Oxford: Oxford University Press, 2007).

Office for National Statistics, 'Measuring National Well-Being: Personal Well-Being in the UK, 2014 to 2015', www.ons.gov.uk/ons/rel/well being/measuring-national-well-being/personal-well-being-in-the-uk–2014-15/index.html.

Osteen, Joel, *Your Best Life Now* (London: Hodder, 2008).

Osthövener, Claus-Dieter, *Erlösung: Transformationen einer Idee im 19. Jahrhundert* (Tübingen: Mohr Siebeck, 2004).

Pannenberg, Wolfhart, *Theology and the Kingdom of God* (Philadelphia, PA: The Westminster Press, 1969).

Pattison, Stephen, 'Can We Speak of God in the Secular Academy? Or, Need Theology Be so Useless?', in Frances Young (ed.), *Dare We Speak of God in Public* (London and New York: Mowbray, 1995), 35–49.

Pattison, Stephen, *Shame: Theory, Therapy, Theology*, (Cambridge: Cambridge University Press, 2000).

Pauck, Wilhelm, (ed.), *Melanchthon and Bucer* (Philadelphia, PA: The Westminster Press, 1969).

Peperzak, Adriaan T., 'Philosophical Presuppositions of the Christian Debate on Salvation', in Rienk Lanooy (ed.), *For Us and for our Salvation: Seven Perspectives on Christian Soteriology* (Utrecht: Interuniversitair Instituut voor Missiologie en Oecumenica, 1994), 133–44.

Pierson, David P. (ed.), *Breaking Bad: Critical Essays on the Contexts, Politics, Style, and Reception of the Television Series* (Lanham, MD: Lexington Books, 2014).

Pierson, David P., 'Breaking Neoliberal?: Contemporary Neoliberal Discourses and Policies in AMC's *Breaking Bad*', in David P. Pierson (ed.), *Breaking Bad: Critical Essays on the Contexts, Politics, Style, and Reception of the Television Series* (Lanham, MD: Lexington Books, 2014), 15–31.

Piper, John, *Desiring God: Meditations of a Christian Hedonist*, (rev. edn, Sisters, OR: Multnomah Books, 2011).

Porter, Roy, *Enlightenment: Britain and the Creation of the Modern World* (London: Penguin, 2000).

Putnam, Robert, *Bowling Alone: The Collapse and Revival of American Community* (New York: Simon and Schuster, 2001).

Quash, Ben, *Found Theology: History, Imagination and the Holy Spirit* (London and New York: Bloomsbury T&T Clark, 2013).

Ranker, 'The Best Movies about Redemption', www.ranker.com/list/best-movies-about-redemption/ranker-film, accessed 15 April 2016.

Ray, Stephen, 'Structural Sin', in Keith L. Johnson and David Lauber (eds.), *T&T Clark Companion to the Doctrine of Sin* (London and New York: Bloomsbury T&T Clark, 2016), 417–32.

Reed, Esther D., 'Redemption', in Gareth Jones (ed.), *The Blackwell Companion to Modern Theology* (Oxford: Blackwell, 2004), 227–42.

Re Manning, Russell, 'Theology of Culture after Postcolonialism', *The North American Paul Tillich Society Newsletter* 28:2 (2002), 25–32.

Re Manning, Russell, *Theology at the End of Culture: Paul Tillich's Theology of Culture and Art* (Leuven: Peeters, 2005).

Re Manning, Russell (ed.), *The Cambridge Companion to Paul Tillich* (Cambridge: Cambridge University Press, 2009).

Re Manning, Russell (ed.), *The Oxford Handbook of Natural Theology* (Oxford: Oxford University Press, 2013).

Re Manning, Russell. 'The Religious Meaning of Culture: Paul Tillich and Beyond', *IJST* 15 (2013), 437–52.

Re Manning, Russell, 'Unwritten Theology: Notes towards a Natural Theology of Music', in Férdia J. Stone-Davis (ed.), *Music and Transcendence* (Abingdon and New York: Routledge, 2016), 65–74.

Richter, Gottfried, *The Isenheim Altar: Suffering and Salvation in the Art of Grünewald* (Edinburgh: Floris Books, 1998).

Rieger, Joerg (ed.), *Liberating the Future: God, Mammon, and Theology* (Minneapolis, MN: Fortress Press, 1998).

Robinson, Matthew Ryan, *Redeeming Relationship, Relationships that Redeem* (Tübingen: Mohr Siebeck, forthcoming).

Rohr, Richard, *Near Occasions of Grace* (Maryknoll, NY: Orbis Books, 1993).

Roper, Lyndal, *Martin Luther: Renegade and Prophet* (London: Vintage, 2017).

Ruether, Rosemary R., *Introducing Redemption in Christian Feminism* (Sheffield: Sheffield Academic Press, 1998).

Ruhmer, Eberhard, 'Notes on Plates', in *Grünewald: The Paintings* (London: The Phaidon Press, 1958), 113–28.

Ruparell, Tinu, 'The Dialogue Party: Dialogue, Hybridity, and the Reluctant Other', in Viggo Mortensen (ed.), *Theology and the Religions: A Dialogue* (Grand Rapids, MI, and Cambridge: Eerdmans, 2003), 235–48.

Ruparell, Tinu, 'Inter-Religious Dialogue and Interstitial Theology', in Catherine Cornille (ed.), *The Wiley-Blackwell Companion to Inter-Religious Dialogue* (Oxford: Wiley, 2013), 117–32.

Ryrie, Alec, *Being Protestant in Reformation Britain* (Oxford: Oxford University Press, 2012).

Sattler, Dorothea, *Erlösung: Lehrbuch der Soteriologie* (Freiburg im Breisgau, Basle, and Vienna: Herder, 2011).

Scharer, Matthias and Bernd Jochen Hilberath, *The Practice of Communicative Theology: An Introduction to a New Theological Culture* (New York: Continuum, 2008).

Schindler, D. C., 'A Very Critical Response to Karen Kilby: On Failing to See the Form', *Radical Orthodoxy: Theology, Philosophy, Politics* 3.1 (September 2015), 68–87.

Schleiermacher, Friedrich D. E., *The Christian Faith* (Edinburgh: T&T Clark, 1928; latest edn, London and New York: Bloomsbury T&T Clark, 2016).

Schleiermacher, Friedrich D. E., *Christmas Eve Celebration: A Dialogue* (Eugene, OR: Cascade Books, 2010).

Schmitt, Pierre, *The Isenheim Altar* (Berne: Hallwag AG, 1960).

Scholes, Jeffrey and Raphael Sassower, *Religion and Sports in American Culture* (New York and London: Routledge, 2014).

Schültz, Daniela, *Quality-TV als Unterhaltungsphänomen* (Wiesbaden: Springer, 2016).

Schweiker, William, 'Theology of Culture and its Future', in Russell Re Manning (ed.), *The Cambridge Companion to Paul Tillich* (Cambridge: Cambridge University Press, 2009), 138–51.

Schweiker, William and Charles Mathewes (eds.), *Having: Property and Possession in Religious and Social Life* (Grand Rapids, MI: Eerdmans, 2004).

Selby, Peter, *Grace and Mortgage: The Language of Faith and the Debt of the World* (London: Darton, Longman, and Todd, 1997).

Selby, Peter, *An Idol Unmasked: A Faith Perspective on Money* (London: Darton, Longman, and Todd, 2014).

Seligman, Martin E. P., *Authentic Happiness: Using the New Positive Psychology to Realize your Potential for Lasting Fulfilment* (New York: Simon & Schuster, 2002).

Seligman, Martin E. P., *Flourish: A Visionary New Understanding of Happiness and Well-Being* (New York: Atria, 2013).

Shaw, Watkins, *A Textual and Historical Companion to Handel's* Messiah (London: Novello, 1965).

Sherry, Patrick, *Spirit and Beauty: An Introduction to Theological Aesthetics* (2nd edn, London: SCM Press, 2002).

Sherry, Patrick, *Images of Redemption: Art, Literature and Salvation* (London and New York: T&T Clark, 2003).

Sherwood, Harriet, 'Nearly 50% are of no religion—but has UK hit "peak secular"?', *The Observer*, 14 May 2017, www.theguardian.com/world/2017/may/13/uk-losing-faith-religion-young-reject-parents-beliefs, accessed 5 Sept 2017.

Siedentop, Larry, *Inventing the Individual: The Origins of Western Liberalism* (London: Allen Lane, 2014).

Sinitiere, Phillip Luke, *Salvation with a Smile: Joel Osteen, Lakewood Church, and American Christianity* (New York: New York University Press, 2015).

Smith, Ruth, *Handel's Oratorios and Eighteenth-Century Thought* (Cambridge: Cambridge University Press, 1995).

Sødal, Helje Kringlebotn, '"Victor, not Victim": Joel Osteen's Rhetoric of Hope', *Journal of Contemporary Religion*, 25 (2010), 37–50.

Spander, Art, 'Mickelson finds redemption' (13 February 2007), www.telegraph.co.uk/sport/golf/ustour/2307676/Mickelson-finds-redemption.html.

Stapert, Calvin R., *Handel's Messiah: Comfort for God's People* (Grand Rapids, MI, and Cambridge: Eerdmans, 2010).

Stendahl, Krister, 'The Apostle Paul and the Introspective Conscience of the West', *Harvard Theological Review* 56 (1963), 199–215 (repr. in *Paul among Jews and Gentiles*, Philadelphia, PA: Fortress Press, 1976; London: SCM Press, 1977).

Suchocki, Margaret Hewitt, *Through a Lens Darkly: Tracing Redemption in Film* (Eugene, OR: Cascade Books, 2015).

Swinton, John, *Raging with Compassion: Pastoral Responses to the Problem of Evil* (Grand Rapids, MI: Eerdmans, 2007).

Swinton, John, 'From Inclusion to Belonging: A Practical Theology of Community, Disability and Humnanness', *Journal of Religion, Disability and Health* 16 (2012), 172–90.

Sykes, Stephen, *The Identity of Christianity* (London: SPCK, 1984).

Tanner, Kathryn, 'Theology and Popular Culture', in Dwight N. Hopkins and Sheila Greeve Davaney (eds.), *Changing Conversations: Religious Reflection and Cultural Analysis* (New York and London: Routledge, 1996), 101–20.

Tanner, Kathryn, *Theories of Culture: A New Agenda for Theology* (Minneapolis, MN: Fortress Press, 1997).

Tanner, Kathryn, 'Cultural Theory', in John Webster, Kathryn Tanner, and Iain Torrance (eds.), *The Oxford Handbook of Systematic Theology* (Oxford: Oxford University Press, 2007), 527–42.

Taylor, Barbara Brown, *Speaking of Sin: The Lost Language of Salvation* (Norwich: Canterbury Press, 2015).

Taylor, Mark Kline (ed.), *Paul Tillich: Theologian of the Boundaries* (London: Collins, 1987).

Temple, William, *Nature, Man and God* (London: Macmillan & Co., 1935).

Thatcher, Adrian, 'Theology, Happiness and Public Policy', in Mike Higton, Jeremy Law, and Christopher Rowland (eds.), *Theology and Human Flourishing: Essays in Honor of Timothy J. Gorringe* (Eugene, OR: Cascade Books, 2011), 251–63.

Theuring, Ashley, 'Salvific Communities and Practices of Resistance: A Feminist Theological Response to Trauma', *theotherjournal.com: An Intersection of Theology and Culture*, http://theotherjournal.com/2015/04/20/salvific-communities-and-practices-of-resistance-a-feminist-theological-response-to-trauma, accessed 15 October 2015.

Thistlethwaite, Susan Brooks and Mary Potter Engel (eds.), *Lift Every Voice: Constructing Theologies from the Underside* (rev. edn, Maryknoll, NY: Orbis, 1998).

Thompson, E. P., *The Making of the English Working Class* (London: Victor Gollancz, 1963).

Tillich, Paul, *The Shaking of the Foundations* (New York: Charles Scribner's Sons, 1948).

Tillich, Paul, *On Art and Architecture* (New York: Crossroad, 1989).

United Reformed Church in the United Kingdom, *Service Book* (Oxford: Oxford University Press, 1989).

Van der Kooi, Cornelis and Gijsbert van den Brink, *Christian Dogmatics: An Introduction* (Grand Rapids, MI: Eerdmans, 2017).

Vanhoozer, Kevin J., Charles A. Anderson, and Michael J. Sleasman (eds.), *Everyday Theology: How to Read Cultural Texts and Interpret Trends* (Grand Rapids, MI: Baker, 2007).

Viladesau, Richard, *Theological Aesthetics: God in Imagination, Beauty, and Art* (Oxford and New York: Oxford University Press, 1999).

Viladesau, Richard, 'Engagement with the Arts', in Mike Higton and Jim Fodor (eds.), *The Routledge Companion to the Practice of Christian Theology* (London and New York: Routledge, 2015), 404–21.

Volf, Miroslav, *Free of Charge: Giving and Forgiving in a Culture Stripped of Grace* (Grand Rapids, MI: Zondervan, 2006).

Volf, Miroslav, *Flourishing: Why We Need Religion in a Globalized World* (New Haven, CT, and London: Yale University Press, 2015).

Volf, Miroslav and Justin E. Crisp (eds.), *Joy and Human Flourishing: Essays on Theology, Culture and the Good Life* (Minneapolis, MN: Fortress Press, 2015).

Washington, James M. (ed.), *A Testament of Hope: The Essential Writings of Martin Luther King Jr.* (San Francisco: Harper & Row, 1986).

Webster, John, Kathryn Tanner, and Iain Torrance (eds.), *The Oxford Handbook of Systematic Theology* (Oxford: Oxford University Press, 2007).

Wikipedia, 'The Big Bang Theory', https://en.wikipedia.org/wiki/The_Big_Bang_Theory, accessed 20 December 2017.

Wilkinson, Richard and Kate Pickett, *The Spirit Level: Why Equality is Better for Everyone* (London: Penguin Books, 2010).

Willetts, David, *A University Education* (Oxford: Oxford University Press, 2017).

Winslow, Luke A., 'The Imaged Other: Style and Substance in the Rhetoric of Joel Osteen', *Southern Communication Journal* 79 (2014), 250–71.

Wriedt, Markus, 'Luther's Theology', in Donald K. McKim (ed.), *The Cambridge Companion to Martin Luther* (Cambridge: Cambridge University Press, 2003), 86–119.

Wright, David F., 'Pelagianism', in Sinclair B. Ferguson and David F. Wright (eds.), *New Dictionary of Theology* (Leicester and Downers Grove, IL: IVP, 1988), 501.

Young, Kenneth, *Chapel* (London: Methuen, 1972).

Z2solutions, 'Big Bang Theory Audience Demographics', http://z2solutions.com/demographics/big-bang-theory-audience-demographics, accessed 25 September 2017.

Zahl, Simeon, 'Atonement', in Nicholas Adams, George Pattison, and Graham Ward (eds.), *The Oxford Handbook of Theology and Modern European Thought* (Oxford: Oxford University Press, 2013), 633–54.

Zahl, Simeon, 'On the Affective Salience of Doctrines', *Modern Theology* 31 (2015), 428–44.

Biblical Index

Names and Subjects Index

1